MESSERSCHMITT ROULETTE

THE WESTERN DESERT 1941-42

by

Geoffrey Morley-Mower

DFC, AFC

ISBN: 1-883809-01-0

Library of Congress Catalog Card No.: 93-085728

Cover Design and illustration by John C. Valo

Swindon Borough Council Library Services	
Askews	
	£16.95

Published by:

Phalanx Publishing Co., Ltd.
1051 Marie Avenue W.
St. Paul, MN 55118-4131 USA

Distributed by:
Airlife Publishing Ltd
101 Longden Road, Shrewsbury SY3 9EB, England

A DEDICATION

We came from opposite ends
Of the earth,
But our father's

Generation had fought
At Gallipoli
And with Allenby

At the storming
of Jerusalem.
I'd always hankered

To be a member
Of that select company,
The hard core,

Who hold out
To the bitter end,
Their bodies, centuries later,

Unearthed by the inner wall
Of the last fortress.
For eight months

In the Western Desert of Egypt
We lived that dream.
One must avoid

Inflated political words
Like "glory"
And "sacrifice."

According to Hemingway
Only the names of places
And of units have dignity.

I agree, but add the names
Of the Australian pilots
Written out in verse

As they deserve
To show respect
Before it is too late;

Ray Hudson
Alan Ferguson
Ken Watts

Ed Kirkham
Charles Edmondson
Ray Goldberg

Colin Robertson
Ron Achiles
Morgan Bartlett

Paddy Hutley
Miller Readett
Kevin Springbett

Wally Gale
Harry Rowlands
And Stan Reid,

The unit doctor,
Who was a Hurricane pilot
Of sorts.

No. 451 Squadron
Royal Australian
Air Force;

July, 1941
To March, 1942;
Qasaba,

Sidi Barrani,
Tobruk,
Sidi Azeiz.

ACKNOWLEDGEMENTS

My first and chief acknowledgement is to David Reid, who was the first to read the original manuscript and who performed the task of editing. He also acted as my agent and has been my indispensable friend throughout. I am indebted to Christopher Shores and Hans Ring for their great work of research in **Fighters Over the Desert**, (The C.W. Daniel Co. Ltd., 1969) which enabled me to identify Hans-Joachim Marseille as the most gallant knight of the air; and more personally to Christopher Shores for supplying his unrivalled collection of air photographs to illustrate this book; to Jack Florey, onetime member of 451 Squadron, for his memories and for photographs from his collection; to the Australian War Memorial for photographs of General Morshead's secret hangars in Tobruk; to the RAAF Historical Section, Canberra, for much assistance and for the nominal rolls of Australian personnel of No. 451 Squadron during the period covered by this book. I am especially grateful to John Culbert of the New South Wales Branch of No. 451 Squadron Association for his help in getting me in touch with surviving pilots.

Nothing has been more important to me in writing this account than the support of my Australian comrades in arms. Ray Hudson's letters were an invaluable source of information to me in the early stages, and I must thank his family for permission to quote from them. Ken Watts has been in communication with me almost from the beginning, has read the first draft, and has been invaluable in comment and support. Group Captain Eric Black intends to write his own book on the siege of Tobruk, but he has kindly given me details of his role in building the secret hangars. Charles Edmondson has taken the trouble to send me the most elaborate account I have received of the squadron's activities in the desert, and his evidence has been most significant in establishing the truth of many events. Alan Ferguson sent me an interesting story of his adventures after being shot down and captured in November, 1941 and also details of his subsequent wartime flying career. Without the help of Colin Robertson I could not have known how General Morshead used his "private air force" after I returned from Tobruk on 12 October, 1941. This is an area that has been completely ignored by historians of the desert war and, as it turned out, he was the one surviving witness. Finally, I thank my wife, Mary, for putting up with my fascination, over the past few years, with battles long ago.

TABLE OF CONTENTS

"Time spent on reconnaissance is seldom wasted."
(British Field Service Regulations - 1912)

Tactical reconnaissance pilots are the unknown warriors of the air war and there are no famous names to conjure up. The Army was always less than impressed by the airmen's contribution to victories on the battlefield and the air force authorities resented the diversion of its precious aeroplanes to the Army. So we weren't popular with anyone, were debarred by unwritten laws from press coverage and treated like Cinderella when the gongs were being dished out. This book is written in the hope that readers unfamiliar with the role of aerial spy will be entertained by our trials and tribulations.

My account has an additional theme. I was an Englishman attached to an Australian squadron and throughout the campaign against Rommel in the Western Desert of Egypt in 1941 I had less trouble with marauding Messerschmitts than I did with our own wild colonial boys.

To prevent embarrassment to living persons I have given fictitious names to two officers who appear under the guise of Willy Whitlock and Ken Dawlish.

I

ESCAPE FROM A BACKWATER
(20th June to 31st July, 1941)

It was one of those unbearably hot Indian days in late June when sensible people retreated to a spot of shade, reclined under a fan and waited for the sun to abate its wrath. But Batts Barthold, our flight commander, was a zealot and he kept us flying fighter tactics till three o'clock in the afternoon when the air was so bumpy that our light biplanes were tossed around like paper bags in the stifling upcurrents.

When we landed I humped my parachute behind him across the hardstanding where the Hawker Audaxes stood in line, cooking in the bright sun and sending off waves of heat as we passed.

"You could fry eggs on this concrete," Batts said, grinning at me. Lean and quick moving, he had many premature lines on his young face and when he smiled he reminded me of an intelligent monkey. He was a good friend of mine, but I planned to leave him though he did not yet know it.

"I'll have to talk to you some time, Batts," I said.

"Come in for a cup of tea after charp* time," he answered. I went to his room at five o'clock. His bearer had already served tea and biscuits on a tin tray and we sat wetly, with towels around our waists, in the oversize officer's mess armchairs, the fan whirring above us like a propeller.

"5 Squadron isn't going to be re-equipped with Hurricanes," I said. "Look at the newspapers. All the front line aircraft they can spare must go to the Middle East. We're stuck in a permanent backwater here. I want to get into the war before it's over.."

"I thought you'd be enjoying your time with Joan," he replied. "But I see your point. I feel edgy myself, living in such absurd comfort, waited on hand and foot by servants while the world goes up in flames. If you really want to go, I'll talk to Air Headquarters. They may appreciate volunteers. We'll be sorry to lose you."

"Thanks, Batts."

No. 5 Squadron had moved from the Northwest Frontier to Lahore, an important city in the plains of northern India (now Pakistan), in the fall of 1940 to begin fighter training. All that winter and spring I had been having an affair with Joan Lettington, the daughter of a major in the Royal Engineers. She had

---

*The word for bed in Hindustani is charpoy. Charp time was the afternoon siesta.

1

a classic profile spoiled - but not spoiled for me - by a slightly too generous mouth. We borrowed her father's old Chevrolet to make love secretly in the two downtown hotels, Nedou's and Falletti's, and by the time she departed for the coolness of Dalhousie, the local hill station, we were engaged to be married. I explained to her that I had to fight the war first and she accepted it as a fact of life, like cancer or the bubonic plague.

The response from Air Headquarters, India, was surprisingly prompt. Just before noon on 15 July, 1941 a chaprassi[1] with the RAF colours in his turban came into the office in No 1 Hangar where I was sorting maps. He saluted and handed me a message slip to report to the flight commander. I knew what it was and ran across the tarmac, past the sun-scorched biplanes to the flight office.

"This is what you've been waiting for." He handed me a signal posting me to Middle East Command. I was to report to the Staging Post, Karachi by July 20th.

"It doesn't say what sort of squadron I'm going to."

"You'll have to take your chance on that. With your bomber background it might be Blenheim."

"Christ!" Blenheims had already earned the reputation of being sitting ducks. They were the daylight bombers the Luftwaffe fighters drooled over.

"What will Joan think?"

"Nothing good."

I called her from the officer's mess that night. Her voice was small with distance."I'm leaving India."

"Oh!"

A pause.

"Where are you going to?"

"The Middle East. I have to be in Karachi by the 20th."

"Can you come up here to say goodbye?

"Darling, there's no time for anything. I have to pack up my possessions and put them in store, hand over my jobs and go."

"Oh, Geoff!"

"I'm sorry. But I really want to go."

"I know you do. But you'll come back to me."

"Of course I will. I'll write to you every day. I love you."

When we had said goodbye to one another I put down the receiver and stared at the wall for some time. I had pressed so hard for this. Why didn't I feel more pleased? What had possessed me to make a song and dance about fighting the stupid war when it was life, not death, that was beckoning

---

1. Messenger

to me? What a fool I am, I said aloud. But it was too late to do anything about it.

We flew from Karachi across the Persian Gulf in a Sunderland flying boat, landing on the confluence of the Tigris and Euphrates near Basra. The next day the heavy boat made its slow progress across the brown emptiness of Arabia, lurching and juddering in the upcurrents, making some of the passengers airsick. It dropped down to the Dead Sea to disembark an officer posted to AHQ Levant in Jerusalem, landing finally on the Nile in the pearly evening light. At the dock I was handed my orders to proceed by rail to Ismailya for conversion to Hurricanes. Conversion, I thought, had a New Testament ring about it, as if I were to be baptized as a monoplane pilot, anointed with Merlin engine oil and therefore permitted to fly at hitherto unimagined speeds.

On the train the next day, crawling slowly across the green Delta, I stared out of the carriage window at the immemorial Egyptian scene. Beside white flat-roofed villages brown men in galabyas hitched up to their waists waded through irrigation ditches, and a huge camel, its head raised in protest, turned a heavy wheel to draw water. All the time I was dreaming of shooting down enemy aircraft, fighting mock air battles in my mind. When I reported to the adjutant at Ismailya, however, he told me I was in a "pool" for fighter reconnaissance squadrons. I comforted myself that I was at least to fly fighters, though I was to be one of the hunted rather than the hunter.

Ismailya, situated on the Great Bitter Lake, was still operating on a peace time basis like the stations in India. An army of Egyptian workers kept it neat as a pin. The lawns and hedgerows were trimmed, concrete posts were painted white and the lofty old-fashioned hangars and Victorian looking barracks gave it an air of stability and civilization. Camouflaged twin-engined Blenheim bombers, some Hurricanes and a variety of training types were lined up on the airfield.

Most of my time in India had been spent flying Westland Wapitis. These were biplanes designed just after the First World War to use up spare parts of the old D.H.9A aircraft. They cruised at eighty mph and like most aircraft of that early vintage had tailskids and were not equipped with brakes. I loved to fly them, knowing that they were the last of their breed and that only in police type actions on the Northwest Frontier of India could such museum pieces still be useful. There had been a profound change in technology over the previous ten years and I was aware that my experience had been with a wood-and-wire world that had passed away. Aeroplanes were no longer designed to look like box kites. Fighters had begun to look like swallows and bombers like pterodactyls.

Next morning I reported to the conversion flight and had my first good look at the Hawker Hurricane. It had the same racy greyhound's look as the

3

biplane Fury which had preceded it and the shapes of the body and tail were similar, but there the resemblance ended. Instead of fabric, sheet metal covered the wings, the cockpit was neatly enclosed by a hood and it stood like a gull on frail retractable legs. In 1934 Sidney Camm, the Hawker designer, responding to general feeling in the aircraft industry that the biplane era was drawing to a close, began to design a monoplane fighter with a retractable undercarriage. R.J. Mitchell at Supermarine had come to a similar decision and had started work on an aircraft that eventually became the Spitfire. In 1934 Rolls Royce developed a more powerful engine to replace the Kestrel which had driven the Hart, Audax and other Hawker models. It became known as the Merlin and was arguably the most successful engine of its time. It was incorporated into the design of the Hurricane, the Spitfire, the Mosquito, the Mustang (P-51) and the Lancaster bomber. The Spitfire turned out to be the greatest fighter, faster, more maneuverable and with better climb; but the virtue of the Hurricane was in its sturdiness, to which many airmen owed their lives. My first impression wouldn't have included sturdiness. To me it looked frail, slim and speedy. For the old Wapiti hand it was a giant step into the future.

When converting to an aircraft, it is normal for an instructor to fly with the student for an hour or so on a version with two sets of controls. For single seater fighters this was not usually feasible; there was, in fact, no dual control Hurricane in the Middle East. I was checked out on a Magister, a low winged monoplane used for primary training, by Sergeant Marshal, a beefy middle aged man with a strong Belfast accent. I must have performed satisfactorily, for he at once introduced me to the Hurricane and sent me solo the same day.

When I was settled in the cockpit and ready to go he climbed heavily onto the step and, looking over my shoulder, gave me some last minute instructions.

"Fine pitch, then open up smoothly to full throttle. You won't be used to so much power. It you open up too quickly you'll feel as if someone booted you up the arse. But don't, whatever you do, throttle back or you'll run out of runway. When you're sure you're off the ground and climbing away, select your undercarriage up and fly around a bit. Get used to the way it handles and then try a landing. Give yourself lots of room. And for Christ's sake, don't forget to put your undercarriage down or you'll make such a nasty mess in the middle of the field."

I taxied round the perimeter track with the hood slid tight over my head and in my right hand the spade "stick" with its prominent firing button for the eight guns in the wings. This was not only my first flight in a modern high speed fighter but also my first experience on a concrete runway. I'd been trained to fly on a grass airfield at Hullavington in Wiltshire and had been operating since then from tiny landing grounds of sunbaked mud in northern India. The concrete looked mighty hard and the legs of the Hurricane a trifle spindly.

4

ESCAPE FROM A BACKWATER

On takeoff I found myself sucked rapidly into the air by the powerful engine, fumbling for the undercarriage lever in the unfamiliar cockpit and worrying about the alarming build-up of speed. The wheels made a reassuring clunk as they locked up. I reduced the engine revolutions to 2400 rpm as instructed and climbed away at 160 mph, a speed only achieved by a Wapiti in a steep dive. In front of me the Rolls Royce Merlin made an impressive noise. The controls felt sensitive and a steep turn could be initiated by the tiniest movement of the ailerons and the merest touch of rudder. I pulled back on the stick and tightened the turn until I as on the verge of blacking out. I resisted the temptation to flip the aircraft onto its back, flew along the borders of the Great Bitter Lake and came in to land.

Reduce speed to 140 mph. Fine pitch. Undercart down.

Clunk!

I made a flat approach, giving myself plenty of room as the sergeant had advised. When I selected full slap the nose went down steeply and I needed more throttle to drag it in. The runway looked weird from the flat angle. More throttle to drop it in over the boundary fence. Now gradually back with the power, back, back. Rumble, tumble, tumble from the wheels and tailwheel and a loud wheeze from the oleo legs. A satisfactory landing but I was still roaring down the runway quite fast. A touch of brake. "Don't hold the brakes on for long or you'll burn the buggers out." Another touch and I could run the Hurricane slowly up to the perimeter track and turn gently on to it with a squeeze of brake and full left rudder.

I had expected a training programme, some night flying, a cross country flight and a chance to fire my guns, but Rommel's pressure on Egypt didn't allow for such rational procedures. I flew six times only, totaling four and a half hours in the air. For my final sortie Sergeant Marshal authorized me to practice aerobatics over the Sinai Desert. I spent forty minutes looping and rolling above a barren landscape where Moses had wandered for forty years.

"That's your last trip," he told me, when I asked to fly again. "You're to report to your squadron."

"What squadron?"

"We don't know yet."

That lunchtime I sat down beside a flight lieutenant with a new DFC ribbon displayed under the wings of his tropical bush shirt.

"I'm Tommy Tucker," he said, turning to me with a friendly smile. "Ex-208 Squadron. I'm instructing here temporarily. I hear you're going to 451, the Aussie squadron."

I was used to wartime rumour mills and didn't take his news very seriously.

"I haven't heard anything yet."

"You're recce, aren't you?"

"Well, I was training for straight fighters but. . . "

"Then you must be going to the Aussies. They need pilots. Tough crowd, I'm told. You'd better watch out for that bunch."

He laughed, throwing back his head at the idea of an innocent Englishman being scragged by the wild Australians.

"They can't be that different from us," I countered.

"Don't believe it. A month or so ago they threw an Egyptian whore out of the fourth storey window of a brothel in Alexandria. Killed her stone dead. They're white savages."

He tilted his chair back, laughing loudly and staring at me. He was tall and boyish with a fair moustache. I began to dislike him for his elegance, his superior tone and the fact that he was pulling my leg. The story of the girl being thrown from a window had reached India and I'd heard it before.

"It wasn't the air force people who . . . "

"No, it was army blokes, but they're all the same. You'll see. They'll have your guts for garters."

The rumour of my posting was confirmed within the hour by the station adjutant and I walked happily back to my room to pack, telling myself that I wasn't at all worried about Australians. I'd known about Australians all my life. My uncle Frank had been an infantryman in the Westminster Rifles at Gallipoli and he had always said they were the greatest hand-to hand fighters on earth. "They out-Turked the Turk," he used to say. So Tommy Tucker was too late to disillusion me about my boyhood heroes. In my anticipatory fantasies they would welcome me, identify me as a friend, drag me off on a heroic drinking spree during which they would get roaring drunk and I would stay sober. I'd left the soft life and military inertia of India less than a week before and here I was on the brink of a great adventure with the compeers of my choice, eager to pit my courage against theirs. Not having ever faced death directly, I had no idea how my guts were going to shape up, but I was full of inflated hopes. My minimum ambition was a DFC ribbon like Tommy Tucker's to pin on my bush shirt when the show was over.

II

THE FIGHTING TRIBE
(1st to 8th August, 1941)

I took off from Ismailya after lunch on 1st August, 1941 in a new Hurricane, camouflaged for operations in the desert, which I was to deliver to the squadron. To get to Qasaba from the Great Bitter Lake region one had to cross the Delta of the Nile at its broadest extent. To the South it is a recognizable river, snaking through an arid countryside with mud-roofed villages lining its banks and feluccas with lateen sails floating on its tide. In Egypt's Delta, however, the river dissolves into a thousand streams, canals and ditches which feed the precious water over a vast area. The line of demarcation between the lush vegetation with its flooded fields and the arid desert on both sides was abrupt and artificial, as if it had been drawn in by hand. From 15,000 feet the irrigated portion looked like a bright green rug, about an inch thick, which someone had carefully spread out to the very edge of the bright Mediterranean. The two deserts on either side seemed to have a paper thin crust stretched tightly over the earth's core like an overbaked rice pudding, burnt brown in patches.

I looked at my map and then down at the extraordinary landscape below me. Aviation maps usually only bear a diagrammatic resemblance to the landscape a pilot sees and it is necessary to puzzle out one's position by hard work and observation. The Delta, however, looked more like a map than the one in my hand, which had the irrigated area painted green and the desert ocher. It was so easy to locate myself that my mind drifted back to the Australians I was shortly to meet.

The only images I had were those provided by Uncle Frank's stories of the long agony of Gallipoli and the storming of Jerusalem by Allenby. Half naked bodies in demoniac activity, streaked with sweat, fed shells into the breeches of smoking cannon while implacable Turks with Asiatic visages advanced steadily upon them, and men with fur felts, the wide Australian bushwhacker hat with one side turned up, crawled on their bellies through enemy lines to cut Islamic throats in the darkness. I assumed that my Australians were going to be tame in comparison to my uncle's but I was looking forward to meeting the sons of those whooping, drunken heroes who had done such great deeds in the earlier war.

Qasaba was easy to locate in the empty terrain west of Alexandria, a cluster of camouflaged tents and vehicles, aircraft widely dispersed against air attack, and a portable windsock hanging limply in the light breeze. The landing strip was indicated by white canvas markers. Against the harshness of the desert the Mediterranean looked incongruously feminine and pretty with its narrow frill of surf.

I landed and taxied to the refueling area where an airman wearing a fur felt beckoned me into place. He was a big redheaded youngster and his khaki shorts were cuffed to expose muscular thighs, reddened with sunburn.

I jumped down excitedly from the cockpit.

"Is this kite for us?" he shouted.

There was a Hurricane running up its engine a hundred yards away and we had to raise our voices to communicate.

"Yes, it is. I'm joining your squadron as one of the pilots."

He frowned and turned away, walking quickly toward one of the large technical tents, abandoning me with my parachute and my small bag of belongings. He'd smiled at me at first but hearing my English accent had turned his back, shouting in the direction of some fur-felted airmen near the tent. It wasn't the welcome of my dreams.

A dust cloud approached, in the midst of which was a battered staff car. The driver, who was wearing an RAF service hat, I'd met once in India. He was Wizard Williams,[1] a senior army co-op pilot from one of the frontier squadrons. An identifiable Welshman with very black hair, blue eyes and a moustache, he had the reputation of being a wit with a gallows humour.

"Halloo!" he said, sticking his head out of the car's window. "I hope you'll like this God-forsaken place. Get in. We have a few of our chaps from India here. The rest are dinkum Aussies. The RAF's not popular in these parts. I'll tell you the whole sad story.

"The Australians don't want us?" I asked rather stupidly. "That airman . . . he just walked away from me."

"He was disappointed, that's all. They're all waiting and hoping for Aussie pilots to fly in. But you won't see too much of that sort of thing. They're good fellows most of them. Let's have a drink." He smiled at me - friendly and conspiratorial. "Let's take one thing at a time."

The officer's mess, a standard wooden hut, easily erected and pulled down, was crowded with bodies for the pre-lunch drink. Regulation collapsible wooden tables had been made into a makeshift bar, with crates of beer piled up behind them and canvas chairs were stacked up against the walls. Most of the officers were standing up and an Australian corporal was acting as barman.

"Gyppy beer, I'm afraid," Wizard said. "They keep promising us the strong Australian stuff but nothing's arrived yet. This is the land of promises - to be distinguished from the Promised Land which is a few miles further east."

---

1. **Squadron Leader R.D. Williams, DFC**

THE FIGHTING TRIBE

He introduced me all around in a Welsh accent, which he used to humorous effect without saying anything memorably funny. His style was ironic and self-deprecating and in the months ahead I seldom heard him speak entirely seriously. His gift for entertaining depended more on the lilt of his voice and the expression on his face than on the words he uttered. On this occasion his affability received little response and they nodded glumly at the announcement of my name. They were all in their late teens or early twenties and I thought they looked harder and fitter than Englishmen. One or two of them came, in fact, from farms in the outback, the products of life under a blazing sun all year round, but even those from the big towns had an open air look about them.

A discussion that my arrival had interrupted resumed on the subject of the Hawker Hurricane and Ray Hudson, a middle-sized titan from Sidney with cropped fair hair and muscled like a gymnast, was a big talker.

"Eight machine guns in the wings," he said wonderingly. "What a waste of fire power. If we were in a fighter squadron we could blast those Messerschmitts out of the sky. Can you imagine that hail of lead, all focused on a small target? We'd smash 'em to smithereens. They'd disintegrate!"

"Steady," said Wizard soberly. He was sucking on a cold pipe and took it out of his mouth to speak. "Better not get too excited about shooting planes down. We're not in the glory business. The army, God help us, tells us what to do. Firing guns in anger isn't our job."

This remark triggered a violent response in Ray Hudson. His handsome face flushed and he glared at Wizard in silence for a second. Then he burst out, unstoppable, righteous, his voice rising above the chatter of the bar with the urgency of rage. "We've got a right to be browned off at what's happened. We were all earmarked in Australia for Hurricane fighter squadrons in the Middle East and throughout my flying training in Rhodesia I know my category never changed. They promised us we'd go to an Australian fighter squadron and now we end up in a recce unit, tied hand and foot to the perishing army. What a blessed let down! Am I right?" There were supporting noises and some muffled cheers from the others.

"Tough titty," said Wizard, smiling dangerously over a raised glass of beer. It was obvious that already there was no love lost between these two.

Ray turned away, fierce and blue-eyed. I couldn't see his face as he spoke but the hut rang with his complaint. "We're volunteers not conscripts and we were promised we'd serve under Australian command. You can't trust Air Headquarters, sitting on their fannies in Cairo. They don't give a damn about us. Pilot Pope's[2] a good guy but we won't have him for long. He's going to be offered up as a sacrifice to the bloody army. It's enough to make you spew."

---

2. "Pilot" Pope was Squadron Leader, V.A. Pope.

"What pilot is he talking about?" I asked Wizard, when the noise level had died down a bit. "Pilot Pope," he replied. "That's his nickname. He's quite a chap. the most experienced army co-op man in the Middle East theatre. He's in the RAF and he's at present in command of this squadron, but the army's after his balls. He's in Cairo today fighting for his life with the staff wallahs. Pilot says he won't allow boys with only half a dozen hours on Hurricanes to carry out deep penetrations of enemy territory. He wants more time for training and he's sticking to his guns. He's quite right, of course, but he may lose the argument. There's a ghastly shortage of pilots and Rommel has panicked the higher ups out of their breeches, so it's become what one calls an inter-service issue. There isn't much love lost between the army and the air force these days, you know. We're all waiting with baited breath to see what happens next. And, as you've heard, there are other troubles. Some of these youngsters aren't exactly keeping a vow of silence about it. Come over here."

He led me to two canvas chairs placed against the wooden wall away from the crowded bar.

"This is the background. Three Squadron - an Australian fighter squadron - has made a helluva name for itself out here. You must have heard of Killer Caldwell.[3] He's a national hero to the Aussies. He's a sort of genius at shooting. Doesn't waste a round. So Ray Hudson and his crew could see themselves doing likewise, shooting down Messerschmitts and getting their names in the headlines of Australian newspapers. Now they're bitterly disappointed. They feel they'll never be heard of again. And I suppose they won't."

He assumed a childish treble.

"What did you do in the war, Daddy? I did reconnaissance for the Army, child."

I laughed.

"I wanted to be on fighters, too," I said. "I was sort of half trained for the fighter role in India. I can see their point."

"So can I," replied Wizard, his face suddenly serious. "The difference is that you're an old soldier compared to them. They didn't volunteer for anything as dull and unrewarding as reconnaissance."

"Are we going to stay with this squadron? I mean, it's an Aussie outfit. Won't they get their own C.O. and more of their own pilots?"

"I don't know. We're here to help out, even though we're not welcome. Apparently they can't find a senior Aussie trained in Army co-op. You know our people from India? They're ex-28 Squadron chaps. Malone, Carmichael and Pat Byers."

---

3. **Killer Caldwell was then Flight Lieutenant C.R. Caldwell, DFC and Bar. He flew with 250 Squadron and afterwards 112 Squadron and later commanded 112 Squadron. His score of victories in the desert was the highest - 20.5.**

"Yes, a bit. I was on the boat with Molly, but didn't see much of him. I met Pat Byers in the hills once."

"Well, they're Army co-op people. The idea is that we can train the others. Most of them have less than a hundred hours total flying, you know. Pilot Pope has made a beginning, or tried to. But he's in serious trouble with the higher-ups and if they kick him out I may be taking over the job, God help me! I certainly don't want it. Pommy bastards aren't too popular with the likes of Ray Hudson."

"Pommy bastards?"

"That's what they call us."

The word "pommy" does not connote anything good, as I soon discovered. It imitates in a derisory way the superior tones of the English upper class, and it is the democratic Australians' response to being dismissed as "Colonials". The word applies across class barriers to all Englishmen, and it has a more hostile edge to it than the American "limey", which merely reflects amusement at the quaint custom of issuing lime juice to British sailors. The bastard, which is usually added for emphasis, carries little weight in itself. Australians can use bastard as an alternative to fellow and a nice man will be referred to as a good bastard. I hadn't heard the term before because, although there were plenty of Australians in the regular RAF, they soft-pedalled their differences with Englishmen and most of them married English girls, settled down in Britain and in time disappeared into the folk, identifying themselves only by the occasional vowel sound or by opening their mouths a shade wider than we do when saying "car park". These wartime volunteer Aussies, however, were not tame. They were fresh out of their own environment and their behavior was as unmodified as their accents.

That afternoon I drew my "bivvy" from stores and set it up among the others clustered around the officer's mess tent. Bivvy is short for bivouac and it was the official designation for a one man tent. They were made of desert camouflaged canvas and stood three feet high and eight feet long, supported by two poles. I had to borrow a heavy mallet and an iron spike to make the necessary holes and hammer the tentpegs into the stony ground. Not everyone chose such private and limited accommodation. Some of the officers lived in a larger version that could take two people, but no one offered me a place in theirs and for the next eight months I slept alone in one of these Boy Scout shelters.

I went to bed that night disappointed by my reception and bewildered by Wizard's graphic introduction to the problems we faced. If I'd thought about it seriously beforehand I might have anticipated that they would resent dilution of the squadron by non-Australians. After all, the unit was 99% Australian and every man jack wanted to make it as famous as "Three", as No 3 Squadron, Royal Australian Air Force was always called. The pilots may have had their own gripe about not being used in the fighter role but the rank and file ground crews saw just as clearly that a unit led by an RAF squadron leader and supported by pilots from outside destroyed their image of themselves as an Aussie fighting force, hell bent for glory. It took all the fun out of the war and they were mad as hell.

Nevertheless I found them attractive as well as scary. They had lots of panache, walking with a swaggering unofficial stride and their way of speaking the English language - to my ear an intriguing mixture of London and Texas - was fascinating. I listened to its lilt like music, getting my tongue ready to imitate it, as I still can. But I knew they didn't view me as a friend and my hackles went up like a street dog at that thought.

Ray Hudson and Ed Kirkham could have modeled for recruiting posters advertising the ideal Australian warrior. Ed was lanky and dark haired but the contrast between them didn't end there. Ray was always in motion, his voice heard above the crowd. Ed was quiet, slow moving and humorous; the kind of character James Stewart used to play in the movies. They were always together. A couple of nights after I came to Qasaba I heard them chatting at the dinner table.

"How'd we get into this outfit?" said Ray loudly. "Who wants to spot for the Army? I want to shoot m'guns."

Ed grinned. He looked down at Ray and lowered his voice.

"Me, too. I wanna' be in Three. Straight fighters. No poms!" They both laughed.

The true size of the problem was not revealed to me until about ten days after I arrived. I got up in the night for a call of nature. It was a walk of several hundred yards to the latrines, a square of high canvas walls with an entrance on two sides. Inside was a row of pails and, separated by ten feet or so, "the bogs", a long rudely constructed wooden platform with holes cut at regular intervals. There was no privacy and by daylight I disliked it intensely, conversation with others on the job being apparently obligatory. Ray Hudson remembers laughing at me as I pretended admiration for the size of my morning dump, but my jocularity was covering embarrassment. I have never been a quick performer and had long become accustomed to studying immortal works during the necessary waiting period between the first and second movement of the bowels. The night was dark and I had to weave my way carefully through the officers' single bivouac tents dotted haphazardly about. They appeared in my path only when I was right on top of them; low camouflaged shapes, slightly paler than the dark sand. By day they looked like moored boats at the turn of the tide, facing all ways. In the darkness it was easy to trip over tent pegs, injuring one's feet and rousing the occupants.

Coming back I heard voices. Two tents had been placed close together, perhaps six feet apart. To converse with one another the occupants had to raise their voices a little. I couldn't identify the speakers except in a negative sense. Neither was Ray or Ed. One of the voices was deep and may been been Robertson, but I couldn't be sure. I stood still and listened.

"Molly Malone's a dimwit," the bass voice said.

This sounded good to my ears and I went on listening.

"Fuck'n wig on his head. He looks like one of the Ugly Sisters in a Pantomime. Talks like a powder puff. His mouth's full of marbles."

"Micky Carmichael prances around like a ballet dancer. His mouth's so tight he can't spit," the other said.

There was a pause.

"Did you see "M squared" with his book of poems? I reckon all the poms are queer."

"Just our luck to miss being with Killer Caldwell and ending up with a bunch of fairy poms who don't know how to fight.."

"Shit!"

There was a lull in the conversation and I continued on my way back to bed. But I couldn't sleep. To be a pom was misfortune enough. I'd digested that one. But to be identified as a homosexual was a disaster. Wizard, Molly, Pat Byers, Micky Carmichael and myself had been sent to Qasaba to give the squadron a backbone of experienced pilots but we could hardly lead the Aussies if they thought of us in those terms.

Molly certainly had a bizarre appearance. A childhood illness had rendered him hairless and he wore a rather crude blond wig which he only removed to don his flying helmet. He had joined the RAF as a university entrant from Cambridge and he had the Cambridge manner, clerical, precise and didactic. Whatever firm virtues he possessed - and Molly was far from a nonentity - it wouldn't be easy, I thought, for him to be accepted by these people.

I noted that there were no derogatory references to Wizard or to Pat Byers. Pat was red haired, freckled from head to toe, and built like a truck. He had been a rugger hero at his public school and his formidable masculinity could not be questioned. Wizard's advantages were also fairly clear. There is something about a Welsh accent that cuts across class and cultural lines. When humor and geniality is added you have a passport stamped for all nations. I learned long afterwards that Welsh means foreign in Anglo-Saxon; and there was a sense in which he was as foreign to the English officers as he was to the Australian. He played on this ambiguity. He was very sly and political, a veritable Welsh wizard, walking unscathed through the minefields left in our path by the brutalities of British colonial history.

Carmichael was tiny, with a mop of auburn hair and he, too, did not impress at first sight. He was a second generation regular officer, whose father was a Group Captain in England. He turned out to be a gutsy little fellow but his rather exaggerated accent - he sounded "that" as "thet" - reinforced the impression they already had that he was an effete member of a decadent ruling class.

MESSERSCHMITT ROULETTE

I stretched out on the hard ground, staring up into the darkness, focussing glumly on our hopeless disadvantages. We wore very wide, long shorts that cut the knee cap. Everyone wore them in India and I had not previously noted how ridiculous they looked. It was the duty of an officer's bearer to see that they were starched to crispness. We had to own half a dozen pairs, for they could only be worn once before losing their shape. In the desert we wore them many days running and washed them ourselves, often in salt water. Even freshly ironed they looked more like skirts or culottes, absurd garments that did not suit the masculine figure, making it appear hippy and feminine. But not more absurd than the oversize RAF solar topi, light, bulky headgear designed to keep out 120 degrees of heat which we had all brought with us from the North West Frontier. The taller people looked topheavy and spindly, all head and hips and stick-like arms and legs. The shorter ones, like Carmichael, looked truly preposterous. Dressed all in khaki he moved around like a giant toadstool.

The Aussies, by contrast, wore abbreviated shorts that emphasized the muscularity of their buttocks and thighs, and on their head they wore the romantic Digger's hat. They really looked like a warrior tribe, athletic, bronzed and dangerous. We considered ourselves to be professional military persons and we were conscious of the fact that our nation had a great fighting tradition, but we were different. No so obviously masculine, undemocratic of speech. Even a very rich Aussie - a machine gun outfit nearby was commanded by a McArthur-Onslow,[3] whose family owned legendary acres of sheep farms - felt obliged to speak as if he were one of the boys. We, on the other hand, had special voices that proclaimed we had been to special schools for gentlemen. We said "awfully sorry" and "frightfully good". All this sounded reedy against the more natural Australian tones, reinforcing the disadvantage of our ladylike shorts and butterfly-catcher hats.

I had been damned for reading poetry and I cursed my own carelessness for that. The only book I'd brought with me from India was W.B. Yeats' **Collected Poems** and I'd walked around with the volume in my hand, even propping it up on the mess table at breakfast time for all to see. It was a shock to be characterized as a cowardly degenerate. Not that I accepted for a second that homosexuals lacked military virtues. A brief review gave the lie to that - the Spartans, Alexander the Great, Richard the Lionheart, General Gordon of Khartoum, Siegfried Sassoon, Wilfrid Owen.

I lay awake for hours that night. At first I thought of seeing Wizard and asking to be sent elsewhere, but the objection to that course of action was that it would confirm the impression that I was a coward and didn't want to fight. It would be interpreted as desertion in the face of the enemy and Wizard would suspect my motives. I went to sleep with the problem unresolved.

I'd just landed from a practice flight the next day when Doc Reid approached me. He was the squadron medical officer, a distinguished

---

3. **Later Major General Sir Denzil McArthur-Onslow.**

surgeon who had given up a prosperous practice to join in the war. He was in his mid-forties, had pale blue eyes and fair hair going grey at the edges. An ex-alcoholic, he sipped away at a soft drink in the mess while everyone else was lapping beer. He looked more like a boxer than a surgeon, with his big chest and shoulders and his springy walk. He was the senior Australian, but even if he had not been so by rank he would have taken precedence by his personality. He looked, and was, formidable. I never saw him angry, though one feared his anger. He gave the impression of immense power in reserve; a sort of bottled-up violence that never rose to the surface.

He put his hand on my shoulder.

"Geoff," he said, "Wizard asked me to talk to the boys about how things are going. You must have noticed they're not exactly thrilled to be a recce outfit."

"Who is?"

I picked up my parachute and we walked together over to the flight tent. It was a small marquee containing a couple of collapsible tables. In one corner was an untidy pile of parachutes. I tossed mine on top of the heap.

"And they'd really like an all-Aussie squadron. Wizard knows. It's understandable."

"I know it too."

"You've heard some talk?"

"Yes."

"I'm telling the boys to keep their hair on. They're disappointed, but we're in a war. We're all in this together. If you hear any piss and wind, let me know. Everyone's got to pipe down and get on with the job."

"I'm bloody angry."

"What's the matter?"

"I heard one bugger say I was a pansy because I read poetry. And I'd like to say that I can't alter the way I speak to sound more manly to an Australian. I'm no bloody pansy."

He grinned.

"Don't take any notice. It's just ignorance. I spent three years in London doing my surgery. I know how you poms go on!"

We both laughed.

"None of these boys has been out of Australia before. We've all got to settle down and respect one another."

"Well, I didn't start anything, Doc."

"Calm down, Geoff. I'll talk to you again."

He walked away towards the officers' bivouac tents and I saw him squat down beside a group of pilots, their heads all turned towards him.

MESSERSCHMITT ROULETTE

III

WIZARD WILLIAMS

I spent a lot of time lying in my tent, smoking one cigarette after another, and thinking about the situation. It was in the days when everyone smoked. Wizard and Molly smoked pipes and all the other officers cigarettes, with the sole exception of Doc Reid, ex-smoker, ex-drunk and man without vices. Tobacco was free for all ranks. All the officers had to do was to ask for a pack when they went to the bar for a drink. The most available brand was "C to C", short for "Cape to Cairo" and often called "Camel to Consumer", which kept me coughing throughout my desert tour.

I couldn't discuss my problem with Molly or Carmichael, for obvious reasons, and I didn't know Pat Byers well enough to confide in him. I felt like a skier who has slipped into an invisible crevasse and it would be a long hard struggle to climb out. I had been disgraced without committing a crime. I liked the Aussies, which made it worse and I had no such prejudice against them as they had against us. I thought they were being grossly unfair. At the same time I sympathized with their desire to have their own people in charge of the squadron and I was amused by the comments of the anonymous voices on Molly and Micky. I didn't, however, want to be included in the overall judgment. It was a false conviction, anyway. Neither of them was a homosexual. Molly was just a cranky upperclass Englishman with a wig. Hard to get the Aussies to see that.

I would have to do something. Deeds not words were the answer. If we'd been a fighter squadron I could have acquired merit by shooting down enemy aircraft, gaining victories and cashing them in for universal respect and approbation. Reconnaissance, whatever that turned out to be, didn't seem to offer any yardstick for achievement that I could use. We had such a flat, unglamorous non-scoring job, flying west into enemy territory to observe "areas of interest" to the army and bringing back the info. How do you build up a reputation delivering routine reports? Dodging Messerschmitts is unpleasant but not really interesting. If you evade successfully, everyone thinks it must be easy. If you don't you're dead! The only thing I could do was to fly as much as possible. The more experienced I became and the more useful I was, the better would be my position in the squadron. I'd try to fly twice as much as anyone else. I'd volunteer for every flight going. With this rather simple response worked out I felt better. I hadn't solved anything but at least I had a plan.

MESSERSCHMITT ROULETTE

Egypt's Western Desert, which is the eastern edge of the great desert of North Africa, is one of the better places in the world to fight a war, for it has only a small and scattered population of Arabs whose dark tents we rarely saw. In other respects it was less satisfactory, being no tonic to the eye, except perhaps after heavy rain when the whole landscape turns into a pattern of shallow lakes. There are no white Saharan sand dunes for the French Foreign Legion Camel Corps to sashay down, as in the movies. It is brown, flat, stony. Any movement of vehicles raises clouds of dust and when the wind blows sand gets into everything. It gets into the eyes and collects in the ears and nose. Shoes fill up and have to be periodically emptied. Every mouthful of food tastes gritty. The occasional escarpment, a problem for tanks and often the scene of the fiercest fighting, is the only relief from flatness. We lay on the hard ground with a groundsheet and a folded blanket beneath us and ate a diet that consisted of easily transported rations - bully beef and biscuits. The canned pressed beef was often mixed with pulverized biscuits to form rissoles, and the anti-scurvy tablets would be piled up in saucers and placed at strategic points on the unstained wooden tables to compensate for the absence of vegetables in our diet. Those who didn't partake, said Doc Reid authoritatively, would get desert sores.

I have not mentioned fleas. They lived in the Western Desert in vast numbers, feeding on God knows what when human bodies did not offer themselves. Everyone had fleas. Pilots and tank crews and army generals had them. Rommel, who often slept on the ground or in the back of a truck, must have had fleas. To rid ourselves of them we would take a truck to the beach a few miles north of the airfield and swim naked in the blue water. Then we'd wash our clothes out. Micky Carmichael even had some special soap that lathered in salt water, but the fleas returned at once, eager to inhabit fresh clothes. My body was covered in tiny puncture marks. They were sand fleas, not the orthodox fat shiny body fleas such as one finds on cats and dogs in Europe. They were small, difficult to locate, and on their own soil completely ineradicable.

We were also plagued with flies. The large number of unburied corpses favoured the fly population and during battles they multiplied. We became used to brushing them away from our faces by a more or less continuous movement of the hands. Some people used the fashionable fly switches, which were essentially a bit of horsehair attached to a stick, but they could get very fancy and expensive. The joke went round that if you saw a person in Cairo waving his hands across his face for no reason, he'd just come in from the desert.

In August, 1941 with Europe fallen to Hitler's armies, the single battlefield open to British arms was this one and even here there was a lull in the fighting. In December, 1940, General Sir Archibald Wavell had launched a skillful attack with the inadequate forces available to him and had pushed the Italians, commanded by General Graziani, back to the Cyrenaican port of

Benghazi, a distance of over a thousand kilometres from Alexandria, thus relieving the Axis threat to Egypt. At this point he ran into technical problems; most of his tanks had to be withdrawn to bases in Egypt for repair, leaving Benghazi lightly defended. American Lend-Lease was in its early stages and there was a chronic shortage of equipment for waging the swift moving war - almost like a war at sea - that the Western Desert permitted.

Wavell's problems were complicated by the constant diversion of men and material away from the all-important desert theatre. Winston Churchill, as he makes clear in his memoirs, was determined to fight anywhere and everywhere it was possible to confront the enemy. He was obsessed with the strategic importance of the battle for North Africa but he nevertheless insisted on British, Australian and New Zealand forces being sent from the Middle East to defend Greece. This was a lost cause. The Germans attacked in strength on 6 April 1941 supported by a tenfold air superiority. It was all over by the 24th and Greece formally surrendered. At Churchill's insistence Crete was then reinforced in an attempt to hold it. It was attacked by overwhelming parachute forces on May 20th - the first time that any major use had been made of this form of warfare - and the final evacuation of our forces took place on May 30th. Five thousand British and Imperial troops were captured. It is possible that Churchill's policy was correct - German losses of paratroopers had been excessive - but it made Wavell's task in the desert impossible. Iraq had erupted under the pro-German, Raschid Ali, who on April 29th had moved to capture Habbaniya, the RAF's main training base. The rebellion was suppressed by a combination of forces from the Middle East and India. Finally, a small force had to be sent to wrest control of Syria from the Vichy French, who had permitted the Germans to establish air bases within striking distance of Egypt.

When German armoured divisions arrived in North Africa in March, 1941 commanded by General Erwin Rommel, Wavell's weakened army was rolled swiftly back and once again there was a threat to the security of the Egyptian base. Churchill became dissatisfied with Wavell, relieved him of his command and sent him to India as Commander-in-Chief. His replacement was General Sir Claude Auchinleck.

In the summer of 1941 many observers of the war thought that Russia could only hold out for three months, when the full force of the Nazi war machine would concentrate on a mopping-up operation in the Middle East. In fact the curtain was rising on one of the most interesting conflicts of the war. It would be waged back and forth, from the environs of Alexandria to the port of Tunis, until the final expulsion of Axis forces from North Africa in May, 1943.

It was during a pause in the fighting, while Rommel was regrouping for his next assault on Egypt, that No. 451 Squadron was formed. Its job was to provide aerial reconnaissance for No. 13 Corps, which at that time consisted of the New Zealand Division and the 4th Indian Division. Only the isolated garrison at Tobruk was seeing fighting and this was mainly bombing and artillery attacks. When Rommel swept along the coast towards Egypt, Tobruk's garrison held out. The little white-walled town with its thirty-five miles of fortified perimeter was manned by the 9th Australian Division and some British tanks and infantry, all under the command of Major General Leslie Morshead, an Australian. German and Italian troops were camped outside the perimeter and Stukas from nearby Axis airfields flew over every day to hammer away at targets, undisturbed by British fighters. An attempt was made, early on in the siege to operate Hurricanes of 73 Squadron from Tobruk, but the proximity of El Adem and the overwhelming German air superiority made it little more than a gallant attempt.[1] They were all shot down, though not all the pilots were killed.

The twenty-five thousand men of the garrison were maintained solely by the Royal Navy and a few merchant vessels, which had to get in and out of Tobruk without fighter cover. Destroyers would steam out of Alexandria or Mersa Matruh and make a dash under cover of darkness to Tobruk harbour, the approaches to which were closely mined with only a narrow channel kept open. The landing crews on the dockside included a picked band of Indian troops who worked frenziedly to get the tanks, shells, spare parts and other necessaries ashore while darkness lasted, so that the ships could be well out to sea before the Luftwaffe began to search for them at dawn. Even then they were often pursued by bombers until they reached their port in Egypt.

In August, 1941 British forces held the line of the Egyptian frontier with Libya. It was called "the wire" because a barbed wire fence ran south from the coastline deep into the trackless waste. A number of small forts, most of them damaged by artillery fire, provided the only useful landmarks. No. 13 Corps Headquarters required regular reconnaissance of enemy territory to ensure that our forces were not surprised by an attack, and No. 451 Squadron, most of whose pilots were newly trained, were to carry out these missions in Hurricanes they were still learning to handle. None of the young Australians had heard a single word of instruction on army co-operation. Pilot

---

1. **Air Marshal Sir Peter Wykeham KCB, DSO, OBE, DFC, AFC has this to say about the air defense of Tobruk.**

"I was commanding officer of 73 Squadron in the spring of 1941, first inside Tobruk and later and Sidi Hanaish. It was a very bad time as we were outclassed by the 109s, heavily outnumbered, and hopelessly placed tactically. Our losses were very heavy, both inside and outside Tobruk. During my six months in command I lost 120 percent of my pilot strength, including four flight commanders.

"We shot down a number of Stukas and 109s. Few of these were confirmed as the battles were always over enemy territory, or over the small Tobruk perimeter. On the whole I think our losses were about the same as our victories, or somewhat more. The poor profit/loss ratio was increased by the fact that we did a lot of ground attacks on airfields, where we lost heavily to German light flak. Our role was to keep up some appearance of participation, so that the army should not feel deserted by the air force, but the heavy cost of this was known, and we were urged to hold out until the Desert Air Force could be reinforced with new fighter squadrons." (Page 222 *Fighters Over the Desert*.)

WIZARD WILLIAMS

Pope, who had protested that the unit wasn't ready to go on full operational status, was removed a few weeks after my arrival and Wizard Williams took over. I only saw Pilot a couple of times and never spoke to him. He was a fresh faced muscular man with one of those big George Washington visages that give such confidence to the troops. He was very serious and dedicated and the thought crossed my mind that he would have been the ideal leader for some simpler situation than ours. A squadron divided into hostile groups and grossly unprepared for its role might do better with a humorist than a hero.

The squadron had got off to a poor start and none of its troubles ever quite went away, but what saved it was the alliance of Wizard and Doc Reid. Even before Wizard was designated CO they began visiting the technical sections together, speaking to the men, demonstrating their solidarity with one another and providing a model of unity to all of us. They spent time in the officer's mess bar, drawing the pilots into discussion by openly venting the operational issues. I don't know whether to credit Wizard with extraordinary political wisdom or Doc Reid with amazing control over his fellow countrymen, but I suspect that their success in pulling the unit into shape was due to a perfect meeting of their gifts.

Doc was a natural leader, a man's man, a pilot as well as a surgeon. He only once referred to his alcoholism in my presence, but part of his charisma was a sense that he'd hit bottom, experienced shame and finally conquered his personal devils. He didn't have the narrow, long-jawed face that looks so well in a fur felt, but for all that no one looked more Australian than Doc did, and his speech was a drawl unmodified by his residence in England.

Wizard, as I've said, wasn't an identifiable pom. He was better educated than most of us as well as being older, having a degree from a Welsh university, but it was not part of his personality to show any indication of superiority. The character he assumed with every indication of naturalness was of our Welsh uncle, a victim of circumstances like ourselves, forced to circumvent the harsh impositions of fate by wit and vigilance. It was not a threatening image and only a heart of granite would have failed to respond.

My memories of those early days are of Wizard seated at the bar, a glass of beer in front of him, talking to Stan Reid about his daily skirmishes with 13 Corps HQ while the pilots stood around listening. When he returned from meetings at corps headquarters, he needed a drink and an audience. He had a gift for informal chat and little as a lecturer. I once heard him address the men and the flavour of his personality was missing. He liked to be irreverent and critical and the pep talk style didn't suit him at all. Doc Reid had probably persuaded him that delivering the news of the day while it was still fresh was good for morale, so the unplanned chats became a regular feature.

21

"I was wooed by the gentlemen at corps today, Stan," he said, "but I kept my knees together like a Swansea virgin. Oh, they were so nice to me. Majors and colonels with their red tabs, beautifully dressed. Maps and plans, neat as you please. But I tucked my skirts around my ankles. Didn't let them see a bloody thing."

His Welsh voice elongated the "o" sounds, so that "wooed" and "so" were almost sung.

"They wanted my co-operation."

He smiled at Doc, making of "co-operation" a long and seductive word. Stretching back in his canvas chair he looked around at his audience of twenty-year olds.

"Our brothers in the army are a little slow of wit. Their brains get damaged, you know, with all that stamping on the barrack square. And I don't believe they've learned much since Waterloo."

Wellington's victory probably didn't mean much to his hearers but he enunciated the word as if it were a magic spell.

Molly Malone was standing up behind him, very serious, not joining in the laughter at the army's expense. He was a loyal army co-operator and slightly disapproved of Wizard's tone.

"Did you manage to see the Brigadier?" he asked.

"Took me to lunch, no less. Glass of sherry. Napkins. A perfect gentleman is Brigadier Horrocks. Smooth as silk. If he slipped a knife in your gizzard you wouldn't feel it till next morning. Didn't have a clue about aeroplanes."

"Did he give us a list of tasks?"

"Yes, Molly. He wanted us to take photographs of the whole Western Desert. I had to tell him there's such a thing as the German Air Force. It is not in the nature of those buggers, I said, to let themselves be snapped, as if they were sitting for a studio portrait to send back to their mums."

Murmurs of "Jeez" and "Stupid bastard" from the onlookers. Wizard sucked on his pipe. He knew that he had everyone's complete attention.

Like a stooge in a comedy act, Doc Reid supplied questions on cue.

"Did you accept anything?"

"Noo! I just let him run on. His next idea was a daily reconnaissance as far as the Tobruk perimeter. I told him there was a string of fighter airfields just south of the coastal road. On a routine basis we'd lose all our pilots before the army made their next push forward."

"What'e say to that?"

He sipped on his beer and wiped his moustache, like an actor filling a pause with stage business.

"Said he understood. He wasn't pulling rank. Just feeling his way. I'll have to watch him like a hawk, though. His staff are hundred percent dimwitted pongos who don't know their arses from their elbows."

Molly pursed his lips at this inter-service blasphemy. Wizard went on.

"I told him our Hurricanes were just a lit-tle on the slow side. And we'll be flying low down. Through the flak, you know. The Jerry fighters won't even have to search for us. The ground gunners will display our pretty tails to them. Like beaters, I told him, flushing out partridge. He loved that. Very huntin' shootin' is Horrocks. Intelligent, though."

"It's a lousy job," said Hudson morosely.

"Here endeth the first lesson," said Wizard, beaming ironically at Ray. "It's not going to be any picnic, young chap."

"But we've got eight guns. We can take 'em on," said Kirkham. He looked over Hudson's head with an unlined, innocent visage.

"That's brave talk," said Wizard. "Young bloods eager to take on the Hun in mortal combat." The term "Hun" was employed in a pejorative sense throughout the Great War of 1914-1918, but by 1941 it had lost its sting and was only used for humorous effect.

"What's wrong with that?"

"Number one, we're a reconnaissance outfit and are meant to return with the dope on enemy movements, we're not encouraged to get involved in vulgar brawls. Number two, the Messerschmitts have near a hundred miles an hour on us in level flight." [2]

"Hundred miles an hour!"

"And diving down on us from God knows what altitude they'd have all the advantage. Forget your dreams of glory, Ed. Put on your red wig and your false nose and learn to be inconspicuous. Save your energy for running away. That's our game, I'm afraid."

"Shit," said Hudson.

Doc Reid was the oldest man present by twenty years, yet he had already established such a commitment to the squadron that no one questioned his function as defender of Australian rights at all levels and this included flying operations. He looked anxious as he asked the vital question.

"Horrocks must have got something out of you, Wiz. What did you agree to do?"

"I said we'd fly as far as Halfaya, Sollum, Capuzzo, just beyond the Libyan border. No long range sorties as yet."

Ah, I thought. Wizard deserves his nickname. Pilot Pope fights gallantly for realistic tasks for our rookies and gets the boot for his trouble. Wizard, however, sits down with Brigadier Horrocks and they agree to charm the breeches off each other. Match drawn! Very funny.

This agreement, in fact, lasted a good while and if it hadn't held I believe we'd have suffered serious losses early on. As it happened, we were able to keep a watchful eye on the strongly defended coastal positions. We became so familiar with the enemy's camps and forts on the Libyan-Egyptian border that we could detect the presence of even small Axis reinforcements.

---

2. **Comparing Messerschmitt Bf 109- F to Hawker Hurricane I.**

If we'd been forced to fly further west we could not have avoided the Luftwaffe airfields - and we weren't ready to tackle enemy fighters at such a disadvantage in height and speed. I was still learning to fly the Hurricane. The cockpit looked cluttered and unfamiliar to me and my use of brakes, pitch controls, undercarriage and flaps were not yet instinctive.[3]

John Herington, in his **Air War Against Germany and Italy: 1939-1943** says that beginning on August 9th a number of sorties were flown to the Tobruk perimeter by No. 451 Squadron, accompanied by strong fighter escort. I don't believe this is accurate. I had just arrived in the squadron and every detail of those days is imprinted in my mind. Ray Hudson has confirmed my impression that it has been misreported. I think it was this issue that Pilot Pope contended with 13 Corps and lost. Wizard was more successful at handling outrageous requests and his greatest contribution throughout was his control of what sorties the pilots flew. He struggled with the army brass to the end, using all his persuasive arts to modify their demands. He was quite alone in this and always dealing with officers of another service who were much senior to himself.

1941 was a bad year for inter-service co-operation. Things had gone pretty poorly for us since 1940, when the British Expeditionary Force in France had been routed by the German tanks and pounded by bombers as they made their way to the northern ports. The soldiers had looked in vain for RAF fighters to protect them. In some areas of southern England where the beaten army was regrouping after the evacuation at Dunkirk, it had become embarrassing and on occasion dangerous to be seen in air force uniform, particularly after dark. The decision to withdraw our few precious fighter squadrons from a campaign that could not be won had been made at the highest national level. When the Battle of Britain commenced in the summer of 1940, this hard decision saved the nation. The Luftwaffe, superior in numbers, threw its full force into an attempt to overwhelm the RAF and open the way to an invasion of England. It did not succeed, but it was a close thing. The honour of the RAF was, for the time being, re-established. During the next year, however, there were more terrible defeats in the Mediterranean. Greece and Crete were fought over before being evacuated, while the Germans, in total command of the air, ceaselessly attacked the retreating troops and sank ships at will.

---

3. **"Pope inaugurated these Tobruk flights on 9th August,"** Herington writes, **"when he made an intensive reconnaissance of the eastern and western perimeter sectors, and fifteen similar sorties were completed successfully before the end of the month, each time strong escorts of fighters being provided."** *Air War Against Germany and Italy 1939-1943* by John Herington, Halstead Press, Sydney, 1954, page 101. Both Ray Hudson and I believe that General Morshead's requests for reconnaissance resulted in this project. It was never carried out, however, because Pope rightly and righteously opposed it. He won his battle with higher authority, but, as so often happens in such cases, lost his job.

It was not the RAF's fault that it was outnumbered and defeated in these battles. Planes were simply not available in sufficient numbers. Lord Beaverbrook, as Minister of Aircraft Production, was doing legendary work in animating and reorganizing the industry and the production of aeroplanes was a national priority, but the rank and file in both the army and the navy blamed the flying boys for not being there when needed. Wizard had to make his case for a cautious use of our resources to army staff officers who tended to believe that the air force was already cautious to the point of being cowardly.

Wizard was very explicit about this at one of his evening sessions. They were not unlike present day TV interviews, with Doc Reid as the interrogator and the pilots acting as an informal panel, interrupting occasionally with a question or a comment.

"Major Hurst was very fierce today," Wizard said. "He thinks the livers of airmen are decidedly on the pale side compared to the juicy purple innards of infantry officers."

"He doesn't get insulting, does he?" asked Doc.

"Noo! A hair short of that. Though a hundred years ago it would have been pistols at dawn. I'd enjoy shooting the bugger at twenty paces."

"What about Horrocks?"

Wizard sucked on his pipe.

"Horrocks saves the day. None of them would dare talk such crap in front of him. But little Hurst was dive bombed in Northern France and we weren't there to shoot down the nasty Germans. He'll never forgive us."

Molly smiled his classroom smile.

"Army co-operation is meant to be carried out in an atmosphere of mutual trust. Their requests should be reasonable and we should surely comply."

"That's what it says in the textbooks," said Wizard, "but too many of these pongos [4] have blood in their eyes. They think we fly through the air with the greatest of ease and don't suffer like the brave soldiers do. This morning one of them wanted to send a sortie to Mechili."

"Where's that," said one of the Aussies.

"A hundred miles past Tobruk. With full tanks we'd never get there and back. Hurst looked at me as if I should have volunteered to go myself and perish in the attempt. He just loves the idea of sending us out to die."

"Well done, Wiz," said Doc, putting a hairy surgeon's hand on Wizard's shoulder.

---

4. "Pongo" is RAF slang for an army officer, and it carries the connotation of being stupid, excessively conventional and classridden, and unwilling to consider the Royal Air Force as a superior service.

MESSERSCHMITT ROULETTE

IV

PANIC AT HELLFIRE PASS
(9 August 1941)

My mental agonies over poor relationship with the Australians were short lived because I began almost immediately to fly on operations and it blew every other trouble out of my mind. It is strange that one can be obsessed with a subject one day and oblivious of it the next, but I think the same process happened to all of us in some degree. The carping and protesting died down as soon as we began crossing regularly over into enemy territory. Our casual talk changed to the various kinds of flak, the dangers presented by enemy fighters and methods to avoid being killed by them. In the presence of sudden death, which we hadn't thought much about before, we had common experiences and common interest drawing us together, assisting in the work of unifying the squadron which Wizard and Doc Reid had begun. I forgot my wounded pride at being rejected by the Aussies as I underwent my first important failure in the air.

Molly Malone, because of his seniority and experience, was designated flight commander. Behind his kindly, rather lofty manner was a very strong personality fired with enthusiasm for his craft. He was eager to teach all he knew and Doc Reid had persuaded the Aussies to listen to what he had to say. Little groups of pilots would gather round him in the flight tent and he would instruct them in the techniques of identifying and counting objects on the ground, the importance of rechecking data that might be significant to the army commander, how to record each item on a knee pad with the time of observation alongside it.

To my mind his whole discourse stank of Cloud Cuckoo Land. Weightless anti-aircraft shells, enemy fighters that didn't kill you but simply moved you five squares down the board to challenge the next throw of the dice, the big prize going to the guy who made the neatest log entries. One point subtracted for every 5% error in totals. Two points for all errors in location greater than one mile. The umpire's decision is final. Unreal!

Early in August he took me out as cover. The squadron we had replaced started the practice of aircraft flying in pairs, one making the reconnaissance and the second weaving behind and keeping a look-out for enemy fighters.

The briefing for Molly's sortie was held in the army liaison tent. It had several tables and many canvas chairs, a chest of drawers for maps and an upright display map of the area as far west as Derna, with little flags marking

German and Italian units. Hugh Davies, a former London stockbroker aged about thirty whose tank regiment was re-equipping at a depot near Alexandria, was the 13 Corps Air Liaison Officer assigned to the squadron. Just before departing for the Middle East he had married a gorgeous blonde actress and on his honeymoon performed sexual prodigies, but south of Benghazi his tank was blown up and he lost one testicle. He told a hilarious story of his recovery in hospital and how with infinite caution he satisfied his anxieties about potency. Apparently one is plenty. He pointed to the situation map.

"Corps thinks things are a lot too quiet these days. Rommel may be working up for another move."

He frowned and then grinned at us, expressing concern and encouragement in turn.

"We'd want to know if there was any increase of movement along the coastal road, of course, particularly around Bardia and Sollum. Concentrations of motor transport and armour. The General is very interested in Fort Capuzzo. It should be difficult to hide tanks in that area. A strong positive or negative would be useful. They're operating an airfield here."

He pointed to a spot on the map near the coast, halfway to Tobruk.

"I know you'll keep a good lookout for fighters."

One of the nicest things about Hugh was his genuine air of concern for our lives. He was upper-class Jewish, had been in battle, and now had a safe job for a while sending other people into danger. On this occasion he was looking agreeably pained at having to send two of his fellow mortals into enemy territory at the risk of their testicles. He was popular for another reason; he did not, like so many army people who had suffered from German air superiority in past campaigns, blame the airmen for their woes.

When the briefing was over, we walked to the flight tent and Molly took the opportunity to prime me on his mode of operation. He smiled seductively, his golden moustache bristling vigorously on his upper lip, contrasting with the mop of dyed and lifeless hair perched on the top of his head. I couldn't help like him and mistrust him at the same time. He treated me like a romantic child who had to be instructed in the facts of life, lest he ruin his prospects and end up in the French Foreign Legion or by emigrating to Canada, the traditional escape routes for failed Englishmen.

"Geoffrey," he said, "We'll do this together and you can see what sort of report the army expects from a recce pilot. I know you have yearnings to be a fighter boy but really they have a boring job compared to us. Waiting around all day, sitting on their parachutes and then taking off en masse like a gaggle of geese. No individuality required. This is far more interesting work, don't you think?"

I suppose he must have said much the same things to the young Australians. I couldn't see Hudson or Kirkham being convinced that flying for the army was better than fighters. It was just his standard gas to the junior pilots. I smiled back but didn't reply.

PANIC AT HELLFIRE PASS

"I'll fly at 4000 feet, which I think is the best height for observation of vehicles. You can easily tell lorries from tanks and tanks from armoured cars at that height. Track marks are helpful too in identifying tanks. We may have to go a little lower down to observe built-in gun emplacements. When we get back I'll show you how I've recorded the data. One has to be neat in one's recording. A good recce pilot's knee pad should be clear enough to be read by anyone without additional explanation. Ideally, if you were shot down and the pad recovered it should render a complete account of your sortie to the army. In this featureless terrain we have to be especially careful about map co-ordinates. We mustn't be content with vague information. The army has a right to know the exact position of enemy forces and precise numbers. I always recheck every item. It's a good habit for a recce pilot to get into."

I listened to him elaborating on the care and precision required of that most exquisite product of Western civilization, the well-trained recce pilot. All this time I was wondering if his reactions would be quick enough if we were bounced by enemy aircraft.

We took off in bright sunshine at about ten o'clock in the morning and climbed. In a few minutes I dropped behind and began weaving, scanning the sky for fighters. We flew parallel with the coast towards the German lines until we saw "the wire", a faint but discernible trace on the landscape below. Molly then turned north towards what I'd already identified in my own mind as trouble. From 4000 feet the desert looked flat, still and empty. It was hard to believe that warring armies were involved in a scene so apparently uninhabited. The blue sea shimmered engagingly in the strong sunlight and was totally devoid of shipping. Molly was aiming for his first reconnaissance point, Halfaya Pass ("Hellfire Pass"), the most noted defensive position in the area and the most easily recognizable of landmarks. The paved coastal road here traverses the plateau of an escarpment and then winds tightly through a pass down to the port of Sollum. Rommel had halted his advance here while he built up reserves for a further push towards the Egyptian Delta. Hugh Davies had warned us of the intense anti-aircraft fire we could expect from Halfaya and I expected Molly to skirt the area.

My first shock came when he flew directly over this defensive position, dipping his wing slightly to observe the ground. A minute later a pattern of large black puffs appeared below and behind our tails. Then the gunners adjusted their aim and the puffs were all around us, above and below and ahead. It was an eerie experience. Over the roar of the engine no sound of explosions could be heard and the shell bursts looked harmless, small black clouds that dissipated in the bright air. I had heard of box barrages in which a number of guns programme a pattern in the sky to catch invaders in a net of fire, so my instinct was to dive at once out of danger. They had estimated our height correctly. Molly was flying at precisely 4000 feet as if he were co-operating in some gunnery exercise with our own troops, and it seemed to me only a matter of time before we collided with one of those explosions.

I pressed my R/T button on the stick for the first time.

"Molly, let's get out of this."

No reply.

"I think we ought to change height."

Nothing. I weaved behind Molly's tail in exaggerated swoops, losing and gaining height in steep turns back and forth. I felt I had to take some evasive action but couldn't do it effectively without leaving Molly altogether. It was no good searching the skies for fighters because there was too much confusion to the eye with the black puffs all round us. We were flying straight through the barrage and Molly even stopped his slight turn and was proceeding parallel to the coast towards Bardia.

Suddenly we outflew the defensive system and were in the clear.

Behind us a flock of dispersing puffs drifted over Halfaya and Sollum. Looking west I could see no dangerous black specs against the sky, no dust clouds marring the desert's peace which would indicate that fighters were taking off to pursue us. In the bright atmosphere the jagged coastline was sharply etched against the dark blue of the sea and the coastal highway stretched like a white ribbon beside it. I said nothing as we turned on to a southerly heading for a while and then north towards the coast. I could see Molly looking out of his starboard window, then his head would drop as he wrote on his knee pad.

As we approached Bardia, a small seaside town west of Sollum, the anti-aircraft fire began again. Molly flew on as if he were sightseeing. He didn't react to the fire with so much as a movement of his wings, keeping his speed steady at 180 miles per hour.

"Can't you see the flak?"

No reply.

"Change height, for Pete's sake."

He might have been deaf as well as bald. The barrage was not as concentrated as over Halfaya but I began to get very angry at being dragged unnecessarily through it. It is common sense that a barrage, which is visible for up to fifty miles on a clear day, is an indication to enemy fighters that their airspace is being invaded. I don't believe the Germans had radar or its equivalent in those early days but they had normal vision. Even if we didn't get ourselves shot down by the guns, we might well be sitting ducks to the fighters on the airfield Hugh Davies had indicated on the map, who only had to follow the traces of our path to pick us up easily. I weaved violently, trying to concentrate on my job of fighter spotting and looking anxiously up the coast to the west for dust clouds.

The gunfire petered out again and Molly turned in a leisurely sweep south towards Fort Capuzzo, just west of the frontier wire. He had not altered his speed and probably had not touched his throttle since gaining height. The sky was clear of fighters. Were we too unimportant to justify a reaction? Had they just landed from a sweep and were refueling? Fort Capuzzo looked dead. It wasn't much of a fort, though you could see the outline of a major building that must have been battered in one of the previous battles. A few tents were visible and perhaps a dozen soft skinned vehicles. No tanks or armoured cars. The wire stretched in a straight line south to Sidi Omar and off into the brown immensity of the desert.

Then, instead of turning for home, Molly flew north and after a few minutes' flight entered again the Halfaya box barrage. This time the gunners were waiting for us and we were soon immersed in an inky mass of explosions. For the first time I could hear the crack of near misses above the engine noise and felt the thumps against the fuselage as they discharged.

"You're not going to go right through this bloody barrage again?" I shouted.

Silence from Molly.

Another near miss rocked me and I heard, or thought I heard, the pattering of steel fragments against the side of the aircraft. The sheer terror of immediate extinction overwhelmed me. I turned my Hurricane on to its back and barreled vertically down through the dense explosions and out into the clear.

Intoxicated with relief, I held my dive towards the earth, leveling out at 100 feet, heading south to the safety of the open desert.

400 mph plus on my airspeed indicator.

Fantastic blur of speed as stone and scrub flashed past. Panic gradually lessening as the minutes went by.

Then something like calm.

Then shame and remorse.

What have I done?

Looking upwards I could see that Halfaya was giving Molly the works. His Hurricane, a dark shape against the sky, moved slowly through a sea of shell explosions.

I turned back towards him, cutting across a German lorry which slewed off the track it was following, men jumping out all ways, falling and running. Heading north, still close to the ground, I saw out of the corner of my eye a soldier making for a mounted machine gun, reaching it, turning it.

Too late!

I poured on full throttle and climbed up to join Molly whose position was indicated by a straggle of despairing rounds following his track as he flew clear of the barrage. With the speed I had built up I seemed to reach him in one movement. I was still angry and my rage was intensified by guilt. My mind boiled with self-justification as I weaved behind him. Should I have flown stupidly on, dutifully covering his tail? No! He had no right to expose us both like that for no reason. The reconnaissance could have been done quite successfully by skirting the defended areas and getting minimal ack-ack. Only by the grace of God were there no fighters around. I wasn't at all happy at having deserted my post in the face of the enemy. That was surely in the worst tradition. Molly would be withering in his contempt and any chance of distinguishing myself in this squadron would be over. Maybe I'd be court martialled. That would fulfill the predictions of some of the Aussies about our courage. It would be an added shame to have let down my own side.

The sortie was now apparently completed to his satisfaction. Molly flew blandly back to Qasaba in a straight line at 4000 feet while I weaved uncomfortably behind his tail composing speeches of outrage and excuse. It was the nadir of my fortunes.

On the ground my aircraft was waved into a dispersal about 150 yards from Molly's As soon as I'd shut down my engine I threw back the hood, tore off my straps and disengaged myself from the parachute, throwing it down to a waiting airman. I jumped to earth, grabbed the chute and ran towards Molly, catching him up as he was nearing the flight tent. He was walking heavily, the two knee pads making a slapping noise at every step.

I stood in his path but he trudged abstractedly past me. He was still wearing his flying helmet. I began shouting at him, unsure whether he could hear me with his helmet still fastened. He smiled sideways at me. Playing cat and mouse, I thought. What was he so bloody pleased about?

At the tent opening he set down his parachute, detached his map and message pad and finally reached for his helmet. His hairless dome gleamed momentarily as he put his wig in place. Then he sat down on a canvas chair behind the table. It was provided with "In" and "Out" trays but both were empty.

"Geoffrey," he said gently, "you have a great deal to learn about reconnaissance. That was a successful sortie, I think. I got everything the army was asking for. I'll talk to you about it - and other matters - when Hugh has debriefed me."

"Other matters?" I said. Christ! He's going to keep me on tenterhooks, prolong the agony and then institute court martial proceedings for cowardice in the face of the enemy. Even if he doesn't go that far the news will be around the squadron in minutes. None of the pilots had anything to do but fly and gossip and this would be a juicy item. I could hear Ray Hudson's scornful laugh. And even worse the voice of Pat Byers, that red haired rugger player with a cutting edge to his tongue. "So M-squared cut and ran! Couldn't take a bit of flak. Left poor old Molly to himself in the barrage. Poor show!"

"Didn't you hear me asking you to change height?": I pleaded.

"Yes." Easy, smiling.

"Then why didn't you . . ."

"I don't need any advice from you on how to conduct a Tac/R sortie," he said, looking down at the map which he'd spread on the table. "Let me show you where we went. And then we can go over the log. You'll be surprised how much information is there. I don't suppose you saw much of the ground. The flak was pretty thick over Halfaya, wasn't it? I lost sight of you for a while."

"I was there," I lied.

"Of course."

I could have howled with relief.

I felt faint and slumped into the other chair, my mind whirling with the ecstasy of deliverance. I wasn't, after all, going to be court martialled, disgraced, the butt of jokes by better men. Molly had been unaware of my desertion. His characteristic engagement with his task would have accounted for that. When he had cleared the barrage there I was, good old faithful!

I sat pretending to listen while he droned on about the identification of gun positions and tank tracks and his estimate of traffic on the coastal road. By the time he'd finished telling me what a great job he'd done my machinery of self justification was in form again. If no one had seen my action, it had not officially occurred. I bounced back, my previous anger returning in full measure. Anger also at my failure of nerve, at my atrocious lie, at my subservience to Molly who, judging by his insensitiveness to danger, was going to be a dead man soon.

"You can shove your report, Molly," I said quietly. "In my opinion you took unnecessary risks. I refuse to fly with you again."

Molly's innocence and virtue stood up well to the occasion. He looked more amazed than hurt.

"I have twelve other young pilots to train. I won't need to fly with you. But you'll just have to get used to the ack-ack, won't you?"

We both got up.

I picked up my parachute and hurled it across the tent. It struck the untidy pile of squadron chutes, dislodging the top one. Both fell to the earth.

I strode out, not looking back.

Riding an impulse, I borrowed a jeep and drove round the strip to Wizard's headquarters tent. It was really a small marquee and had a partition in it, so that Wizard had a separate office but was not entirely cut off from his adjutant, Bill Langslow, who sat at a table to the right of the opening. Bill was sometimes called "Fanny" because of his over precise manner. He'd been a bank manager in Australia and by middle age his experience had given him an old maidish air. He had an irritating habit of sitting at his desk with a fur felt on his head and the strap round his chin as if he were going somewhere, which he wasn't. I brushed past him and entered Wizard's section saluting perfunctorily. He beckoned me to sit down.

"What is it, Blower?"

Some wit on the North West Frontier had nicknamed me "Blower". I have a loud voice which increases in volume under stress or alcohol and Wizard had picked it up.

"I've just come back from that sortie with Molly and the man is a lunatic," I said. I told the story, omitting my dive.

"I'm not going to fly with him again. I've told him so."

Wizard spoke soothingly as he grinned at me over his paper strewn desk.

"Recce isn't a science, you know," he said. "I don't think any of us know what we're doing yet. I certainly don't. Last year in the Wavell campaign they started out with Lysanders, got them all shot down by Italian CR42s, so they added a Hurricane for escort. It didn't work. The Lysanders still got shot down."

He grinned and spread out his arms in a gesture of mock despair.

"Then they tried a single Hurricane. Fast and sneaky, they thought. Didn't work because the poor buggers couldn't do two things at the same time. They were shot down while diligently counting motor transport. Now we've ended up using two Hurricanes on every sortie, but where it will end who knows. Molly has his ideas on how to do a sortie, you have yours. I'm more inclined to be cautious, like you. Anyway, you won't be flying as cover again, will you?"

This turned out to be the end of the matter. Molly bore me no ill will, being protected from insult by his own certainties. He believed in the doctrines taught some years previously at the School of Army Co-operation, Old Sarum, much as a fundamentalist preacher holds to the literal truth of the Bible. His whole emphasis was on precise reporting suitable for exercises, when the "enemy" fighters shoot you down by reporting your aircraft letter, or the umpire tells you over the radio that you have been a casualty of ack-ack fire. It was out of whack with the realities of war.

On the day after this flight, 10 August, Molly took Ray Hudson out on a similar mission.[1] In the course of the recce Ray saw a Henschel 126, a light plane used by the German army for recon and communications. He at once attacked it and shot it down. Molly didn't join in the kill. Ray thought he disapproved because it wasn't "British" to shoot down an unarmed plane but I interpret it differently. I think Molly disdained everything that diverted attention from the gathering of information for the army. He was a purist.

His courage was not in question. Perhaps he would have won high awards flying bomber missions in which the dangers are statistical and the necessary qualities are steadfastness and resolve. I'm sure he wanted recce to be something that called for his own qualities. But it didn't. It was the aerial equivalent of being a spy and the virtues of a spy are prudence and cunning. A spy also needs courage but it is not that of the legendary hero, like Richard the Lionheart, cutting his way through half a mile of Saracens at Acre. Apart from his unfortunate hairlessness, Molly was of sturdy build and ruddy limbs and might have fitted into Richard's armour; but his heroism was all wrong and most of what he taught was misleading.

To this day I have not forgiven myself or him. He had discovered my weakness and broken me, without ever knowing that he'd done so. I was

1. "10th August, 1941; the squadron (No. 451) had an early success when P.O. Hudson on reconnaissance near Bardia, shot down an Hs 126 flown by Major Heymer, commanding officer of the Luftwaffe's reconnaissance unit." *Fighters Over the Desert* ,Christopher Shores and Hans Ring, Arco Publishing Co., C.W. Daniel Co. Ltd.,New York, 1969, page 50.

besotted with Yeats that season and had tried to see myself as a romantic figure, casting derision upon supersession of breath. I was fond of murmuring the opening lines of "An Irish Airman Forsees his Death" for consolation.

> *I know that I shall meet my fate*
> *Somewhere among the clouds above;*
> *Those that I fight I do not hate,*
> *Those that I guard I do not love.*

It seemed to fit my situation beautifully. I really didn't hate the Germans, nor did I love the Egyptians. But at the sticking point I'd failed, as Yeats might have done, I thought, (knowing nothing about him at the time), if he'd suddenly found himself in a heavy barrage. I still respected courage above everything but Molly had given me a sickener for the stoic, mindless variety. I had to rethink my position.

On the positive side, I did get experience of two of the major threats to a reconnaissance pilot - heavy anti-aircraft and small arms fire - and I thought compulsively about it all the time, like a sickness. Heavy A.A. had to be avoided completely. Fly lower. 2000 feet. Lower even. Out of small arms fire and too low for the big guns. Better for observation of camouflaged items, anyway. If fighters appeared, dive to ground level and, if attacked, go into maximum steep turn. The Me. 109 had an advantage in speed but it also had higher wing loading. It would have difficulty getting inside the Hurricane for a deflection shot. I tried to work out pockets of safety or of relative immunity to which I could escape under various conditions. Once inside enemy territory I would increase throttle and fly close to full bore, weaving and changing height constantly to make myself a hard target for the ground gunners. The hell with writing on a knee pad! My head wasn't going down for minutes on end like Molly's. I would record directly on a map, which I'd switch from my left knee, where it was conventionally strapped, to my right side. And I'd keep a good look out. I would not trust my covers to spot fighters. How many brave, dim-witted, half asleep pilots might there be in the world to offer my hide to a section of Messerschmitts screaming out of the sun?

MESSERSCHMITT ROULETTE

V

THE LULL
(11 August to 3 September 1941)

Molly pressed on with his programme of indoctrinating the Australians. He had all the self confidence of a 19th Century missionary to the savages who has given up the comforts of home to teach the unwashed how to live. He took them out one by one and scared the living daylights out of them. They didn't react with the same panic and rage as I had. They were straight out of elementary flying school in Rhodesia and in a mood to be further instructed by "an expert in his field", as Doc Reid had seriously described him.

To my amazement it didn't take him more than a few days to establish his credit and to be accepted by them, wig and all. They may have thought he was crazy, and I doubt if many of them followed his foolhardy ways when they flew off by themselves but they had to respect him. In war, courage is the only valid currency. Everything else - rhetoric, charm, even organizational ability - is scrip. A coward, however brilliant, cannot lead men into battle. So Molly, against the odds, became the first of the RAF pilots to gain acceptance. I don't believe he was in the least conscious of his triumph. In his view he was giving instruction in correct procedures, followed by practical demonstration in the air, to pilots who knew nothing about army co-op. It was a peacetime programme, out of date the instant the war started, transferred with great authority to the Western Desert in 1941.

One Australian put himself out to be friendly. This was Corporal Coffey, the mess steward, who presided over the bar. He was extremely well built in the way one associates with heavy exercise, like rowing or gymnastics. You couldn't miss his rounded calves and his big thighs showing below the abbreviated Australian shorts. In contrast he had a rather pretty face, with a mass of honey coloured hair. He may have been a bartender in civilian life. His whole attitude was brisk and professional, as if he were accustomed to the role. He greeted approaching officers like the proprietor of an English inn. When stocks were low, he entertained us by parodying his own style.

"Well, gentlemen," he'd say, "We recommend some nice, thin Gyppy beer today. Supply is limited of this delightful beverage, though."

A pause. A beaming smile.

"First come, first served!"

One evening I was the only officer in the bar tent for a while, and he told me of his longing to go to England.

37

"My mum was from Liverpool. I think I'd like it there. Australia is so crude. I'd like to speak the way you do."

He was washing glasses and came towards me wiping one with a cloth.

"If there's anything special you'd want from the bar, I'll keep it back for you. What cigs do you prefer?"

"Anything but those damned Rhodesians."

"I'll save you some Players."

He was as good as his word, always tipping me off when attractive items appeared in stock. The occasions were rare enough, which made them more touching. I knew I had a friend in Corporal Coffey, and at this time he was the only one.

General Auchinleck was making preparations for the next offensive, which was to be called "Operation Crusader", as if the Germans under Rommel were a Paynim host. Its object was to relieve Tobruk and drive the enemy out of Cyrenaica. To promote this a railway was under construction along the coastal road out of Alexandria at a point seventy-five miles west of Mersa Matruh. A pipeline was being laid close to the railhead and 30,000 tons of munitions, fuel and other necessaries of war were being stored in the forward areas.

Meanwhile there was little enemy air activity and our first tentative sorties encountered none of the dreaded Messerschmitt 109-Fs that we had been warned about. To confuse German reconnaissance the British Army made dummy airfields with dummy fighters and bombers standing around in dispersed positions, giving a formidable impression from the air. There was one at Fuqa, halfway between El Alamein and Mersa, that looked more real than the genuine airfield a few miles distant. Clusters of dummy tanks, looking very foolish at ground level when their canvas fluttered in the breeze, stood in dummy depots in the hope that the Luftwaffe photographic aircraft would be deceived into thinking our preparations for future battle were more advanced than they in fact were. Every street boy in Cairo knew we were short of armour and awaiting shipments from Britain but there was a madness for deception and concealment in the Middle East that added a bizarre element to the war.

After breakfast on 11 August Wizard drew me aside and suggested we fly together on a recce of the Halfaya-Sollum area that was planned for that day.

"I'm all fingers and thumbs with these modern aircraft," he said, grinning and pulling at his black moustaches. "I was getting quite respectable at flying the biplanes. I could cope with those nasty little toe brakes on the Audax and remember to wind out my radiator when the oil temperature went up. I'm getting too old to change. The Hurricane is so complicated with its flaps and retractable undercarriage and variable pitch bloody propeller. One slip and you've made a proper clot of yourself. It'll be as much as I can do to cover your tail."

So we went out together, me leading. He had been taking over command of the troubled squadron from Pilot Pope and conferring daily with his inquisitors at No 13 Corps HQ. He needed to chalk up some operational hours, as he told me, but didn't want to make an idiot of himself with one of the Australians in his unpracticed state.

It was a bright day with the sun high in the sky and making few shadows on the desert floor. Some broad tracks made by tanks and lorries in the previous campaign were traceable, growing faint in places where months of blown sand had filled in the crevices. There were no topographical features to guide me, so I timed myself to turn north short of the wire. Climbing to 1000 feet I weaved towards Halfaya, seeing the red escarpment ahead and noticing that tracks, large and small, were spreading like giant spider's webs over the gently rising ground. I had been briefed to report movement and was just noting the position of a small convoy of trucks on my map, my head momentarily down "in the office", and when I looked up again the entire landscape seemed to have disappeared and I found myself flying through a speckled sea of shell explosions, some of them dangerously close. This was my first experience of light "ack ack", as we used to call it, using the alphabetical code of the First World War. The explosions turned into white cloudlets and it was quite a pretty sight. I turned away, diving steeply, and was soon out into the clear. Wizard's aircraft was weaving above me. I pressed my R/T button to speak.

"Sorry," I said. Wizard did not reply.

Skirting the area and climbing to get out of range of the guns I could see the entire position, a plateau pockmarked with shell craters through which ran the paved coastal road. On the southern and eastern slopes you could see the heavy gun positions with their tall sandbagged towers. I was busy counting and identifying vehicles on the highway when the heavy flak, big black puffs that Molly had valiantly ignored, began to bracket us. I dived away, edging back to observe at a lower height, retreating once more when the flak became too thick. I found it quite possible to see what I wanted to without flying smack over the defended area.

We were just out to sea near Sollum, getting a little flak from the harbour defences - it looked like a fishing port, but the only boats I could see were a couple of dinghies tied to the dock - when Wizard's voice broke it.

"Look to the west. That may be a fighter section taking off."

Twenty miles away, just inland from the line of red cliffs, a telltale line of dust smudged the surface of the desert. It looked to me like more than one aircraft taking off. Our whole business, I thought, was interpretation of dust clouds, fighters taking off from desert strips, trucks wearing a well used trail to powder, tank tracks churning up the surface like a sausage grinder.

We didn't say much about it on the ground. I gave my report, which Hugh said was similar to the day before, and Wizard made some rueful comments about there being no safe height to fly. In retrospect, however, this was the beginning of our partnership. In the months ahead all the powerful figures on the RAF side of the equation were to go and Wizard and I were alone.

In the middle of August I flew my first photographic sortie. Some of our Hurricanes were equipped with cameras, three of them, mounted to the rear of the pilot. The massive old fashioned air cameras, designed for a larger platform than the frail Hurricane, weighed the tail down so badly that the nose would rise in flight even with the elevator trim fully forward. On these aircraft thick elastic cords fastened the stick to the dashboard, relieving the pilot of the physical effort of holding the nose level by main force. To climb, the pilot didn't have to move the stick from its position of maximum dive. Half a notch on the elevator trim and the aircraft would lurch upward as if released by a giant hand. This effectively turned a racehorse into a carthorse. The very thought of encountering fighters while flying one of these overburdened, unbalanced aircraft made one nervous.

Hugh Davies was in his most sympathetic mood. If he had a fault it was in knowing us too well and being too close to us emotionally. He knew what heights were worst for flak and he shared our perhaps ill-founded belief that light ack ack was less lethal than the heavy stuff. He knew where the Luftwaffe airfields were and where the box barrages were to be encountered. He sat at his table with maps in front of him, his black tank beret on his head and his beak of a nose, sun-peeled at the tip, projecting like the prow of a ship. The photographic NCO, Sergeant Buxton, who was in the RAF and ran the mainly Aussie section, stood beside him.

"The Corps Commander is anxious to get a good look at the Bardia area while the German fighters seem to be taking a rest," he said. "It's a strong point, and the port is still in operation for small ships. The flak isn't so bad, is it? I mean, not so bad as Halfaya? You'll only be flying through the barrage for about four and a half minutes by my reckoning. On each run, that is."

"What height?"

"Six thousand feet. I know that won't please you. It's a good height for the German 88 Millimeters!"

"I want to fly as fast as possible," I said, "to get it over quickly."

"I'm sorry, Geoffrey," Hugh said, "It's all been worked out for a hundred and eighty. That's a good speed from the photographic angle. All three cameras will be clicking away, producing a sort of instant map of quite a wide strip of territory. When the film is processed by the photographic interpretation team at Corps HQ, they can look through their stereoscopes at the prints and see everything on the ground in relief. They can tell a Mark IV tank from a Mark III. Even the height of a telephone pole. It's amazing."

I thought 180 mph was ghastly slow but suspected that there might be some technical reason that dictated it. Anyway it was too late to argue.

THE LULL

"And if I fly too fast or too slow," I said, "The overlap on the films won't be correct and they won't be able to interpret it and I'll have to do it all over again."

"You took the words out of an ALO's mouth." [1]

"I hope the 88s don't guess my speed straight off."

I walked away thinking of ways to minimize the risk. I settled on approaching from the sea, climbing quickly and getting that dreadful thirteen and half minutes of straight and level flight over before the fighter boys were after me. As for the barrage, I could do nothing but endure it.

Everything went according to plan. There wasn't a cloud in the sky. I climbed to 6000 feet just short of the coast and locked on a heading of 240 degrees at 180 miles per hour. The sweat ran down my cheeks under the flaps of my helmet. We were flying right into the barrage and in a minute the black puffs began to appear. They were low and behind us to start off with, then the gunners got our correct height and moved their fire forward. Suddenly we were flying through a storm of explosions and the ground was totally obscured when a cluster of shells burst close. I could do nothing but hold course, twisting my head around from side to side and scanning the sky for fighters to keep busy. I felt pretty foolish and hoped the Jerry gunners understood that I was taking important photographs and not just flying through this shit for the fun of it. The Sutton harness and the buckles of my parachute straps were bunched on my shoulders, chafing my neck. Four and half minutes on the first run, then turn and back through the fiery furnace.

My cover, Paddy Hutley, broke in.

"Fighters port three o'clock."

I saw them. Six in loose formation, maybe 5000 feet above, heading our way. I felt the joy of release. Anything was better than the prison bars of those photographic tracks. I turned over and spiraled down. No option but to head south and lose them in the desert. At 100 feet with brown earth, shrub and salt flat flashing past, still weaving, with my head turning with every weave to cover my tail, I could see no sign of pursuit. Had they missed us? Were they out after someone else?

On the ground again, I felt an extra stickiness under my shirt and reaching in with my hand withdrew it covered in blood. Fifty-five minutes of moving my head back and forth to cover the sky, rubbing my neck against my parachute harness and cockpit straps, had made bloody furrows where the neck meets the shoulder and rivulets had run down my chest and belly. After that experience I took the precaution of placing pads between the straps and my body, but they were difficult to keep in place and I would bleed again. A sore neck was part of my life in the desert.

---

1. **Air Liaison Officer, always an army officer representing the Corps Commander.**

The next day Hugh Davies grabbed me just before lunchtime.

"I've got the Brigadier 13 Corps in my office. He wants to meet you. He's pleased with your photographs. When he turned up here unannounced I thought he was going to put the curse of the seven Protestant bishops on us but apparently all's well. I'll be trotting him along to the mess."

So, over a drink, I met Brigadier Brian Horrocks who later became a corps commander and was afterwards famous for his television commentaries on the war. He was in his mid forties, going grey, patrician. He would have looked well in a toga. We sat down in canvas chairs and sipped Egyptian beer. Wizard and Stan Reid joined us.

"That was a nice line overlap," he said. "The information we get from you people is absolutely invaluable. Just want to say that."

He smiled. He had a world-weary, conspiratorial smile. We're all in this dreary business together, the smile said.

"I was interrupted on the last leg," I said.

"So they told me. Didn't matter. All the stuff was there. I must say it can't be much fun for you chaps, hanging around being shot at and then being chased off."

"It isn't."

"We really appreciate it. Williams fights hard to save your skins." He smiled one of his conspirator's smiles in Wizard's direction.

"He's not going to let the silly army get you all shot down," he added. Horrocks knows the whole story, I thought. And he's letting Wizard know it. "Silly Army" was a dig at us. But I couldn't detect malice under the charm. He just understood the competing interests of Wizard and his own air liaison staff and he wanted us to know that he knew.

For Brigadier Horrocks it was probably a routine visit. He'd asked one of his staff to check on photographic work and to give him a pilot's name. He must have gone round all his units with the same intention; saying nice things, exercising his gifts, sending the message that 13 Corps cared for its people and appreciated what they were doing. I had done nothing spectacular and knew it but it was warming to be thanked from on high.

By the end of August I had flown thirteen sorties and no longer felt that I was a novice. Three newly trained RAF pilots arrived in the third week of August - Ken Whalley, Graeme-Evans, and "Masher" Maslen. The first two were short and skinny and "Masher" was tall and stooped. They looked rather odd together and did not, to my eye, compare well with the Australians. But I had little time to go beyond first impressions. They were kept busy practicing flying on the Hurricane aircraft while I was piling up my operational hours.

At the same time six South African Air Force pilots were posted in. They were newly trained, except for Captain Murray Gardiner, a tall saturnine lawyer, aged twenty-eight. He had flown Hawker Audaxes in the East African campaign against the Italians and was wryly aware that he was now entering the real war. Murray was strikingly handsome, moved slowly and deliberately and possessed great philosophic humour in times of crisis, a quality that soothed and amazed me. His grip on his own South Africans was absolute. The other pilots were Bill Andrews, Pete Campbell, Tommy Thomas, Pete Haddon a hugely muscled fellow with his white blond hair cropped like a convict whom we called Smithy.

The pilots were now neatly but not happily divided into three separate groups, belonging to different nations, different services and whose uniforms varied in shade and cut. South African shorts were even more abbreviated than the Australian ones and they still had army ranks - second and first lieutenant for pilot office and flying officer, and captain for flight lieutenant. Their uniforms were noticeably of better quality, brightened by some touches of scarlet on hatbands and rank tabs and they spoke a more guttural English with some strange clicking sounds that may have had their origin in an African tongue.

Naturally the Australians responded with gloom to the further watering down of their pilot strength by poms and "black troops", as the South Africans were playfully called. I overheard Doc Reid arguing with an obviously disgruntled group of airmen, all sitting cross legged in a circle around him.

"This is 451 Squadron, Royal Australian Air Force," he was saying, emphasizing Australian. "I promise you we'll soon be an all Australian squadron, but until we get our boys over we've got to support the pilots we have. It's not their fault. They're the ones who'll be doing the job. . ." His voice, quiet but urgent, beat on until I was out of earshot.

Most of our reconnaissances were of a routine nature covering the defensive positions on the Libyan border and were repeats of what, I suppose, were daily or perhaps twice daily check-ups for the Corps Commander. Once I was sent to report movement in the area of Sheferzen, an old fort down the wire, thirty miles southwest of Sollum. It was an uneventful flight into the desert wastes, presumably laid on to make sure that Rommel was not pulling a fast one by a thrust from the deep south. I made one reconnaissance of the Italian camps at Sidi Omar, twenty miles southwest of Halfaya. On this occasion I flew a circuitous route at low level, timing myself carefully and popping up to do my recce, getting some light ack ack that was wide of the mark. I was getting practice at making myself a difficult target.

To occupy my time between sorties and to stop myself worrying unduly about the fate of the squadron with its open enmities and potential for breakdown, I volunteered for every flight going, from aircraft test flights after routine inspections to picking up equipment from depots in the Delta. Our squadron runabout was a yellow painted Westland Lysander, a product of between-wars thinking on army co-operation, eventually displaced by fighter types. It was a high wing monoplane with a fixed undercarriage and a huge cockpit canopy for all-round observation which had been designed as a replacement for the Hawker Audax in 1934 and was introduced into squadron service in 1938. The specifications had required an unobstructed forward view, docile handling characteristics, good low speed control and the ability to get out of confined spaces. W.E.W. Petter, the Westland designer, produced a brilliant monster of an aircraft. It had a chunky cantilever undercarriage from which stout V-lift struts held the wings in place.

The fascinating thing was its ability to fly slowly under control. It was equipped with every kind of flap and slot to prolong steady airflow over the wings and so sustain flight. With lots of throttle it could stagger along at speeds as low as forty-five mph. The intention had been to design a machine fast enough to evade fighters and flak and slow enough to turn itself into a sort of helicopter when observation was safe. Unfortunately it was just too slow. Its ability to land and take off from very small fields made it an ideal vehicle for dropping and picking up agents in occupied France and in that role it became famous. I loved to fly it and got endless amusement out of practicing short landings and takeoffs.

Flying it over the green Delta, always a sight for desert-sore eyes, was a delight; lots of room in the cockpit, a big view and a steady platform. It was on a flight to Heliopolis on some errand that I first saw the Pyramids. I circled round them in some amazement; three of them, one the great pyramid of Khafre, with the eroded Sphinx nearby. I had always imagined them surrounded by desert on all sides, but they were only a few miles from the Nile and the centre of Cairo. When I thought about it, I realized that my idea of their isolation had been based on Shelley's Ozymendias.

> *Nothing beside remains. Round the decay*
> *Of that colossal wreck, boundless and bare,*
> *The lone and level sands stretch far away.*

I made a habit of going through the Flight Authorization Book, which was kept in the flight tent, to count the number of sorties each pilot had made. Some of the Australians who had arrived in July were well ahead and Molly, because he was still taking out rookie pilots, had totted up a good score, but by hanging around when the army requests came in I was catching up.

At the very end of August the pleasant conversations with Horrocks landed me in trouble. Because he knew me and had said something about my work he made a special request that I do some more photographing of the critical frontier areas. Wizard represented this to me as somewhat of an honour. I would have volunteered for ten reconnaissance missions to avoid one photographic trip, but because of the train of events, which were mildly flattering to me, I could hardly protest. I carried out two sorties on successive days, 30th and 31st of August. The first one was a line overlap of the Sollum-Bardia-Halfaya area. The second was a long run down the wire from Sollum to Sidi Omar. Both involved prolonged flying at steady speed and height over Rommel's major defensive positions.

THE LULL

The Hurricane was not designed to take such heavy, awkwardly shaped objects as cameras and it was a sight to see the modifications that the riggers had performed in the narrow space between the rear of the cockpit and the tail. It was a crude carpentry job, a "lash-up", and the spars looked too frail to support the dense, spiky mechanisms, facing downwards at differing angles from the large hole cut in the underside of the fuselage. I always hated to see the side panels off and the photographers with their heads inside, making last minute adjustments. Unlike riggers and fitters, who get dirty on the job, the camera crews looked neat and clean. They spent their time in a tidy section with a dark room and little tongs to pull the dripping film out of the developing fluid.

The middle camera faced directly down and the other two were angled to cover the areas on either side of the aircraft's path. A timing device opened and shut the lenses at the correct intervals for the speed flown. The pilot simply had to press a button to start the whole thing off. If the wings tilted at all, an incorrect tract of country would be photographed. If the speed was too great or too little, the timed overlap would not work out right, causing problems for the interpretation team. Everything had to be precise, with little margin for error.

To give an idea of the problem, the flight on 30th lasted one hour and forty-five minutes. Estimating the time to and from the target area as thirty minutes each way, this meant that I flew for forty-five minutes through those three barrages, unable to drop a wing slightly for fear of ruining the overlap. Strangely enough, with the cameras all clicking away, the spoiling effect of the explosions, which of course appeared on the film, was not serious. On 31st the flight time was even longer - two hours and ten minutes - and I must have been eighty minutes on the task, which included passing several times through the 88 mm barrages at Sollum and Sidi Omar.

On September 3rd Horrocks asked Wizard for a final mission. This was to consist of runs over Gambut, Fort Capuzzo and Sollum, thus completing his picture of the frontier defences. In the light of what happened a few weeks later when the Luftwaffe came out of hiding, it seems incredible that I should have been permitted to get away with such blatant invasions of enemy airspace. Certainly it must have given 13 Corps a false impression of the risks involved in such operations. The Hurricane was not a large plane and perhaps did not present much of a target to the anti-aircraft guns. Statistically one might be unlucky to receive a direct hit, even in the middle of a box. I really don't know. I had no special revelation that the shells bursting all round me were destined to miss me, I had no confidence that the enemy fighters would continue to ignore me, and I had other worries, too.

Ken Whalley was thin and small, with white-blond hair and a long pointed nose that was always red at the tip and raw at the nostrils. He reminded me of a white mouse. He also looked a bit like the bust of Voltaire by Houdon, but there was nothing Voltarian about him, except perhaps his nervousness. He was to cover me on this trip and it was his first operational flight.

At the briefing he didn't seem to be concentrating, his pale watery eyes staring out of a white face and his hands fluttering about. As we walked towards the flights I tried to calm him down.

"You're nervous," I said.

"Yes."

"Well, it's your first go. Everyone's scared at first, but it wears off. All you have to do is to hang on to my tail and scan the sky for fighters. I'll be looking around as well, don't you worry. If any trouble comes our way, we'll beat it. I'll turn away steeply and dive, so watch for that."

"OK," he murmured glumly biting his lip.

He seemed so upset that I wondered whether he could fly properly. I wanted to shake him up, comfort him and strengthen him all in one gesture. I also wanted to explain to him what was in the forefront of my mind. "What are you afraid of, Whalley?" I wanted to say, "Death? Death isn't the real issue. The real issue is whether we can keep our end up with the Australians. They don't think much of us. We talk funny. Most of us don't look as strong or fit as they do. As a group they're convinced that Englishmen will fight their wars with Aussie blood if given half a chance. We can't afford to be white-faced and trembly. They have to admire us, Whalley. We have to lead. Fly the sorties. Look confident. So put on an act, damn you. We're on stage in an Australian play with South African overtones. We're stage Englishmen with silly accents and trousers that look like skirts. So play up, for Christ's sake!" But there was no way of saying this. I was just talking to myself.

Our Hurricanes were close together, so I stood and watched him as he climbed into the cockpit. Then I stood on the step, leaning over his shoulder, reminding him of his long range tanks and how to turn them on when the fuel in the main tanks got low. This was probably unnecessary but I felt sorry for him and thought that the least I could do was to make him feel that this was a normal flight and that the routines he'd been taught still had value.

Whalley's flying style irritated me from the start. His listlessness showed in the way he lagged behind my tail. Most covers weaved in a regular pattern behind the lead aircraft and it gave one a feeling of security. Ken did little weaving and merely stood to one side and well back. As we made our way towards the Sollum area I called him up a couple of times.

Just off the coast, pointing towards the bay of Sollum, I began my climb to 6000 feet and was soon locked into my gridiron pattern. The guns on the ground, surprised by my sudden appearance, were a little slow to open up but by the time I was over the centre of Sollum the barrage had reached full bloom. At the end of my first run I turned and flew obediently back over the barrage. Ken Whalley drifted farther behind. As I glanced back I could see a storm of explosions through which I could barely make out the shape of his Hurricane.

THE LULL

"Ken, don't lag behind."

"Roger."

He edged up a little through the murk of shell traces which expanded in the bright air and formed a thin layer of grey cloud behind him. A hopeless case, I thought. A dead man if ever I saw one.

I had nothing else to do on these missions beyond holding my speed and direction and keeping my wings level, perversely making myself the most predictable of targets for the 88s, so I spent my time on the fighter search. All I could see as I turned my head was Whalley's aircraft doing nothing much behind me. I wanted him to move, damn it! I looked at the flat, brown desert to the west where the Luftwaffe airfields lay, at the hard edge of coastline and at the blue sky, peppered with shell explosions. We seemed to crawl across this nasty, dangerous space with imperceptible motion. I could do nothing but fly as accurately as possible, but Whalley was free. Why didn't he swoop and soar as I would have done? I'd have been happier if he'd carried out loops and rolls.

"Get weaving, Ken," I said.

"I can see all right."

"Are we all clear?"

"Yes."

"No dust clouds?"

"No."

He was twenty. A child, I thought. My two years seniority seemed like a century of experience. I had a mental image of his thin face and his mop of white hair. A weasel, too bewildered to look after himself properly, much less me. Lagging behind like that he was asking to get hit by a shell aimed at the lead aircraft, for even in a planned barrage most shells fall behind the target. Whalley didn't see that. Some people don't have a strong instinct for danger. Molly was obviously such a one. Ken Whalley, in a paralyzed sort of way, was another. I envied and despised them both in one impulse of irritation. Personal danger doesn't bring forth generous thoughts in me. I knew my feelings were unreasonable but the whole situation, 6000 feet above the German army, taking photographs in a clapped out Hurricane, burdened with long range tanks and three heavy cameras, was out of some old pilot's nightmare.

These hours remain in my memory as the worst I ever spent in the air. Fear is a strange thing. If you are busy, it is often not felt at all. Flying fast, close to the ground, catching all kinds of small arms fire, I can remember no unpleasant feelings. Most reconnaissances gave me so much freedom of choice in height, speed, flight path and manoeuvre that I almost enjoyed the prospect of pitting my wits against the known dangers. There was always a compensating thrill associated with doing something well, or as well as I knew how, that neutralized feelings of panic. Photographic missions, however, did not occupy one's energies. The minutes dragged. There was little to do but endure the Russian roulette of the barrages and wait to see if some fighters came along to pick you off.

When I'd finished the last run over Sollum the accumulated tension led me to perform a wild descent at maximum power. As I made for the coastline I could see a convoy making its way in an easterly direction along the road towards the German front line. There were about twenty trucks - we called them soft skinned vehicles in the jargon of army co-op - and they looked very attackable. I had not used my guns before and had even thought of them as useless or at best of use as last resort. Eight .303 calibre machine guns were mounted in the wings, a formidable fire power that had excited Ray Hudson. I moved the selector on my control column from "Off" to "On" with my thumb and aligned myself with the paved coastal highway. It was an afterthought and I must have left it too late for a good attack. When I held the button down and raked through the convoy, I was so close to the ground that I had the impression of the whole world blowing up in my face. All I could hear above the noise of the engine was the "Trr Trr" of the guns and I felt some mild vibration; but on the ground was an earthquake, multiple explosions and great clouds of smoke rose up at me as I swept overhead.

Turning steeply to look back, I could not believe that my single action could have had such a stupendous effect. I glanced around guiltily to see if a squadron of Blenheims was overhead carrying out a bombing attack, but the sky seemed empty. Almost all of the trucks had exploded. It looked as if a giant's hand had scattered them. No longer in neat formation, they lay wrecked and flaming in a disorderly cluster, some on their sides in the ditches and others, further away from the road, facing back the way they had come, depending, I suppose, on the reaction of the drivers when the tempest of lead hit them. Explosions were still going on and I saw men running into open ground. I couldn't wait to see more but I headed out low over the sea on my planned safety exit. Whalley was taken by surprise and hadn't joined in the attack. His voice crackled over the radio.

"You knocked that lot for six," he said.

"Fuck'n oath," I replied, in imitation of the Aussies, very cool. But my feelings were confused as I raced across the waves and turned east to the safety of our own lines. Behind me the cloud of smoke had reached 1000 feet. It may have been a munitions convoy bringing shells and mines to the defence system and that would account for the violence of the explosions. My later attacks on ground targets left burning wrecks but nothing so volcanic as this first time. I was both disturbed and elated. I had never wanted to be a bomber pilot and disliked the notion of actually killing people, but reconnaissance flying was a masochist's delight and didn't suit my taste either. There was something humiliating about having to be as nervous as an antelope on a lion plain in order to survive our saucy penetrations, and photographing through an 88 millimeter barrage was as dispiriting as being whacked at school. It was glorious to strike back. I wanted to do it again.

THE LULL

By the first week of September, a month after joining the squadron, I was feeling slightly less tragic about the pommie issue. Molly had led the way, pursuing his path with godlike self confidence, as unconscious of the minefield of hostile Aussie thoughts as he was of the 88 millimeter barrages he led them through. Those who flew with him may have thought him a fool but no one could think him a pansy.

Calling in to Sick Quarters one day to pick up some adhesive tape for my neck, Doc Reid saw me and led me over to his tent for a chat. Unlike the other officers, he lived in a bell tent and slept in a camp bed. Two oil lamps, one sitting on a crate by his bed, the other tied to the tentpole, enabled him to work after dark. There was a metal RAF issue desk and a cabinet of drugs and medicines beside it. He sat down on his bed and beckoned me to the only chair.

"How's it going, Geoff?"

"Better, Doc," I said. "I think they're still disappointed at not having an Aussie skipper, but Wizard's doing a good job. They seem to accept him."

"He's a marvel, old Wiz. Molly's a card, too. The boys are growing to love 'im."

"God knows why! He's a maniac."

"Yeh. I heard you complained to Wizard. But the boys are eating him up. Gee, I'd like to fly with the squadron and see for myself how it is out there. I've flown over a thousand hours on biplane types. I was too young for the "Fourteen-Eighteen" and now I'm too bloody old for this one."

"And you'd like to have a go at the Hurricanes?"

"I can taste it."

"Perhaps Wizard'll let you have a try. They're an easy kite to fly."

"I've been studying the handbook. One of these days he'll weaken. By the way, we heard from R.A.A.F. HQ today that they can't send us more Australian pilot replacements. I've arranged a meeting with the senior NCOs this evening to let them know that we're not going to be an all Aussie squadron till next year."

"Next year! I hope I'm alive next year."

"You will be, Geoffrey."

Doc grinned showing his teeth in a crescent like a shark. He turned and laid back on the bed, revealing a barreled chest and powerful arms as he put his hands behind his head.

"I heard some of the boys talking about you," he said. "They said you were right."

"Right" in Australian parlance, means genuine.

"No one mentioned powder puffs?"

"No. I think we're beginning to pull together."

It was good to hear a confirmation from the best informed source in the squadron that Molly's heroics were improving our image. Even better to hear that I was "right with the boys." Doc Reid was being kind, however, and

49

I knew that the process of acceptance was only just beginning. The technical airmen who fussed over our Hurricanes as we set off on operational sorties had been the first to show warmth, naturally enough. They were "their" aeroplanes taking off to encounter the Hun and we were flying them. But the Aussie pilots only waved and grinned, keeping themselves to themselves, still a select group at mealtimes and impenetrable to outsiders in their clump of tents separated by fifty yards from the rest of us.

VI

MY BROTHER THE SPY
(3 to 8 September, 1941)

On 3 September Wizard sent me on four days leave. On the morning of that day I flew a practice artillery reconnaissance with a nearby gunner regiment and only heard the news when I landed. There was a Hurricane to be ferried back to the Delta for a major inspection and one to be collected on the day of my return, so it worked out neatly. I rushed to my tent to search for clothes to wear in the big city but my best khaki uniform had been stuffed into the parachute bag I used as a pillow and was both dirty and rumpled. I decided to go as I was.

From Heliopolis, a busy airport near Cairo, an RAF truck ran me into Shepheards. It was one of the great hotels of the world, standing on a broad street and overlooking a reach of the Nile. In peacetime I would have hesitated to enter its noble portico unless generously supplied with cash, but by 1941 it had become an officers' billet for the British, Australian, New Zealand, French and Polish units fighting in the desert and the price of a room was commensurate with what an officers' mess would charge anywhere in the region. The marble lobby was on the grand scale and set the tone of sybaritic splendour. One could sit down at a marble table under the domed ceiling and be fussed over by hotel servants dressed in white galabyas and scarlet cummerbunds. All around were people in uniform. Middle East Headquarters was a few yards away in Garden City, so there were red staff tabs and hatbands to be seen. The Free French officers with their romantic kepis were the best dressed, and they had a great advantage in this city where the upper classes had been speaking French since the time of Napoleon's occupation. Polish officers with their shaven heads and stiff military courtesy looked as if they had strayed in from Prussia by mistake.

Out on the street there was a variety of human types. At the bottom of the social scale were the brown skinned, good tempered Egyptians of the peasant class - the fellahin - with their simple white garments, sandals and a raggedy turban. A middle entrepreneur class, many of whom wore red fezzes on their shaven heads, were augmented by people of Greek, Italian and Syrian stock. It was a meeting place of nations and I had never before seen such a range of desirable women. They varied from blonde Scandinavian types through every kind of European mixture, to Arabian beauties with large dark eyes and jet black Sudanese with exquisite straight noses and strongly defined Negroid lips. Sitting outside Groppi's, a popular restaurant on the

MESSERSCHMITT ROULETTE

French model with tables on the pavement, I watched the girls go by. The fashion in those days was for knee length skirts and a goodly display of nether limb. The high heels favoured a wading motion, as if the air they moved through had the consistency of a liquid. I found this very seductive, but they were separated from the British soldiery by national sentiment as well as by language and they were not friendly.

Under the 1936 treaty between Britain and Egypt we had retained the right to station troops to guard the Suez Canal zone, but there was an uncomfortably colonial atmosphere about our presence. Shepheards Hotel and the Gezira Club, with its polo ground and tennis courts, were annexes of imperial power and privilege. Although the average Egyptian preferred us to the Italians who had been threatening to replace us, there was little anti-German sentiment. The Egyptian upper classes and the officer corps were opposed to our presence, so it was not surprising that after the war, in the revolution of 1950, the first buildings to be gutted were Shepheards and the Turf Club. Egyptian women, therefore, were for show; unless you went to the "Bosphore", a night club with an immense dance floor and several sections for different kinds of entertainment, the most popular being belly dancing. Here the high priced whores were available. A few brothels catered for the troops and "Mary's" was the officers' whorehouse.

Coming from two years on the borders of Afghanistan, I stared like a country cousin at all this French refinement set against the backdrop of an old Arab kingdom. I also looked like a country cousin. My clothes, washed in salt water and unpressed, looked far from elegant. At Qasaba I had been issued with a light Australian made battledress jacket on which I had never bothered to sew my wings or rank tabs. I had become fond of this ugly garment and continued to wear it in Cairo with an open necked shirt and "desert boots", the untreated leather half boots worn by everyone in the squadron. I was aware of myself as a front line fighter and wasn't displeased to look like one, separating myself from the Middle East Headquarters staff - the "Cairo Warriors" or "Gabardine Swine", as they were called - whose uniforms were immaculate and whose shoes were polished. I couldn't have been the only one of my kind around because military policemen would glance at me - ill clothed and of undetermined rank, only to be identified as an officer by my faded peaked hat - and then look away. No doubt they had been instructed not to hassle obviously operational types.

My brother Ken, older than me by three years, had been in Cairo for six months and I phoned him as soon as I settled in my room. We had always been very close. As schoolboys our master plan was to walk round the world, starting in Europe and traversing the back of Asia, through Tibet to China. Needing money to fulfill the dream, Ken joined the investment department of Schroder's Bank in the City of London while I joined the RAF as a short service pilot to earn the gratuity of four hundred pounds on completion of four years service. After my departure to India, however, he began to find the City intolerable and in an apologetic letter he told me that he must set forth alone. At the outbreak of war he was in Greece and had an adventurous time getting home to join up in the army. He was now a spy in the British Intelligence Corps.

We met in the great lobby of Shepheard's and our appearance contrasted sharply with that of the Gabardine Swine. Ken had a dirty white double-breasted jacket over black drainpipe trousers and he looked sinister and Levantine. He was about six feet tall with curly hair, a great forehead and an outsize mouth which showed all his teeth when he smiled. His sleazy clothing was explained by his cover story. He was posing as an Irishman of the rebel sort who had been stranded in Egypt by the war and was short of cash. To make his entry into the community of spies the Egyptian police had been persuaded to arrest him and to put him in jail alongside a number of people suspected of collaboration with the Axis Powers, as well as a mixed bag of petty criminals, pimps and prostitutes. Loudly talking against Britain, he soon found himself a contact. When he was released, he was welcomed into a society of Greeks, mainly shopkeepers, who were working for the Germans.

My room at Shepheards was large and luxurious. It overlooked the Nile and had a little balcony., It was also equipped with a sofa, two armchairs, a washstand and a bidet. It even had a writing desk. On my last night Ken and I settled in with some liquor and talked till dawn.

Ken was restless and eager to get out of Cairo. He was waiting to accompany a commando in an attack on the Greek mainland. The soldiers were to destroy coastal installations, and Ken was to be picked up by a partisan group which had asked for liaison with British forces in the Middle East. The operation had been held up until a submarine could be made available.

"My Greek is good enough to fool a German," Ken said, brushing aside the dangers of clandestine war, which I privately feared more than death in the air.

We began the evening by writing a joint letter to our parents. The German invasion of Russia which had started in June, 1941 was progressing swiftly, and some military observers were anticipating a Russian surrender, after which the British position in the Middle East would become untenable. The letter was to inform them that we would be joining the underground resistance to Hitler in Europe if that happened and they were to make no attempt to contact us.

I rummaged in the desk drawer and found a few sheets of hotel writing paper. A nice touch, I thought. From the old world luxury of one of the great hotels of the Middle East we announce our doom. I could see myself hanging by the wrists from a hook and being flogged by a sturdy young collaborator, while the sneering pansy Gestapo officer smoked a cigarette through a holder at a discreet distance, waiting for me to break. O shoot me down in flames, Lord God! Permit me to land with a positive thump. No hospitals, last words, funeral cortege. Instant dissolution. I wasn't cut out to be one of Robin Hood's merry men. Ken was.

It is hard to realize now, history having unfolded more benevolently, the gravity of Britain's plight in 1941. How could we have known that Hitler's proud armies would be engulfed, as Napoleon's had been, by that potent combination of iron national will and killing cold? No one in his right mind could have conceived of a folly like Pearl Harbor, which brought the United States into the war on our side. All we could see at the time was the pathetic example of the conquered nations of Europe and the likelihood of our own people falling into the same pattern of shameful servitude and heroic resistance. Churchill on trial for war crimes. Torture and firing squads for resisters. Storm troopers goose stepping up Whitehall. Heil Hitler!

I posted the letter next morning in the forces mail box in the lobby at Shepheards.

VII

ROMMEL'S PROBE
(8 to 14 September, 1941)

The day I had gone on leave to Cairo, September 3rd, had been a day of battle in the air. Just before midday twelve Macchi 200s, some G-50s and Messerschmitts attacked L.G.05, a strip near Sidi Barrani where a Hurricane unit, No. 1 Squadron of the South African Air Force, was situated. Seven Tomahawks took to the air in response, intercepting twenty-seven Fiat G-50s which were flying in to attack at 150 feet above the desert floor. Three of the Fiats were shot down and some damage was done to Hurricanes on the ground.[1]

Oblivious to these goings on, Charles Edmondson of No. 451 Squadron was out on reconnaissance. He was the shortest of the original Australians, stocky and dark haired. I'm tempted to say that he was always smiling, though that is only an impression. Better to say that he was the most consistently cheerful of all the squadron pilots. At the beginning of his desert tour he ran into technical problems, force landed once and did not take to the Hurricane like his compeers Hudson, Kirkham and Robertson. However, Charles was made for the long haul, and he ended up the war leading his own squadron of low level attack aircraft, earning himself a D.S.O.

Edmondson's job was to check on movement of transport and tanks in the area of Fort Capuzzo. His cover was Sergeant Miller Readett, an Australian who had been trained with him in Rhodesia. Charles was circling Capuzzo when the German and Italian aircraft, which had been delivering the raid on Sidi Barrani, were flying back to their bases. This is his account of what happened, from a letter to me dated 1990.

"I was skirting Capuzzo out of ack ack range when I saw the shadow of an aircraft moving swiftly across the sand below me in the other direction. A quick glance up and I noticed a black cross on a yellow fuselage. I gave a warning to Miller, instinctively banking in the direction of the 109 already on Miller's tail as the two of them went into a steep climbing turn. A few hundred feet above at 10 o'clock two more 109s were boring in. I got off a couple of wild bursts and then continued to press the firing button, but all I got was a hissing sound. At the same time it dawned on me that I was literally surrounded by dozens of the enemy. Miller was already on his way down in

---

1. An account of the Italian and German strafing of the Sidi Barrani area is given in *Fighters Over the Desert*, page 52-53.

flames. I "pulled the tit" (emergency boost control) and dived for the deck. It was some time before I realized I was not being pursued. My escape was not as miraculous as it sounds. They must have been short of ammunition and probably fuel as well."

Miller Readett was the first squadron casualty.[2] On 6th September the Italians strafed Sidi Barrani with six G-50s and again on the 7th with twenty-two G-50s and some Messerschmitt Bf 109s. The raid caught our fighters on the ground and at least twenty-one aircraft on several airfields in the vicinity were burned out or damaged.

When I flew back to the desert from Cairo the squadron had moved from our base landing ground at Qasaba. It was now operating from an advanced airfield, L.G. 75, thirty miles south of what had once been the pleasant little fishing port of Sidi Barrani. It had originally been held by the Italians and was shelled by our navy and subsequently fought over during the Wavell push of December 1940. From the air it looked more like partial excavations of an ancient city, rather than the ruins of a modern village. A street near the coast had been cleared of rubble and numerous trucks were always parked there, for the area was filled with military camps, dumps, vehicle parks and airfields. The beach at Sidi Barrani was therefore, a focal point for recreation.

Every day a group from the squadron would go off to the beach in a truck. The unpolluted Mediterranean was as clear as glass and it was a joy to discard our soiled clothes and achieve a temporary cleanliness by soaking our shirts and underclothes in the salt water, leaving them to dry in the sun. They went as stiff as boards, but it was better than nothing.

I have a photograph pasted in my log book of the RAF contingent on the sea shore. Molly appears wearing his Indian solar topi over his yellow wig. He is not wearing anything else. When he went in to swim he took off his hat and wig, but modestly kept away from the rest of us, replacing both articles as soon as he was out of the water. We all respected his privacy. His pudendum was on the top of his head and he was permitted to protect it like a maiden.

On the 12th and 13th of September I flew reconnaissances of the frontier region. On the second flight I saw for the first time, large numbers of enemy aircraft, and there was more activity on the ground as well. Over Sollum, my old photographic area, MEs were patrolling at 25,000 feet. A tented camp with perhaps five or six hundred vehicles had formed north of Sidi Omar and I was greeted with an alarming display of light flak, the red and green tracer leaving scary patterns across the sky. Six Stukas were flying at 1000 feet south of Capuzzo.

---

2. "Two Tac/R Hurricanes of 451 Squadron were intercepted near Sollum by three Bf 110s of III/ZG 26, Sergeant Readett being shot down." *FIGHTERS OVER THE DESERT,* page 53

ROMMEL'S PROBE

The Western desert is flat, stony and negotiable by motor transport without benefit of roads. It opened up all sorts of possibilities to opposing generals, since there were few positions where infantry could stand and fight; whereas armoured divisions, broken up into smaller units of tanks and supporting artillery, could attack from any direction. Their mobility considerably lessened their chances of being cut off or taken in the rear. Rommel was rightly considered the outstanding tank general the Germans possessed and he was operating in a terrain where armour could seldom be challenged.

Twenty-four hours later, on the moonlit night of 14 September, Rommel made one of the sudden and unexpected moves for which he was famous. He despatched an entire tank division, 21st Panzer, across the wire. One of his intentions was, apparently, to destroy British dumps of fuel and ammunition which had been built up close to the Libyan frontier in preparation for "Crusader". Another motive may have been to exercise his tank arm before the battle began in earnest. He gave the operation a poetic code name, "Midsummer Night's Dream", though it was long past midsummer when the plan went into effect. During the next few days No. 451 Squadron got its first taste of mobile warfare.

On the morning of the 15th I was asleep in my three foot high bivouac when someone banged on the canvas an inch or two from my face. A gruff voice with an English Midlands accent was shouting at me.

"The CO wants to see all officers in the flight tent, sir."

I stuck my head out. It was a soldier from the A.L.O. Section, a tank beret on his head, standing to attention.

"Why?"

"Jerries advancing, sir. There's an emergency."

Dressing was rudimentary and swift. Socks. Pull on my khaki shorts and desert boots. I slept in a shirt. Grab my battered hat. I ran all the way and was there in under two minutes. Half the pilots had arrived and were standing around smoking. I lit a "C to C" and took the first drag of the day. Hugh Davies was pinning a map to one of the display boards and Wizard was about to speak. He sat on one of the wooden tables in his usual ironic good humour, his Australian hat on the back of his head.

"It looks, chums, as if Rommel has played another of his sneaky tricks. Advancing at night, you know. Un-British, but you can't trust the Hun to behave like a gentleman. They say a hundred tanks are over the wire. Hugh has drawn a line of advance on the map."

He pointed to a broad arrow which began between Sollum and Sidi Aziz and passed fifteen miles south of our airfield.

"At present they're not heading directly for us, though prudent chaps might pack a panic bag, just in case he turns north. Jock Campbell has been ordered to step back and avoid battle until we know what Rommel's after. So it's going to be a busy day, chums. No one thinks it's going to be shit or bust, but keep your running shoes on."

57

MESSERSCHMITT ROULETTE

Brigadier Jock Campbell was the commander of the 7th Support Group, which stood directly in the line of Rommel's advance. He had a reputation from the previous Wavell campaigns as a heroic tank captain. He was also the inspirer of the "Jock" columns - fast striking groups of tanks and mobile infantry.

Pilots for the first sortie had already been briefed and engines were running up in the dispersals creating their usual tornadoes of dust. I had been detailed to fly the third recce and I rushed to the mess tent to eat my breakfast, but everyone else had the same idea. As a result it took longer than usual to get fed. Toast, margarine, canned jam and corned beef fritters. The toast was soggy and cold, the margarine tasted like axle grease, but the bully beef was palatable enough, though as a staple it had long ago become wearisome. In the Western Desert we ate to live, like prisoners doing time.

Hugh Davies was in a state of glorious excitement. Survivor of two tank disasters, he was the resident expert on this kind of warfare. He sat at his folding table, black tank beret on his head, jumping up from time to time to adjust his situation map. He was packed to go, his staff car and driver at hand.

"They can move at ten miles an hour," he said grimly, "so they could be here by two o'clock. Wizard's ordered all sections to be mobile in case we have to beat it."

The Hurricane I was allotted had some technical defect and I waited around all morning for it to become serviceable. At lunch I sat next to Pat Byers. I didn't know him well. In fact the only protracted conversation we ever had was in India, when we were both on a navigation course at Risalpur. We were alone in the mess bar and he was eager to talk about the affair he'd been having with an army officer's wife whom he'd met in the hills that summer. All I remember is his description of sexual intercourse which was, at the time, a closed book to me and therefore of special interest. One of the expressions he used to describe the terminal ecstasy was "going like a machine gun". It was a vivid metaphor, but I had no experience to help my imagination. Questions bubbled to my lips. Did they go to an hotel? Did he machine gun her on the marital couch? They remained unanswered questions because other officers came in and we never took up the subject again.

Pat was looking unusually worried.

"What's wrong?" I asked. "Is Rommel headed our way?"

"No. Hutley and Rowlands were shot down this morning."

"I didn't know."

"There were MEs all over the shop on my detail," Pat said. "And these fellows were totally inexperienced. Rowlands only had five hours on a Hurricane. What can you expect?"

"Bad luck," I said for want of anything else to say, thinking of my own chances out there.

58

ROMMEL'S PROBE

Pat grunted and remained silent for the rest of the meal.

I got airborne about one o'clock. It was a glorious summer day. The visibility must have been fifty miles. The column was estimated to be thirty miles away and it would only take minutes to reach it, so I didn't climb above 500 feet and flew a zigzag path watching for fighters. The Panzer division was a yellow scar across the featureless landscape. A tail of supporting vehicles, mobile 88mm artillery and refuellers followed the armour. Tank tracks threw up billows of dust obscuring detail and making them difficult to count. Ten minutes after I arrived Maryland medium bombers flew in to attack the column, escorted by Hurricanes. Messerschmitts very high up, looking like a swarm of gnats on a summer eve dived on the bombers. The role of aerial spy is not a glamorous one and I felt quite smug and unheroic, popping up to 500 now and then to check on progress while the battle raged overhead.

There was great tension in the Squadron all day. Groups of pilots sat in the mess tent drinking tea and discussing the non return of the two Australians. My reaction was to steer clear and keep busy. I volunteered for any flying that was going and spent the rest of the afternoon delivering a Hurricane for its routine inspection at our base landing ground at Qasaba and fetching back a serviceable one. It must have been six o'clock when I taxied in, handed over the kite to a servicing team and walked up to the mess for a drink. Wizard, Doc Reid, Molly, Hugh Davies and Pat Byers were in session, looking serious. Wizard, who was on the outskirts of the group, spoke to me.

"Horrocks wants a late sortie. Rommel has turned back and seems to be crossing the wire again. But it may be a feint. The old soldiers at Corps Headquarters don't trust the bugger. I've been objecting to a late sortie because it's too dangerous with the Luftwaffe out in full force. Unnecessary too because Rommel's taken a tremendous pounding all day and is obviously going back with his tail between his legs. But Horrocks pulled rank. Pat Byers has volunteered to do it.

"I can't see how a couple of squadrons of medium bombers could possibly stop a tank force of that size," I said. "Maybe Horrocks is right."

Wizard laughed and made an ironical victory sign.

"The Marylands caught them refueling. Absolute luck. Ed Kirkham says there was black smoke a mile high. Carmichael's just come in and says they may have lost half their armour. They're toddling off home now. I don't see the necessity for another sortie."

It was extraordinary, I thought, that Rommel had not co-ordinated his refueling with the Messerschmitt squadrons. Or maybe he had, but our fighters had driven them off. We didn't know. We were the eyes of the army and knew nothing of our own fighter and bomber operations at all. Beyond, of course, what we could actually observe for ourselves. Later on I became very uncomfortable about this.

Ray Hudson, who had been detailed to cover Pat, came in, his handsome face set in frustration.

"My kite's unserviceable," he said. "The sergeant's going to get another checked and re-fueled. It'll take twenty minutes."

"I've got to go," said Pat.

"But you can't go without me," said Ray, pleadingly. "For Christ's sake, it can wait twenty minutes, can't it?"

"I'm going now. A cover won't be much help."

Pat was leaning forward in his canvas chair, talking quickly in his characteristic splutter. His round face was red with sunburn.

"We've all done a sortie today," he said. "You can't see a bloody thing out there when the sun gets low. A cover wouldn't do much. I'd have as good a chance on my own."

"If it's going to be tricky out there, you need two covers not one," I said. "Wait a bit and I'll come too."

I didn't mean my offer very seriously. I was just arguing for safe procedures. Pat stood up, smiled, waved his hand at us and walked out of the tent.

Pat took off at six twenty for a sortie that should have taken thirty minutes at most, for the column was less than forty miles from our landing ground. Ray Hudson took off in pursuit a quarter of an hour later. By 7:30 neither had returned and Wizard came into the dining tent where I was eating to ask me to fly a back up sortie. Horrocks was adamant that the Army Commander must know the position and direction at nightfall.

"Don't kill yourself to count anything," he said, apologetically. "Just check that he's on his way home. I wish I'd stopped Pat from going without a cover."

"Easier said than done, " I replied. "Pat was in a dramatic mood."

I took Ken Whalley with me, thinking that if two Australians had gone to their eternal reward, it might be equitable to offer a couple of Englishmen. I was full of morbid thoughts, feeling like an understudy who is informed at very short notice that he is to play "Hamlet".

The problem of a late evening sortie in good weather was that the position of the sun, low down on the horizon, made it difficult to see the fighters. They could hang up in the sun and have a good view of intruding aircraft while being invisible themselves. Staring into the sun was counter-productive. My logbook entry reads, "Evening TAC/R 1 hr 15." and my penciled annotation "Jerries return to wire." The comparative length of the flight, from a landing ground only fifty miles from the Libyan border, shows the caution with which I approached it. What I did was to pierce the wire well south of the area of reconnaissance, get up sun as far as I reasonably could in the empty desert, and then fly back towards the column down the well worn track called the Trigh Capuzzo. The sun was by this hour so low on the horizon that I had a fairly good view of the western sky in the fading light. I stared anxiously into the blankness for fighters but could see nothing. Perhaps they were satisfied with shooting down Pat Byers. Was the show over just as the understudy was entering stage left? Underneath me the desert was dark purple and I could see the column, a long pink-tinged dust cloud to the north, still heading west towards the frontier. In the distance it looked like a giant slug undulating across the vast lonely landscape. I approached gingerly, still fearing the deceptive quality of the evening light.

"I don't see any fighters, do you, Ken?"

"They've all gone home, sir."

Whalley was inconsistent in his form of address. With a civilian disregard of military convention he sometimes called me "Geoff" and at other times "sir".

I flew by the column to make a count. There were sixty-four tanks among the more numerous soft-skinned vehicles and I saw again, at closer quarters, the long barrels of the 88 millimetre guns, drawn by stubby tractors. With the host in such turbulent motion I didn't expect to be shot at and they seemed to take no heed of our presence overhead. Close up, I could see that they were strung out in several straggly lines and many of the trucks were following independent paths.

Colour was leaking away from the scene and the sun no longer tinged the dust they threw so abundantly into the air. The leading tanks were just riding up to the faint line of the Libyan frontier. Rommel's probe was over. I turned steeply towards the darkened east and made for home.

It became almost dark as we flew back. I turned on my navigation lights so that Ken Whalley could see me. Slow on the uptake, he didn't respond by turning his own on.

"Turn on your nav lights, Ken," I said.

"OK, Geoff."

His lights flicked on, looking very bright and close. Six oil flares had been laid out to mark the landing path and we got on the ground without fuss. Few lights were showing on the base. Most people turned in when it became dark.

When I swung down from the cockpit Hugh Davies was there with his staff car.

"Glad to see you made it," he shouted. "Is it still heading west?"

"Yes. It's just crossing the wire, heading for Capuzzo. I've marked the position on my map."

"Thank God for that. I'll get on the blower to the Corps."

"Did Pat get back?"

No. Ray Hudson went after him but couldn't find him. Ray got back about an hour ago."

Wizard, Molly, Doc Reid and a few other anxious souls waited up in the mess tent, hoping to hear the engines of Pat Byers' Hurricane overhead and chewing over the day's excitements. We all knew he'd been shot down, though. There had been a strange atmosphere about his sacrificial gesture, as if he'd foreseen his own fate and seized the opportunity to prevent the involvement of another pilot.

I was dog tired and, after half an hour, I left them to find my bivouac.

Two days later, just as dawn was breaking, I was awakened by the sharp crack of a Bofors anti-aircraft gun situated fifty yards away. I scrambled out of my tent to see two Messerschmitts motoring in to our strip as if to make a landing. They were below 50 feet, flying slowly. The other seven guns of our airfield defenses opened up a second later at these sitting targets. MEs could not be mistaken for friendly aircraft. They were smaller than any plane we flew and typically screamed across the sky with a high pitched engine noise that was quite distinctive. On this occasion their noise was muted and they lost height steadily, heading straight into our landing area. Gunfire petered out when they were too low to attack without risking damage to our parked Hurricanes. Half way up the strip a dark object fluttered to the ground. Then the MEs opened up their engines and snarled off, weaving violently, followed by a pattern of Bofors shells whose white puffs curtained the dawn sky.

The squadron commander's car drove slowly down the strip and we saw Wizard get out and pick up the package. I ran across to the mess where the cooks were already active, dishing out mugs of weak tea to the assembled officers. Seeing the dainty shapes of these gnatlike aircraft flying slowly through our Bofors fire to drop something that did not explode was beyond our comprehension. We hardly exchanged a word, staring at Wizard's distant figure in the half light.

When he eventually drove over he was all smiles, holding a handwritten sheet of paper over his head in ironical imitation of our least popular politician.

"You won't believe this, gents," he said. "I feel like Mister bloody Chamberlain bringing peace in our time! I'll read it out to you. It's signed by the Messerschmitt flight commander."

However, when Wizard began to read the message his face became grave and his voice, more Welsh than ever, took on the cadences of a chapel preacher.

WE ARE SORRY TO REPORT THAT LT. BYERS WAS SHOT DOWN ON SEPTEMBER 14 BY AIRCRAFT OF THIS SQUADRON. HE WAS BADLY BURNED WHILE ESCAPING FROM THE COCKPIT. HE IS NOW IN DERNA HOSPITAL AND WE HAVE HOPES FOR HIS RECOVERY. WE WISH TO EXPRESS THE REGRETS OF THE LUFTWAFFE.

ROMMEL'S PROBE

A cheer went up. There were some expressions of amazement. Then we dispersed in a subdued manner to our bivouacs. We all feared burning above every other disaster. The main fuel tanks of the Hurricane were in the wings, a foot or two on either side of the pilot's cockpit; two wells of highly combustible liquid sloshing about asking to be ignited by a passing cannon shell. We were reminded of their proximity every time the aircraft was refueled. An airman would sit on the wing, unscrew the cap, and set the nozzle of the refueller in the tank. The worst case we envisaged was when a Messerschmitt raked through the wings, setting both tanks ablaze. Then the pilot had to extricate himself from the cockpit through a tunnel of fire, the speed of the aircraft acting as a bellows and forming blowtorches on either side of him.

The sudden ending of Rommel's probe surprised five Ju 87B pilots who had landed near Maddelena out of fuel and were captured on the ground by British armoured cars shadowing the retreating column. RAF pilots were at once sent up to fly them back to our lines. This incident caused hilarity and rejoicing throughout the British forces in the Western Desert.

A couple of weeks later, when I was away from the unit, the message-bearing Messerschmitts returned. I wish I could say that our anti-aircraft defenses held their fire in homage to a chivalrous foe, but the guns were under orders and belted away at the slow flying targets. Another package was dropped and the Messerschmitts disappeared (to everyone's relief) unharmed. This time the message was that Pat had died of his injuries and to once again present the regrets of the Luftwaffe.

The affair left the squadron stunned. It was such an extraordinary courtesy, almost medieval in character. It made nonsense of our built-up hatred of the Germans. It even made hard feelings impossible. World War I was fought in the infancy of the flying era, when merely taking to the air was an adventure and every landing in those unstable early biplanes a threat to life and limb. Out of that conflict a tradition of respect for the enemy's courage and skill had grown up between the German and British air forces. Only the most daring spirits turned up for those first tourneys in the sky; and when a pilot fell to earth the victor did not triumph over him. When Baron Manfred Von Richthofen was shot down on April 20, 1918, his body was buried with full military honours, six RAF pilots bearing his coffin on their shoulders. As late as September, 1941, this feeling was clearly not dead.

We did not realize, nor did the Germans, that September, 1941 was to be a turning point in the war. Hitler was saying that England's neck was to be wrung like a chicken, and many Germans may have felt secure enough in the final outcome of the war to harbour genuine sympathy for their British cousins. When the Americans declared war in December the balance of forces changed so dramatically in our favour that it is unlikely such a gesture could have been repeated.

MESSERSCHMITT ROULETTE

Of all the episodes in my war this remains the most amazing, and over the years I have tried to imagine the face and bearing of the Luftwaffe officer who risked his life and the life of his wingman on two occasions simply that Pat Byers' fate should not become a mere statistic. Whoever he was, I thought, he was determined to personalize the conflict and to put his own imprint on the passing tragedy.

In 1992 while examining a copy of **Fighters Over The Desert** by Christopher Shores and Hans Ring, I was finally able to identify the Luftwaffe messengers. This brilliant collaboration by two historians, one English and the other German, contained a day by day summary of air activity throughout the campaigns in North Africa. Here I found the following entry.

"Lt. Marseille intercepted a Tac/r Hurricane of 451 Squadron, the pilot, F/Lt. Byers being taken prisoner. "(P. 54)

In the appendices of the book Hans-Joachim Marseille's extraordinary career of 158 victories, 151 of them in the Western Desert, is recorded. He was twenty-one and a Hauptman in the famous Messerschmitt squadron I/JG27 when he shot down Pat Byers. A year later he was dead. I am pleased to be able to add this grace note to his history, for it is a moral certainty that it was Marseille who dropped the messages. Not only was he crazy enough to fly through our anti-aircraft defenses, who else would have had the motive for delivering a message about Byers except the man who had destroyed him. Eduard Neumann, the Kommodore of I/JG27, describes the Luftwaffe's attitude towards the RAF:

"It may be a little difficult for most people to understand today that the British flyers always enjoyed our respect and sympathy. This is more conceivable if one knows that in German pilots' messes in peace time the old veterans of World War One always spoke of the British pilots, of air combat with them, and of the British fairness in the most positive way. Many German pilots could speak English better than any other foreign language and were thus always quickly on good terms with the captured pilots. We endeavoured to be as hospitable as possible in order to make their passage into captivity a little less bitter. (**Fighters Over the Desert**, p. 223)

The feelings of brotherhood expressed here do not aspire to the level of Marseille's quixotic missions, but he was no ordinary pilot and no ordinary man. There are basically two kinds of successful fighter pilot. Ray Harries, an RAF pilot whom I knew well and whose reputation was made in the crowded skies over England, told me that his technique was to get in behind the target aircraft "close enough to be in danger of chewing his tail off with my prop" and then press the gun button and "fly through the bits!" This may have been a humorous exaggeration but it describes an aggressive attitude that does not depend for its success on accurate shooting. The other kind of ace, much rarer, is the deflection shooter who uses brilliant judgment in aiming his guns at a point in the sky where his enemy, a microsecond later, is going to pass through. Marseille, like "Screwball" Buerling, the Canadian ace, and "Killer" Caldwell, the Australian, was of this kind. And the German system encouraged the building up of victories to the credit of a single expert pilot, just as the RAF rules discouraged it. Under the RAF rules kills were shared, leading to the award of fractions of kills; and over enemy territory the difficulty of establishing a kill, which required other witnesses or the evidence of wreckage, were magnified. The consequence was that Allied aces, like Caldwell (20 1/2), "Imshi" Mason (15 1/2), and Peter Wykeham (13) had lower scores than their actual kills. However, Marseille's wingman flew a hundred sorties with his leader before claiming a victory of his own. Rudolph Sinner, a pilot in I/JG27, explains how this could happen:

"The air war in Africa favoured the "experts" to a high degree. The wing men, "Kaczmareks" and No. 2s had only a small chance to gain any victories. The majority of the victories of the German fighters were the result of surprise attacks, during which in most cases only the formation leader was able to fire. Such quick sparrowlike attacks were seldom followed by a dogfight . . ." **(Fighters Over the Desert** p. 233.)

All this does nothing to diminish Marseille's extraordinary record over eighteen months of combat with minimal rest periods. When he was killed it affected the morale of the entire Gruppe, which had to be withdrawn from the front line for a month.

His greatest deeds, only revealed by the patient work of scholars and the accident of my own involvement as an eye witness, were almost private and purely compassionate. He must have had an easy shot at Pat's lone Hurricane, diving out of the sun, steady in the evening air. As he watched the aircraft go into its blazing descent to earth and the struggles of the pilot to extricate himself, he must have felt both guilt and compassion. Did he visit Pat in his bed at Derna Hospital? I think so. Did something in Pat's deplorable condition or the courage of his responses touch him so deeply that he felt obliged to act as he did? We will never know the details, but the facts as they stand do him more honour than his 158 victories in the air.

Marseille died in almost as uncomfortable a way as Pat Byers. On 30 September, 1942, flying to intercept a formation of Allied fighters, one of the glycol lines in his ME developed a leak, filling the cockpit with nauseous smoke. He was unable to see ahead and was choking on the fumes; so, with his usual decisiveness, he announced to the ground controller that he was bailing out. He opened the cockpit hatch, released his straps and turned the aircraft on its back to fall clear. As the Luftwaffe court of enquiry established **(Fighters Over the Desert,** page 254) his forward visibility was so poor that he did not realize that his aircraft was in a slight dive. The consequence was that on exiting the cockpit he struck his head on the tailplane and was rendered unconscious, never pulling the ripcord of the parachute that might have saved his life.

Paddy Hutley and Sergeant Rowlands both survived. Hutley managed to crash land his shot-up plane and was rescued by our armoured cars. He was back in the squadron the next day. Rowlands, after being pursued for many miles by Messerschmitts, landed his Hurricane in one piece at Bir El Thalata. He had cannon shell wounds in both legs and had lost a good deal of blood. He was rushed to a military hospital in the Egyptian Delta and did not return to the squadron.

VIII

TOBRUK
(16 September to 12 October, 1941)

On September 9th General Sir Alan Cunningham was appointed as commander of what was soon to become the 8th Army, comprising 30 Corps and 13 Corps. 30 Corps consisted of the 7th Armoured Division, 1st South African Division and 22 Guards Brigade. 13 Corps had the New Zealand Infantry Division and 4th Indian Division, supported by Matilda and Valentine tanks. The 4th Armoured Brigade, equipped with the new Stuart tanks from the USA, was expected to be operational soon.

Wizard gave us the general drift of events in his bar sessions and Hugh Davies, restlessly pacing his ALO tent, was eager to fill in further details from the rumour mill, including names and unflattering biographies of the tank colonels. His situation map was becoming quite detailed, with little flags for units in place and long lists of formations due to arrive. He was expecting to go back to his regiment for the next clash of arms.

"They're re-equipping now," he told me. "I wish to God they'd hurry up and call for me. Masses of tanks are being unloaded in Egypt and once the engineers check them out the balloon's going to go up. I give it a month. There's bound to be a decisive tank battle beyond the wire. Probably outside Tobruk somewhere. My guess is that we'll attack as soon as the 9th Divvy has been relieved."

Tobruk had been a problem for Rommel since April, 1941 when he had failed to capture the fortress and was forced to continue his advance into Egypt with this "sally point", as Churchill called it, at his back. Its position athwart his coastal lines of communication and the high morale of the garrison, which suggested that at any time it might break out and harry his rear, forced Rommel to keep twice as many soldiers outside the perimeter of Tobruk as we had inside it. The Australian public became deeply involved with the unfolding drama, and the commander, General Leslie Morshead, became a national figure.

In August, 1941 however, there was a change of government in Australia. Mr. Robert Menzies, who had always been a strong supporter of Britain's conduct of the war, was forced to resign and he was replaced by Mr. A.W. Fadden who took the view that Australian troops should be withdrawn from Tobruk "to satisfy public opinion in Australia." According to Winston Churchill's account of the matter in **The Grand Alliance**, Mr. Fadden was anxious about "the decline in health resistance" and "the danger of a catastrophe resulting from further decline and inability to withstand a determined attack". Churchill protested to no avail. It was a classic example of the Gallipoli syndrome; the fear of huge Australian casualties unaccompanied by equal sacrifices by other British and Commonwealth troops. The notion of a decline in health and fighting spirit within the garrison was a big joke, as the 9th Division was in fine shape and very conscious of its role in giving the Germans their first bloody nose of the war. But the Mediterranean Theatre had been the scene of many recent military disasters and Australian troops had been heavily involved in all of them. There was a case to answer. Unfortunately General Auchinleck had sent the 50th British Division to Cyprus when that island had seemed to be threatened with an invasion on the model of the successful German assault on Crete. But Crete had been too costly for the Germans and Cyprus remained a haven for the rest of the war. Nevertheless the apparent safety and inactivity of a British division there seemed scandalous. The outcome of this regrettable dispute was that a hard pressed Royal Navy had to begin the dangerous task, night after night, of taking the Australian 9th Division off and landing in their place two British brigades and a brigade of Free Poles.

On the afternoon of 17th September I flew Hurricane V7779 back to Qasaba for one of its routine inspections and collected a serviceable aeroplane from Acker Kerr, our squadron engineering officer, who usually stayed at the base camp. The word Acker was slang for an Egyptian piastre and it was a nickname often applied to pay clerks. Acker, however, acquired his sobriquet because his initials were A.C.K. He was a major asset to the squadron, an ex-Halton apprentice, master of his profession and well liked by the Australians. He looked like Ray Hudson's elder brother with his blue eyes, lick of golden hair and sturdy physique. He was as important to the technical health of the unit as Doc Reid was to its physical health. I didn't see much of him because I was always forward and he was always back, so he hardly comes into this story, but to most of the Australian technical staff, numerically nine-tenths of the total strength, he must have represented the RAF more immediately than the pilots did. Whenever I saw him I thanked God that he was with our divided, unsteady squadron. He might so easily have been sent to some fat cat RAF fighter outfit where the only snags were technical ones.

When I returned in the evening Wizard was waiting for me in the dispersal with his battered staff car.

"Anything up?" I asked.

Wizard put on his long suffering face. "Morshead's getting nervous about his perimeter," he began. "He's always been slightly pissed off at having no air recce up there. Now he's thumping the table. He thinks some of Rommel's beautiful tanks might build up and punch a hole in his defences while his relief troops are trying to find where the latrines are. He needs an aircraft inside the fortress to work for him. I thought you'd like to go."

"You bet I would!"

TOBRUK

I couldn't believe my luck. This was the glamour job I'd been waiting for. Something to keep the Aussies at bay. Any one of them would have sold his breeches to go to Tobruk.

"The main airfield at Tobruk," he went on," is unusable. The Hun gunners can turn on a bombardment at will. So they've built a new strip on the escarpment overlooking the harbour, and a couple of heavily camouflaged hangars. The reconnaissance job will be very local, mostly checking out the perimeter for old Morshead. The strip, they tell me, is pretty short. Middle East HQ can lend us a Magister. What do you think?"

It didn't sound right to me. The Miles Magister was a primary trainer. In fact it was the first aeroplane I flew at Anstey in 1937, when our "entry" was being weeded out for serious flight training and we were still in civilian clothes. It was a two-seater monoplane, maximum speed eighty-five mph. Very manoeuvrable. Would land on a sixpence. No problem concealing it. Just throw a tarpaulin over it. I tried to imagine crossing the Tobruk perimeter and flying over the enemy lines at fifty feet . A good machine gunner would have me. 500 feet? Small arms and light flak would both be in range. And the pissy little engine would not be powerful enough to move me quickly out of trouble. I'd jam the throttle forward against the stop and nothing would happen. I'd flick into a steep turn and stay on the same spot. If the fighters caught me it would be like offering them a stationary target. My evasion procedure would resemble that of a fly in a bottle.

"I'd prefer to take a Hurricane, Wizard, " I said quickly. I didn't want any more discussion of Magisters."

"I thought somehow you'd like that idea. Pity. It's only very local flying, you know. You'd never be more than ten miles from base."

I explained my point of view in politer form than my private thoughts.

"Well, it's your decision. The strip is just long enough for a Hurricane if you land short. I'll crack off a signal to say that you'll appear tomorrow at noon sharp over the harbour at 500 feet with your wheels down. I'll ask them to fire a green Very light, signaling permission to land. The Tobruk defences are trigger-happy after all these months of seeing nothing but enemy aircraft. Be careful not to cross the coast until the natives show friendly signs."

At mealtimes we sat at long wooden benches to eat. That evening I was slinging one leg over preparatory to sitting down when Ray Hudson came in behind me and slammed my shoulder.

"You're going to Tobruk!"

"Yes." He slammed my shoulder again.

"Lucky bastard, but good on yer."

"Thanks."

After the unappetizing meal of warmed up bully beef, mashed biscuits and hot tea I walked back to my bivouac in a daze. Things were looking up. That night I slept on the stony ground like a dead man.

MESSERSCHMITT ROULETTE

To my surprise Wizard insisted on escorting me to Tobruk for this important mission. We took off at 11 AM, which was much too early but I couldn't afford to be late for my noon appointment. There were scattered white clouds at three thousand feet and the sea was lapis lazuli, mostly light blue with darker patches of cloud shadow and flashes of gold where the sun struck the white horses. It was 11:40 when I positioned myself directly north of Tobruk and I had fifteen minutes to wait before I began my entry. I couldn't see much point in Wizard hanging around too, so I waggled my wings. He waved his hand at me and turned steeply on to an easterly heading, gaining height a little. At two hundred feet I could see the coast as a brown blur. I hoped Tobruk was somewhere there.

At five minutes to the hour I stopped circling and headed south, peering anxiously for a landmark. Some white houses on the escarpment above the harbour were the first to appear clearly, then suddenly the white Mediterranean to wn, poised enchantingly over the blue water, looking peaceful and civilized like an Italian fishing village. I slowed up, put down twenty degrees of flap and lowered my undercarriage. A green light went up from a mole. Then another. I began to waggle my wings slowly and deliberately for the benefit of the trigger-happy gunners. Everything was going to be all right.

I flew low over the town, curious to see how badly it had been damaged from the pounding both sides had given it over the previous twelve months. Tobruk in peacetime must have been a pleasant place to visit; a sleepy North African town with a single hotel, probably run by a Greek or Maltese family. A market. A small steamer to bring goods from Derna and Benghazi, and a few local fishing vessels to operate from the little harbour. The narrow streets between the flat-roofed buildings would have been crowded with Arabs, veiled women and the occasional regal figure of a nomad, leading an overloaded camel.

From the sea it had looked jewel-like, intact, the walls shining white against the red escarpment; but this was an illusion due to my low angle of vision. Looking down I saw that only the skyline remained. The town was a shell, with roofless houses and deserted streets. The only movement to be seen was at the docks where a body of Australian infantrymen were forming up beside a line of trucks. Glancing inland, I could see a busy network of crisscrossing tracks and the faint outline of the defensive fortifications beyond.

The landing strip to the east of the little town was easy to identify. It ran parallel to the coast and was in some places only fifty yards from the sea cliffs. It seemed too short for regular use by Hurricanes, but a temporary windsock fluttering above a truck told me I had plenty of breeze to work with. I aligned myself, put down full flap, and got on the ground as soon as possible. A man was waving at the end of the strip and I gunned the motor to reach him quickly. He jumped on a truck and still waving vigorously led me a hundred yards or so down a broad sloping track that curved left into a large jagged cleft in the escarpment. Here were the so-called underground hangars, angled slightly in towards one another to fit into the flattened area at the apex. I could see the familiar shapes of RAF mechanics' tool boxes in the corners. Work benches had been set up in the rear of one hangar against the rock face.

As soon as I'd shut down my engine, six airmen ran me into the left hand hangar at a run. I looked up at the tubular steel structure with its heavy canvas covering, enjoying the sense of instant concealment.

A truck rumbled up the steep track from the town and halted in a cloud of dust. A RAF officer with wings on his bush shirt jumped out and ran up to me, hand extended. He looked about thirty-five, with thick black hair and a narrow face full of energy and humour. I had imagined myself to be the only pilot in Tobruk and was momentarily discomfited.

"I'm RAF liaison to General Morshead," he said. "Glad you arrived safely. You look surprised to see me."

He was wearing the three broad stripes of a wing commander. I was, in fact, doubly surprised. He had a pronounced Aussie accent.

"You're an Australian, sir," I said.

"Yes. An Aussie in the RAF. What do you think of that? I'm Digger Black to everyone around here."

We drove down the escarpment to the town. There were some distant explosions. I felt the scene was slightly unreal, like a dream sequence or a stage set. The prettiness of the North African coast line. The neat shape of the harbour with its mole. The sun glittering on the navy blue sea. The white ruined town.

The drive down was agonizingly slow. The only smooth sections of the meandering track ran across slabs of red rock which ended in axle-pounding drops to the next slab. Reversing and manoeuvering was necessary to edge through defiles cluttered with debris and pockmarked with shell craters.

We drove slowly through the narrow rubble-strewn streets of Tobruk, where some of the buildings gave the illusion of being undamaged. A Christian church with a broken statue in its courtyard seemed to have survived the bombs but there was no sign of glass in the windows, or anywhere else, in fact.

General Morshead's HQ was built into the cliff behind the harbour. The entrance was a simple corridor leading directly into the interior of the escarpment. It was a hundred feet long, lit by naked electric bulbs and leading to huge metal doors guarded by a sentry. Then more corridors, the walls dripping moisture which formed puddles underfoot. More doors. Finally we came to the H.Q. itself, a cluster of comfortable looking offices and an operations room with a wall map showing troop dispositions.

The General suddenly appeared in the doorway of his office and put out his hand. I had intended to salute in the conventional fashion but his gesture outmanoeuvred me. He gave Digger Black a brief smile but did not ask him into his office. He beckoned me to a chair and shut the door. Apparently this was to be a completely private interview. He was of medium height, broad, probably in his fifties. His dark hair was cut very short and he wore some World War I ribbons on his bush jacket. His air of authority wasn't at all military. His manner was more that of the boardroom. No big smiles or little jokes to put me at my ease, as Horrocks with his establishment charm might have employed. He had something of the raw power of Stan Reid. Perhaps he's an Australian type, I thought. He looked at me intently without smiling.

"You're here because I can't see far enough beyond my perimeter, particularly in places where there's a depression." He pointed to a wall map. "A considerable force of tanks and artillery could build up . . . " He rose to his feet and pointed out two positions. " . . .here and here . . . and we'd only know about it when it was too late. While the relief is under way we're going to be especially vulnerable. I don't have any worries right now but I'll call you when I need you. Meanwhile could you do some work for the artillery?"

"Yes, sir."

"Our boys have been frustrated for some time because the enemy can use spotting aeroplanes which sit out beyond the perimeter and train their guns on ours. We haven't had that privilege for months, as you know. They've been getting some direct hits on our gun emplacements that way. It'll give them quite a boost to have a spotter of their own and get a bit of old-fashioned revenge. Have you been trained for that sort of thing?"

"Yes,sir," I said.

I hadn't, as a matter of fact. My log book shows one flight, which I've recorded as "Practice Arty/R", on September 4th, the day I flew to Heliopolis for my short leave with Ken. I covered Micky Carmichael on a shoot with local gunners. I was aware of the basic technique and considered it largely common sense.

"I'll get the gunners to contact you through Digger Black."

He stood up. This time I saluted. As soon as I passed into the outer office, half a dozen senior looking army officers were ushered into his presence. He seemed to be a busy man. Not a very expansive type of person but confident, relishing his job.

A Hurricane is not designed to carry personal luggage. However, in a half filled parachute bag I had a change of clothes, long trousers for the evening cool, a pullover, my blue service hat and shaving kit. The inclusion of my best uniform hat, now much battered and sun-bleached, was an afterthought. Back at the squadron I hadn't much use for head covering and I'd ceased to wear a hat. The Aussie airmen who prepared, re-armed and refueled the planes were informal in their manners. I can't recall one of them ever saluting me and thus the need to wear a hat diminished to a vanishing point. It wasn't deliberate rudeness on their part. It was their democratic style. They would occasionally call me "sir' but that salutation has been in the English language since the Norman Conquest. I had brought my hat with me on this expedition, of course, to salute General Morshead and this had now been accomplished.

At the army store I was issued with a new bivouac tent and a steel helmet and was advised to dig myself in by nightfall. I was given a spade that had seen better days and a rusty iron spike for dislodging pieces of rock. Everyone slept, worked and ate below ground. A sixty pounder siege gun lobbed shells into the fortress all day. One heard it fire off many miles away, a distant plop. This was followed by a rising whistle as it ascended to its maximum height. A pause. Then one heard the scream of its acceleration as it plunged towards the earth and the heavy crump when it struck. It was called "Bardia Bill" because it was located east of the perimeter in the direction of Bardia. If it wasn't in action people would say, "I wonder what's happened to Bardia Bill?" At first I used to listen to it all the time. In a few days, like the rest of the inhabitants of Tobruk, I only thought about it when it wasn't firing or when the shells got too close. Fortunately the enemy never suspected that an aircraft was being operated from Tobruk. If they had done so Bardia Bill might have been put to more effective use.

There was a gunner's all ranks mess a mile inland from the airstrip and there I ate most of my meals, which were compounded of the same standard rations, no better, no worse than back at the squadron. One of the minor discomforts was the twenty minute walk before the first gulp of hot tea in the morning. At the outset I enjoyed instant fame as the only pilot to land in Tobruk since No. 73 Squadron, also flying Hurricane Is, was wiped out trying to defend it from air attack in the early days of the siege. Some of their glory necessarily rubbed off on me. Crowds of soldiers would gather round me to ask questions. Was I going to shoot down some Stukas? How many more Hurricanes were coming? When was I going to fly? I tried to explain that I was just spotting for the General but this piece of information never got through to the ranks who insisted on their own myth. From first to last I was "that fighter pilot" who was going to challenge the Luftwaffe against fearful odds. Two tall bespectacled officers - a great many British gunners seem to fit that description - sat with me as I ate and asked me the same questions. They cottoned on, however, to my real function in Tobruk, offering daily suggestions as to how I should be used and debriefing me informally after each flight.

That evening I set up my bivouac tent near the edge of the escarpment from which I could see the sea and the town and harbour to the west. It was a nice view and I took comfort from its normality. At night I could see the black shapes of vessels as they entered the harbour through the swept channel. I asked permission to go into the town one night to watch the relief troops as they disembarked but there was a prohibition on sightseers. This hazardous operation was carried out by the navy with almost no casualties, and though it wasn't a famous victory it had the effect of one. Tobruk was a symbol of defiance, an isolated garrison whose very existence required extraordinary skill and courage to maintain. The fact that its defenders were relieved successfully, under attack by bombers and submarines, gave a lift to all the British forces in the Western Desert. In Tobruk itself that elation was felt stronger and earlier than elsewhere. It was part and parcel of the spirit of 1941, when Britain itself was a beleaguered fortress and we all tended to think of holding on rather than of victory.

The steel helmet they had given me I superstitiously refused to put on. It remained throughout my stay in Tobruk covering one of the tent pegs of my bivouac. Equally superstitiously I did not dig myself in, choosing to sleep above ground and take my chance with Bardia Bill and the Stuka raids. In retrospect I can see that this was foolish, because the biggest danger in a siege is not being hit by a shell or a bomb; it is having your head sliced off by spent anti-aircraft shell fragments. During a bombing attack our big 3.7 inch ack ack guns would belt away and the air would be filled with the musical shrieks of nose caps as they descended murderously to earth. I was vaguely aware of this but considered myself Messerschmitt bait and privately took all bets against falling to lesser evils. I had been issued three blankets. I made a depression for my hip and lay on two of them, keeping the third for covering. In Libya it is still warm in September.

A section of Bofors light anti-aircraft guns had been detached to guard my Hurricane and were dispersed over a slight rise in the ground on the landward side of the strip. I had just finished erecting my bivvy and had set my few possessions under cover when Tony Barrett, the lieutenant in charge of the guns, walked across and took me off for a drink. He was properly dug in, the owner of a network of man deep trenches, his living quarters protected by a metal sheet. His runner was also his batman, a wizened Highlander named McNamee, who cooked and cleaned and provided services. This was high living by desert standards, everything neat and tidy, tea and coffee available on request. Tony injected a romantic fervour into his job of guarding me and my Hurricane from harm and we became friends for life. When we both had time off we would swim in a little cove west of the town. It had a hundred yards of sandy shoreline between harsh red cliffs and was as deserted as a private beach. These were pleasant hours, swimming naked and walking to dry off in the sun.

On 20 September Digger Black passed me a message that the Australian gunners would like me to go to their mess for dinner. I accepted and was picked up by their CO in his staff car. He wore a felt and had one of those angular, beaky faces that are typically Antipodean. The mess was crowded with officers and there was an air of celebration that I put down to their imminent evacuation to Egypt. It turned out to be something else. As soon as drinks had been poured, the CO rolled out a map on the mess table.

"We want you to do something for us," he said, with a big smile. A cheer went up from the assembly.

"Blue Nelson will tell you all about it."

Blue Nelson, whose ironical Australian nickname identified him as a former redhead, was a large balding man of about forty. He was in great form, more from natural excitement than from alcohol.

"We've been firing at these fuck'n Jerry gun positions since May."

He pointed to two places outside the northwestern section of the perimeter defences.

"A couple of weeks ago they had a spotter, flying out of range of our ack ack on their side of the perimeter. Neat little German observation plane. Fieseler Storch. We couldn't do a damned thing about it. They got a direct hit on one of our gun positions. Killed four of our blokes. We've got a perfect line on 'em but our range is a little off and they're so well dug in that a small error will miss them. We need a direct hit, really. We've been praying for a plane to spot for us. Morshead told us you were coming. Now's our chance to get even before we go."

More cheers.

After dinner we locked up the details.

"We'll want to bracket the bastards one at a time," said Blue. "The twenty-five pounder is a pretty accurate weapon. We'll pitch our first shell beyond the target. We'll do that deliberately, so that you can give us a correction below the target. Once we've got it bracketed, mathematics will do its deadly work. Then we'll switch immediately to the other position, so that you won't have to hang around too long."

The evening ended noisily. "Waltzing Matilda" was sung. They were making a dent in the unit booze before their departure. A good deal of the casual chatter was about Rommel's attacks on the fortress the previous April. It was news to me. I had thought the fortress was impregnable. But while I'd been poodle faking in India, they'd been fighting for their lives in this arid outpost.

"I didn't know Rommel pierced your defences," I said innocently.

Blue Nelson grinned.

"Easter Monday it was. He threw his tanks across the perimeter, followed up by infantry and artillery. Didn't get too far that time. Then he had another try on 30 April. You remember that?"

He turned for support to his mates, who nodded, gestured or grunted assent.

"That was the big show. He broke through along the line of the Acroma road from the west. Must have advanced a couple of miles. We threw everything we had at him. Knocked 'im back."

Boozy cheers from the company.

"Good old 9th Divvy," said someone. "We taught the bastard a lesson."

It was hard to believe the morale in this unit. They were defending a fragile position fifty miles beyond our front lines, yet they'd inflicted the first setback of the war on the German Army. My awe deepened a notch. It was an unknown victory. Only after the war was over did we learn that Rommel's defeat was so bad - 1700 casualties - that the German Supreme Command in the Mediterranean reprimanded him for reckless wastage of lives and forbade him to attack Tobruk again.

We'd planned an early start in the morning to avoid interruption by Stuka raids. I got up early, forgoing breakfast, and checked radio communications with the guns at 7:30 while the Hurricane was still in its camouflaged hangar.

At eight o'clock I was scrambled. The RAF airmen of the servicing team who had been transported to Tobruk by sea a few weeks before, pushed the aircraft at a run on to the relatively flat area between the two hangars where a starter trolley had already been placed.

I taxied at full speed on to the strip, very conscious of the occasion.

General Morshead's private air force takes to the war torn air above the beleaguered fortress!

Sudden appearance of invisible Hurricane from non-existent landing ground, overlooked by two Luftwaffe airfields!

First entrance of helmeted stranger, bent on vengeance for Aussie lives!

To make the most of the surprise element, I turned at once towards the perimeter after take off. At 300 feet I headed straight for the enemy guns. They were surprisingly easy to identify. Big castle-like shapes, neatly constructed of sandbags, rose out of the flat desert. Long gun barrels poked out of narrow openings in each structure. A pattern of faint tracks joined the gun positions to each other. Behind them a broader track led to the paved El Adem road.

My throttle was wide open and my speed relative to the earth was high. This was not good for observation of shot, but I had no intention of slowing down. I retreated to the line of the perimeter defences and gave the initial order.

"Fire"

A few seconds later I saw a white puff go up a hundred yards beyond one of the enemy gun positions.

"Drop two hundred. Left fifty."

I turned again to keep the guns in sight and found myself slashing across the defensive earthworks, my wings vertical, into a snowstorm of light ack ack. I swooped and climbed, weaving my way back to the safety of our own lines.

A crescent of cotton wool explosions marked my erroneous path.

Clearly it wasn't safe out there. Tobruk was something special.

All this took seconds. I was vague on how long it took the 25 Pounders to reload. Should have asked them.

"Fire," I shouted.

TOBRUK

I could see Al Adem glinting to the south. Some hangars. A little cluster of airport buildings. Everything seemed quiet in that quarter. I couldn't locate Sidi Resegh from my altitude. It was just a strip and had no permanent buildings but I knew the Messerschmitts were there. Dust clouds would warn me if a section took off.

The next round was only fifty yards from its target. A single correction had been sufficient. In a matter of minutes the second target was engaged and bracketed.

"All right, son. That's the ticket. You can go home now."

"Roger."

But I didn't want to go in. I watched for a few minutes as Blue Nelson's mathematics did their deadly work and destroyed both guns. I didn't want to think about the men trapped in the downfall of their sandbag castles. As smoke cleared I could see how badly reduced they were. That's what the German Fieseler Storch had done to the Aussie guns. Revenge indeed!

I was contemplating a short recce of the immediate area to see if I could find anything of interest to General Morshead when dust clouds began to appear from the direction of Sidi Resegh. Safe within the perimeter I gained height. A section of fighters were taking off away from me. I decided not to stick around. I turned back, reduced speed, put my wheels and flaps down and slid into the strip. The truck was there, an airman waving at me to follow him. I roared down the bumpy track and wheeled left under the safety of the camouflage netting. When I stepped from the aircraft I looked at my watch. Twenty-five minutes. It hadn't seemed that long. I walked outside the cover into the sun. The MEs were at 3000 feet and driving straight out to sea, pursued by black and white explosions from our anti-aircraft defences. They must have assumed that I'd flown in from Egypt and that I would escape out to sea. I watched them wasting good petrol searching for me.

A day or so later the gunner regiment was packing up to go. I lunched with the CO and got many slaps on the back. A Polish 25 Pounder regiment had already disembarked and handovers were taking place. The Polish chaplain, hearing that I was a Catholic, asked me to join them at Mass the following Sunday.

My previous experience of Poles had been at school, where we had three Prince Radziwills. The eldest of them was the fiercest. He was six feet in height, had a long face, a thin hooked nose and his dark blond hair was brushed back unparted from his forehead. One evening during Prep, a period for study monitored by a prefect, I whispered to the boy at the next desk, a thing forbidden by the code. Whereupon Radziwill Senior, who was on duty, knocked me nearly unconscious with a blow to the head, giving me a lasting suspicion of foreigners! Boys who had enjoyed the Radziwill hospitality in Poland reported that, after passing through the gates, they motored six miles before reaching the castle! Whenever I see a Dracula movie I think of the Radziwills.

MESSERSCHMITT ROULETTE

The chapel at the back of the town where the Poles gathered for Mass had no roof and the windows had long been blown out. But it was a cleared space and the congregation of gunners stood throughout the service. Unlike the English soldier, who bawls discordantly, the rank-and-file Pole is musical, fitting his voice naturally into harmony. They made a throaty, textured, sad sound. I felt a wave of European feeling, seeing the blunt faces of the Polish peasantry once again showing up to do their historic duty. It wiped from my mind the image of Radziwill as the representative Pole.

Mid-morning of September 27th I was sitting in Tony's dugout drinking tea provided by the ever attentive McNamee. It was a special pleasure to drink it freshly brewed from the pot. The dark and dangerous looking liquid dispensed from oversized urns back at the squadron was very different. If you were lucky to get an early cup it wasn't so bad, but ordinarily one had to accept a stewed mixture that tasted bitterly of tannin.

"This is a great cup of tea," I said, looking at McNamee.

"Thank ye, sirr."

"McNamee created this refuge," said Tony. "He filched the chairs and a table from somewhere. I don't inquire too energetically about that. He found the piece of steel for the roof that keeps out shell splinters. Where did you get that McNamee?"

"It was aroond, sirr," he replied, disappearing up two stairs into the open air.

"Scrounging is a great art. The Highlanders are past masters. I'm not bad at it myself. This strip of carpet was lying around. No one wanted it. Doesn't it give a homey touch? Getting wine and whiskey requires Byzantine diplomacy. Luckily I have friends in low places."

Ten minutes later we were interrupted by McNamee who stuck his head through the small opening and shouted three words at us.

"Stuka party, sirr."

"See you later," said Tony, grasping his tin hat and struggling up the steps.

He rushed off to "tighten" his guns and to prepare a hot reception for the raid. I sat on top of his metal roof and watched. They were attacking some positions to the south of us and I had the circus in perfect view with no danger of bombs dropping nearby to distract me. It would have been impossible to have choreographed a better air show. Ten Stukas in line astern formation peeled off, one after the other, to execute their slow dives, the air counterpointed with explosions from the anti-aircraft defences. The third plane to descend was hit at the beginning of its dive just as it paused, head down like a falcon, a menacing black shape against the blue. It continued its dive, smoke and flame pouring from it, until it crashed with a violent thump less than a mile from where I sat. Black oil smoke mixed with red dust rose slowly from the corpse, making a smudge on the landscape. Bombs rained down as the remaining

TOBRUK

Stukas peeled off for their attacks, the impacts marked by pinkish clouds which dissipated quickly.

At the top of their dives they appeared almost fixed in space, their protruding undercarriages painted awkwardly against the sky. The weird noise began while they still gave the illusion of waiting, hovering in a vertical attitude, taking aim for their plunge to earth. It was a disturbing sound, getting louder and higher pitched as their speed increased, ending in a screech as they pulled out and flew off almost sedately from the target area. They had looked like eagles descending, but they departed like crows. The whole performance had the same delight to the eye as watching pelicans dive for mullet. It was beautiful and theatrical and, incidentally, pretty useless militarily. The Tobruk garrison was well dug in and few casualties were sustained. It was an attempt to weaken the morale of the defenders; a threatening gesture rather than an effective instrument of war. The Stuka was designed to dismay civilian populations and to proclaim the overwhelming power of the German Reich. Its great successes were over undefended cities like Rotterdam. The situation at Tobruk, with its cocky, unafraid garrison, showed up its weaknesses as a bomber. One could see that it was three quarters theatre of terror and one quarter business. McNamee had called it a "Stuka party," and there was a connotation of contempt in the appellation.

When Tony arrived back, exhilarated at having his guns in action, I mentioned the impressive war cry of the Stuka.

"Sirens," he said.

"What?"

"They've sirens fixed on them to make that dreadful noise. The idea is to scare the pants off us. They don't know that we enjoy the target practice. We don't shoot down many though. The 3.7 boys got him. They were a bit high for us, weren't they, McNamee?"

McNamee nodded wisely.

"Ay, sirr. But if was guid to see one of the bastards go doon."

In spite of his apparent satisfaction with my work, Morshead only used me on four occasions during the three weeks I spent in Tobruk, the other three missions being reconnaissances. I was very disappointed and groaned inwardly as the days went by in idleness. I had hoped to bring back a heroic tale which might ward off Australian insults and I had dreamed of spotting a division of tanks about to attack Tobruk at its weakest point. In my imagination the General would thank me with tears in his eyes for saving the fortress and recommend me for the freedom of the cities of Perth and Sydney! But if he would not let me get airborne there was no chance of glory. I remember crossing the landing strip each morning from my bivouac on the cliff's edge and waiting around glumly for transport to take me to the gunner mess for breakfast; listening for the wheeze and crump of Bardia Bill and thinking of borrowing a spade and digging myself in; considering being sensible and wearing my tin hat. Deciding not in both cases. Swimming with Tony in the afternoons and grumbling about Morshead as we walked, naked like savages, up and down the little sandy bay.

My first reconnaissance on 4 October was much like the others, though I must say I cherished thoughts of the historical significance of this flight, my personal briefing by the General and the strangeness and secrecy of the event. There was no cloud, a light wind and the air so dry and clear that contours and shapes on the ground stood out in exaggerated relief. To find tanks I needed to fly between 500 and 1000 feet, which was the "sucker" altitude at which every kind of light anti-aircraft guns and small arms were within range. I made out to sea, turned east, and began my recce by cutting in behind the Italian units that were parked close to the perimeter. Dense flak came up at me immediately, following me all the way round. Parabolas of bright red and green tracer shells pumped up like a slightly disorganized fireworks display. I struggled, weaving and changing height, through this striped environment which distracted my eyes from the ground. There was a temptation to watch the rounds as they rose slowly towards me, but their initial sluggishness was an illusion, for an instant later they would be flashing murderously past my wingtips. From the height of 1000 feet I could see El Adem with several aircraft sitting in front of the main hangar.

When I'd finished checking the perimeter I gave myself a respite from ground fire by diving to fifty feet as I followed the desert track to Acroma. There was plenty of traffic going both ways, kicking up dust trails which made the route easy to follow. The closest to a tank threat was an armoured car painted in dark camouflage moving at about four miles an hour towards Tobruk. Some kind of flag was hoisted on a pole, perhaps a radio antenna, and several crew members were sitting on the turret. At Acroma I prudently skirted the camp, avoiding most of the ack ack. I made an accurate count of vehicles and tents, then flew across it at fifty feet to see if any evidence of tanks might turn up at that height. Men ran wildly from the path of my aircraft and it was clear from the large number of bodies that it was an infantry base camp and Rommel's armour was elsewhere. Flying back by the sea route was tranquil, as if the war had suddenly been switched off and there was just the joy of being in a fast flying machine, skudding innocently over sparkling blue water.

Morshead listened without comment to my description of the infantry and artillery positions outside his perimeter and to my meticulous count of vehicles at Acroma. As I rose to leave he told me that I was to be relieved by two pilots from the squadron and that I could plan to fly back on the 12th. This was very bad news for me, since I'd begun to see myself as the pilot within the fortress until it was finally relieved. Tony and I spent that evening boozily cursing the poor judgment of higher-ups who didn't know when they were well off.

On my final sortie on 11 October a bombing raid on Tobruk began just as I was returning, low down over the water. All I could see from my altitude was the 3.7 barrage. I kept out to sea for half an hour, very frustrated, watching my petrol gauges empty. When I crept back to the harbour entrance the barrage was withering in the open sky. Soon it would dissipate, leaving a faint smudge in the atmosphere, like the grin left behind by the Cheshire Cat. I waggled my wings to express peaceful intentions and a green Very light went up like a benediction from one of the ruined buildings on the wharf. The sudden relief hit me like the third glass of champagne. I opened my throttle fully, built up some speed and flew over the town performing a series of rolls.

A minute later I was on the ground, racing towards the lead-in truck at the end of the strip. When I shut off the engine and slid back the hood I saw Tony Barrett running down the slope that led to the netted crevasse, shouting at me. I tore off my helmet.

"What?" I yelled.

"Geoffrey, you demon pilot, you. You shot down an aircraft."

"No, I didn't."

"You did some some victory rolls. Was it one of the bombers or a Messerschmitt?"

"Oh, Jesus!"

"What's the matter?"

"Oh, what a clot I am!"

During the Battle of Britain pilots had begun to carry out victory rolls as a sign that they'd shot down enemy aircraft. It was good for civilian morale, and newspapers encouraged it. While I was exulting overhead it had flashed through my mind that my aerobatics might be misinterpreted, but I couldn't restrain myself. Now I was going to pay for it.

"Tony," I moaned, "I was pleased to get back safely after the raid and I did a slow roll."

Tony looked at me, his eyes steady with sympathy, a sentimental bulldog.

"I'm afraid they'll all think you shot one down."

"Oh, my God! Hide me."

He took me to his billet and hid me. I crouched in the corner of his living space and listened to Tony's explanations as the noisy, tired trucks toiled up the escarpment and eventually stopped outside his hideaway, men disgorging and asking for the boy who'd shot down the Jerry. They came from all over Tobruk, with beaming faces and grateful hearts. I skulked out of sight, unable to stop my ears from hearing their glad greetings and Tony's sad denials.

"Just wanted to say how good it was to see one of our boys got back at 'em."

I'm afraid he didn't," Tony would say. "He was doing aerobatics."

"Give that pilot a slap on the back."

"Sorry. He's a recce man. He was doing a sortie for General Morshead and it coincided with a bombing raid. He just turned the plane on its back."

81

MESSERSCHMITT ROULETTE

"I've brought a bottle of whiskey for that RAF pilot."

In my own defence I'll say that it was an easy mistake for me to make, though I can't forgive myself for making it. Throughout my short flying career I'd made idols of the great aerobatic pilots. It was natural. They were the peacetime equivalents of Ball and Mannock. "Batchy" Atcherley, one of the twin brothers who became post-war air marshals, was already famous, not only for his skill but for his eccentricity and recklessness. He had toured the U.S.A. competing with the American stunt men, and his strong aristocratic personality had lent itself to the legend. In the peacetime air force junior pilots were forbidden to perform low down, but in the Western desert I found myself free from all restrictions. Within a month of joining the squadron I had developed a "split-arse" take-off procedure. Once my wheels were off the ground and the undercarriage was locked up I would hold the aircraft down, build up speed, and then turn on my back at about a hundred feet before climbing away. My covers were all aware of this and kept clear.

I justified it in my own mind by arguing that recce pilots didn't have much fun. They didn't celebrate victories, like fighter pilots; they didn't have the horrible satisfaction of seeing a city in flames like the bomber boys. The one genuine thrill was the realization that we'd got away with another sortie. We'd penetrated enemy airspace; we'd brought back useful information; we'd cocked a snook at their whole defence system. So when I returned from a recce I reveled in the freedom to do what I damned well pleased, with no duty pilots or other authority figures to report my violations of flying discipline. I used to dive low and fast over base, pull up vertically until my speed dropped off to 140 mph, ease over in a half loop, hold it for a second on my back and put the undercarriage down - (tricky stuff, that. The undercarriage going down upwards, see!) - and then roll out level. At that point I'd put down full flap and turn steeply in to land. If I'd worked the location of my vertical climb correctly it was a neat performance and took about as much time to execute as it does to describe it. No one in the squadron commented on my post-sortie antics. No one followed my example. The younger pilots may not have had sufficient confidence to put on a public display, while Murray Gardiner and the pilots from India were too mature to be interested in such frivolity. I was just silly enough to think it was great fun.

This time, however, my excitement had betrayed me. I lay low that evening and took off at first light the next morning for Sidi Barrani, eager to get away from the embarrassment.

After the war I searched the official histories for some mention of General Morshead's secret landing strip and hangars, but either the writers were unaware of their existence or thought them too unimportant to mention. I wrote to Digger Black (Group Captain Eric Black) in 1990 and he told me that the idea had originated with him. He worked out the details with Bill Morle of the Australian Military Engineering Service in Tobruk and sold the scheme to Morshead. Authorization was needed from Headquarters Middle East in Cairo and, to get this, Black left Tobruk on a destroyer, **HMS Defender**, to argue his case. The destroyer was sunk by the Luftwaffe on its way to Alexandria, but he was lucky enough to be picked up by one of the ships in the convoy. He saw Air Marshal Tedder, who approved the project, and Black took the dangerous journey back to Tobruk to resume his job as air advisor to the general. The hangars were constructed by the 2/7 Royal Australian Engineers. Luckily official photographs were taken and I am indebted to the Australian War Memorial, Canberra, for providing them.

I have always been puzzled that Morshead used me so little. My guess is that he received an authoritative signal, based on intelligence gathered as a result of the breaking of the Enigma code, that Tobruk was unlikely to be attacked directly at that time. This would explain why he sent me on counter battery work at first rather than reconnaissance, and why his interest in my reports was lukewarm. I was replaced in Tobruk by the young lions, Ray Hudson and Ed Kirkham, who arrived on the minelaying cruiser HMS **Abdul** not long after I departed. They had hoped to fly the two Hurricanes that had been shipped in with them. However, the aircraft never became fit to fly and they returned to the squadron by sea. Other pilots from No. 451 Squadron flew in after that, but I had no details of their activities until I wrote to all surviving members in 1990. Charles Edmondson reports that he flew a Hurricane to Tobruk in October, 1941, and left it there in one of the hangars, departing by sea the next day. Colin Robertson writes that he flew with Ron Achilles to Tobruk on 25 October and stayed until 2 December. Together they carried out twenty-six searches of the perimeter, almost one per day. This was, of course, the period prior to the British advance into Libya which began on 18 November. Clearly, as the campaign developed, Morshead became vitally interested in the information provided by his secret air force. Digger Black's great scheme had finally paid off.

MESSERSCHMITT ROULETTE

IX

I BECOME AN AUSSIE
(12 October to 21 October 1941)

On the day I landed back at L.G. 75 from the Tobruk detachment a truck filled with crates of beer had arrived from Alexandria. We often spent weeks without booze in the desert and the announcement of supplies was usually the occasion for a party. Drinking began in the middle of the afternoon. The Aussies took no heed of the conventional wisdom that the sun should be over the yard arm before indulging and at least one of them didn't make it to the evening meal. It was a euphoric moment for me because for the first time I found myself being fully accepted. The obvious reason for this was the undeserved prestige of my Tobruk mission. Even though it had been something of a holiday, the idea of landing in the fortress, being secreted underground and being personally briefed by the Australian commander, had a heroic ring about it. They were hungering for an all-Australian squadron and all-Australian victories in the field, but an all-Australian siege was better than nothing and I had been part of that.

I thought it might be a long night, so I ate first, read Yeats and walked around the strip, joining the party in the bar about seven o'clock. The tent was crowded with bodies, many sprawled out on the ground for want of chairs or benches. The illuminations was poor. A couple of oil lamps standing on the wooden tables gave out a flickery yellow light. Against the crude camouflage of the tent, khaki shirts surmounted by sunburned faces gave a curiously muddy impression. Limbs and faces lifted out of the murk and subsided again like Dante's lost souls.

It was already noisy. The twang of Australian voices predominated and I enjoyed listening to the unfamiliar rhythms and the liquid, natural sounding diphthongs. It was a virile version of English and gave an impression of energy, in spite of the big drawls. They pronounced the golden word "day" as it was spoken by our Anglo-Saxon forefathers when they rowed across the cold seas from Jutland. They wouldn't be amused to know they spoke like Saxons, I thought. They pronounced "yes" as "yeah", which ironically is a proper form. The modern "yes" is a cut down version of "yea sothlice," yes truly. But they weren't trying to speak correctly, if there is such a thing as correct speech. Best of all they weren't tempted to imitate the effeminate quack that passes for standard English. They were rebels, felons, exiles. A new nation.

Colin Robertson was squatting on the ground, talking of the rigours of sheep farming in New South Wales. "If you haven't dipped sheep," he was saying, "you don't know what work is. It used to take the better part of a week. When I was fourteen, still at school, my father turned me out with the men. Kept me out there the whole week working like a slave, dipping sheep from early morning till after dark and then beginning again before it got light. It's a filthy job and you can't relax or the stupid bastards'll run away. 'Sheep farming is hard work,' father would say, 'and you've got to learn that early on in your life!'"

I remember that particular speech of Robbie's so well because directly he'd finished holding the floor they fell on me. Beer was pressed into my hands, toasts were drunk to "M Squared" and arms went round my shoulders in affection and appreciation. I was a long lost brother, a prodigal returned, one of the boys.

"He's a pommy bastard!"

This was Doc Reid, sober as a judge but smiling widely. A roar of supportive laughter went up. Wizard then approached with Bill Langslow, whose long face was creased with goodwill. Bill was holding a box out of which he pulled a new fur felt.

"Geoffrey," He said, with great formality and sweetness, "I here confer on you, by virtue of the consent of all dinkum Aussies present, this token of membership in Number 451 Squadron, Royal Australian Air Force."

He placed the felt hat on my head.

"He's a fuck'n Aussie!" someone bellowed.

There were screams of laughter and more backslapping.

I wore the felt, feeling happy and foolish and not at all Australian. Then I remembered a Music Hall ditty my father used to sing. It must have been a relic from the previous war. He would hunch his shoulders and swing his arms and render it in a stagey baritone. He was a terrible ham and I took after him

I rose to my feet, did a little Music Hall shuffle in the space available, and sang:

> *Is 'e an Aussie*
> *Is 'e Lizzie?*
> *Is 'e an Aussie*
> *Is 'e,*
> *Eh?*
> *Is it because 'e is an Aussie*
> *That 'e keeps you busy, Lizzie?*
> *Got you dizzy*
> *'As 'e Lizzie?*
> *'Is 'e an Aussie*
> *Is 'e,*
> *Eh?*

It was well received. I could do no wrong that night. Most of the pilots had never heard it before, but elderly folk like Doc Reid, Bill Langslow and Blue Thyer burst themselves laughing and demanded an encore.

I BECOME AN AUSSIE

Success doesn't often come in such dramatic form, but I'd worked for it. Not everyone was presented with a fur felt hat, particularly in a formal way. Knocked sideways by the symbolism of it all, I didn't want to go to bed. I lapped up the strong Australian beer, listening to myself being happy. Most of the pilots had started drinking earlier and passed out or disappeared noisily to their bivouacs. The survivors were Wizard, Maslen, Doc Reid and myself. We talked contentedly into the night.

Some time during that evening I gave Wizard an account of my stay in Tobruk. I was drunk enough to confess my slow roll over the town and its embarrassing consequences. He grinned fiercely, loving it. Nothing pleased him more than blunders, bloomers, balls-ups and disaster.

"Clot!" he said, affectionately.

That's my absolution, I thought. I got off easy. One Our Father and one Hail Mary!

"You ought to go on leave for a few days," he suggested. "See your brother. Get the sand out of your lungs. You don't want to get too tired out."

"I'm not tired," I said.

"I've had you promoted to flight lieutenant. You can put up your tabs tomorrow."

Just before midnight I climbed boozily into my bivouac. I was dirty, flea-ridden and the sore on my leg caused by lack of vegetables was bothering me, but I was a happy man. Troubles due to the heterogeneous make-up of the Squadron were far from over, but I felt my own position was secure. Now all I had to do was survive.

The next day I borrowed some rank tabs from Jasper Brown and flew to Cairo in the Lysander, landing at Heliopolis and taking a routine military bus to the city centre. I was booking in at Shepheards when I saw Hugh French, my cousin, looking typically dashing in a Hawes and Curtis sports jacket, fawn trousers and a yellow polo-necked sweater. I hadn't seen him since 1937 when I had joined the RAF and he had set off to find his fortune in Hollywood. I didn't even know he was in the Middle East. Hugh had been raised in our household and was like a senior older brother - the wackier one! He had spent several years acting in films as the stereotype British stuffed shirt who always lost Barbara Stanwyck to Robert Taylor.[1] I still see him sometimes on black and white re-runs on afternoon TV. He had returned from America to join up, but the army medical board had found him unfit for military service because of "flat feet." He quickly formed an E.N.S.A.[2] concert party (equivalent of the

---

1. After the war, Hugh formed his own agency and represented major stars, such as James Mason, Richard Burton and Elizabeth Taylor. He also produced films, notably "The Young Winston" which brought him into friendly contact with the Churchills. On Sir Winston's death he accompanied Sarah Churchill, the actress, to her father's funeral in Westminster Abbey.
2. Entertainments National Service Association.

American U.S.O.) and had just arrived in Egypt to make the rounds of the front line units. Marilyn Williams, a tall shapely American girl, was the lead singer; there were female dancers, and Norman Hackforth (Noel Coward's pianist) provided the music. Hugh was master of ceremonies and sang in his deep baritone. It was a terrible show, Hugh said, but the troops loved it, joined in the songs and whistled at the scantily clad dancers.

Ken was soon contacted and the family reunion was in place. I remember little of that evening except the happiness. We drank gin in Hugh's bedroom, sitting on huge black trunks filled with theatrical gear, then sallied forth into the night. We laughed at everything; the nightshirted Egyptians, the belly-quaking dancers and the German agents whom it would be Ken's sad duty to kill if Rommel ever succeeded in capturing the city. These individuals were courteously introduced by my brother the spy, and we couldn't contain our mirth. Hugh had always been the magic man, the practical joker, the undisputed lord of misrule and on this night of glory he surpassed himself. I couldn't find my own room and slept contentedly on the carpet at the foot of Hugh's bed.

The next day Ken and I took a train to Luxor on the Nile south of Cairo where we gawped at the temples of ancient Egypt and walked through fantastically painted tombs in the Valley of the Kings. Ken was learned in Egyptian history and gave long lectures that did not for an instant bore me. I thought at the time that I had never been so happy. When I returned to the Squadron on 21st October I was still on the emotional mountain top which had begun with my coronation with an Australian fur felt.

X

AN ADVENTURE IN ARMOURED CARS
(21 October to 23 October 1941)

I flew back to the desert from Heliopolis as passenger in a Lockheed Electra of RAF Transport Command and was dropped off at Bagush, an airfield in the vicinity of Qasaba. I had to wait around for several hours before a communications Anson was available to ferry me up to L.G. 75. The next day I flew my first sortie as a flight lieutenant. It was a routine Tac/R of the frontier and took one hour and five minutes. No trouble.

While I'd been away in Tobruk, however, the Squadron had been less fortunate. I heard the details from Ray Hudson long after the events took place and this account necessarily reflects his views. Toward the end of September Wizard experienced great pressure from 13 Corps Headquarters to double up on reconnaissance sorties. It was feared that Rommel might make a major attack across the wire, combining it with a sideswipe at the temporarily weakened Tobruk. We didn't have enough pilots to sustain an effort of this magnitude, so Wizard asked Group Headquarters for reinforcements but none could be provided. A solution was found by attaching several pilots from No. 33 Squadron, an RAF fighter unit, on a temporary basis until the panic was over. They were not trained to carry out reconnaissance but were used as "covers" only - that is, our recce pilots led the sorties and the fighter pilots, who also flew Hurricane Is, weaved behind them protecting their tails. Everyone thought it would work but it turned out disastrously. Within a space of two days three of our reconnaissance sorties were intercepted by patrolling Messerschmitts and in each case the No 33 Squadron pilot was lost. The scheme was quickly dropped.

What went wrong? Hudson thought that the fighter boys were too aggressive for the job. We had become accustomed to penetrating deep into enemy territory low down, where we were at a hopeless disadvantage to the Messerschmitts which had both height and speed in their favour. At the first sign of trouble we fled. But the fighter pilots didn't share that feeling of inferiority. They had encountered MEs before under more equal circumstances and had downed them, so they stood and fought. They should have fled too, but their training and experience forbade it. It was an atrocious waste of three lives.[1]

Pressure from 13 Corps, however, continued to mount. There was a requirement to reconnoiter the whole coastal strip from Bardia to Tobruk, past most of the German fighter airfields. Wizard had a conference with all

89

the pilots present in which he stated the problem and suggested that the safest way to perform the task was to use the element of surprise. Instead of programming a series of sorties throughout the day, twelve aircraft would begin a simultaneous reconnaissance sweep from a position just east of Tobruk to the Libyan frontier.

Ray violently objected to the scheme as tactically worthless and he got into a shouting match with Wizard. If it were to be done at all, Ray said, the approach should be from the sea to avoid detection. Wizard wanted to come in from the empty desert to the south and he won the assent of the majority. In the event Wizard led this large formation of Hurricanes to the start point and they fanned out to commence their separate tracks home. "Sure enough," Ray wrote, "every German and his dog was waiting for us." They broke up, each Hurricane pursued by fighters, but miraculously no one was shot down. Micky Carmichael was the only casualty. His plane was hit by cannon shells, one of them grazing his skull. The others returned to base shaken but unharmed. Micky was restricted to ground duties by Doc Reid and never flew with the Squadron again.

On 27 September Graeme-Evans had flown out with P.O. Lowther of 33 Squadron and they were attacked over Bardia. Lowther shot down one of the Messerschmitts, but they were outnumbered and eventually both of them were shot down.[2] On October 10th Molly Malone went on a reconnaissance of the Sidi Aziz area and was shot down in flames by anti-aircraft fire. Charles Edmondson, his cover, reports that "Molly went into what appeared to be a flat spin. He had in fact, as I realized later, been hit and possibly killed outright. I pulled up, for we were below a thousand feet, and banked to keep him in view. There is something about that orange red flame and belching black smoke that remains indelibly stamped on the memory - along with the graceful curve of light flak, rising slowly at first and then flashing past with its own special BOK BOK sound."

Molly's death was a bad blow to me personally, for I had never really made up my tiff with him. He was a kind, brave, intelligent, pedantic fellow whose qualities did not fit him for the sneaky trade of recce pilot. I could just

---

1. "3 October 1941. Two days later II/JG 27 had their first combat and claimed to have shot down three fighters. In the morning six Hurricanes of 33 Squadron escorted a Tac/R machine of 451 Squadron over the front. Near Buq Buq they were jumped by seven Bf 109s around noon and Sergeant Lowry was shot down by Uffz."

"5 October, 1941. II/Jg 27 was again successful, three Bf 109s jumping four Hurricanes of 33 Squadron over Sidi Omar, which were again escorting a 451 Squadron Tac/R Hurricane ... Reuter shooting down PO Lush and Sergeant Seamer at 1040 hours, both pilots becoming POWs. Page 56, *Fighters Over the Desert*.

2. The same story of the loss of Graeme-Evans and Lowther is told in *Fighters Over the Desert* but with the added information that they were shot down respectively by Hpt Newmann and Obt Homuth (page 55) Kommodore Newmann confirms that he met a pilot he had shot down, at Derna, just before this pilot was transferred to prison camp in Europe. It is not clear whether this was Lowther or Graeme-Evans.

see him flying across the Azeiz defence system, circling, ignoring the concentration of tracer shells, head in the cockpit making tidy notes on his knee pad. "I saw the flak, Geoffrey," I could hear him say, in his clerical lecturer's voice, "but I chose to continue counting a convoy leaving Azeiz in the direction of Capuzzo. It is important to concentrate on accuracy when reporting for the army. You're altogether too harum-scarum, now. Aren't you, Geoffrey? " A smile. [3]

Yes, Molly, I am. Also a survivor.

The effect of Molly's death and Micky's wound was to eliminate the senior RAF flight lieutenants from the scene and to leapfrog me into a prominence I couldn't have envisaged two months before. From the beginning I had been carrying on my own competition with the Australians and trying to do my bit to improve our decadent image, but now I felt wholly responsible. Wizard had too many duties and could not out-fly the opposition. I had to do that, and persuade others to join me. I wasn't anywhere near so worried about the South Africans who were fewer in numbers and as much strangers to the Aussies as we were, but both parties had to be watched and outflown, operationally speaking. There was plenty for me to think about because, in response to Wizard's requests, we'd at last received an influx of RAF pilots. Ian Porter and Hugh Walford had their flying training in Rhodesia. A more experienced group on their first tour of operations included "Jesus " Evans and Dave Strachan. Evans had acquired his nickname because of the look of suffering on his rather Levantine visage. He reminded me of one of El Greco's saints, with his long face, huge dark eyes and no chin. Dave Strachan was a well-built rugger type with a very straight back and protruding buttocks. Jasper Brown, Willy Whitlock and Ken Dawlish were recce pilots who had been in the Wavell push and were doing a second tour of operational flying. In some strange way, according to unwritten rules that already seemed to obtain in our divided unit, the seniority of Brown and Whitlock and even their previous operational experience did not challenge my position at all. Conditions were changing rapidly. Only six months previously they had been using Lysanders for reconnaissance and were being chased off by Italian biplanes!

Sid Cooper was an army co-op pilot from India who had been scheduled to arrive in August but was delayed by sickness. As soon as he reported in, Doc Reid grounded him and he never flew with the squadron. He stayed on, I think, because he was a friend of Wizard's and could help out with the administrative burden. He had a large purple birthmark covering one side of his prominent nose and spread out on to his cheek. Like many ugly men he was a comedian, knew the words of rude songs and he got on well with the

3. Charles Edmondson, in an account of the action he sent to me in 1990 has this to say about Molly's style: "Molly's tactics were simple in the extreme. First, disregard all those foolish notions about low flying, descend to a few hundred feet at the most and stooge leisurely around anything that captured his interest. It surprises me that he did not put down occasionally to interrogate the enemy personally, or at least to check on the accuracy of his elaborate notes and sketches."

Australians. Even Ray Hudson liked him and didn't resent his presence in a non-flying role. I breathed a sigh of relief over this.

After the disruption caused by Rommel's probe, the main British activity consisted in establishing dumps of fuel, ammunition and other supplies in forward areas and organizing units for the planned advance. There was also a great search for water. One day at lunchtime Doc Reid introduced me to a tall gangling fellow, a real dinkum Aussie. It is too mild to say he wasn't wearing military uniform. With his crumpled felt on the back of his head and his almost ragged clothes he looked like the survivor of some desperate exploration of the outback. I didn't catch his name and asked him to repeat it.

"Don't worry about me name, cobber," he drawled. "Everyone around here calls me the well-boring bastard!"

He was an independent operator, with his own heavy equipment and perhaps a couple of men with him, following his instincts for water to supplement the 8th Army pipeline, which stopped short of the railhead near Mersa Matruh. He always said he could smell water. I met him again several times, because as the army moved up he did too, drilling hopefully and perhaps successfully in the seemingly arid wastes.

There was sporadic German air activity but we saw little of our own fighters, although there were rumours of air battles over the Tobruk convoys and claims that many Stukas and Ju 88s had been shot down. Daily reconnaissance continued and we noticed a steady build up of tents and vehicles at Sidi Omar, Fort Capuzzo and Fort Maddalena which suggested Axis preparations for an advance. Over the frontier area, however, we encountered little opposition. It was almost as quiet as it had been in August when I'd flown all those photographic sorties.

On October 23rd Smith and Thomas, both South Africans, went on an early morning recce and were bounced by MEs. Smith escaped but Thomas, from whom he was separated in the subsequent melee, did not return. I saw Smithy in the mess at lunchtime and asked him what had happened. He was a big good-tempered man with swelling muscles who looked like the village blacksmith. During the summer months I remember noticing how the material of his shorts clung to his massive upper thighs like a second skin. He had a strong South African accent, sounding his r's in a guttural fashion and sharply clicking some of his consonants.

"We were approaching Bardia, jong [young fellow]," he said. "Not a bloody Jerry in sight. I thought it was going to be a quiet sortie. Then a section of Messerschmitts came from nowhere. I dived down to the deck and streaked out to sea. Tommy turned the other way and they followed him."

"You didn't see him go down?"

"No." He grinned ruefully. "I was busy on my own account."

"He might have got away."

"If he was all right he'd have come back by now. It didn't look good for him with all those fighters belting after him. Poor bastard!"

He pronounced it "borstard." Usually cheerful, Smithy was upset. He hung his head over his plate of cold bully beef.

An hour later Sid Cooper came to tell me that Wizard had called a meeting. I found him surrounded by the South Africans who had an air of hectic gaiety about them. Even under desert conditions they were a smart bunch. The material of their uniforms was of better quality and they wore flashes of scarlet on their shirts and hats. The Aussies were deliberately relaxed in their dress but the fur felt gave them an advantage. The RAF had democratically adopted the same battledress for officers as for other ranks and it made us look dowdy in comparison. Sid, Masher and I looked like orphans, I thought.

"I've got word that young Thomas has force landed," Wizard was saying. "It was a wheels down landing, so the kite is O.K. No bullet holes, apparently.

"Where is he?" I asked.

"West of Fort Maddalena. He ran out of fuel. Tunt!"

Wizard was not a swearing man. Perhaps a chapel upbringing forbade it. He did, however, have a tendency towards unparliamentary language. One of his euphemisms was "tunt," enunciated with great precision, both dentals getting their full value.

"On the German side of the wire?"

"On the German side. The Cherry Pickers were on patrol in the area and one of their armoured cars picked him up."

The 11th Hussars were called the "Cherry Pickers" because they had won a famous victory in the Peninsular War after picking cherries.

"How's Tommy?"

"He's fine. He's staying with the aircraft."

"There are some Italian troops at Maddalena," I said.

"Actually," Wizard replied, smiling knowingly, "Germans and Italians. But not too many. The 11th Hussars are willing to take some ground crews and petrol through the wire so that we can fly the kite back. I need to consult with Murray Gardiner."

"Gone to Qasaba for spares," someone said.

"Damn!"

He turned to me with his best smile.

"There's an aircraft at stake. We're too short of them to take any unnecessary risks. Tommy may be all shook up at getting lost. He's waiting for you somewhere west of Fort Maddalena."

I had a mental image of Maddalena and the cluster of tents, trucks and armoured cars I'd recently seen from above. I remembered the Italian ground fire too. Surely they'd spotted the Hurricane going down. It could well be a trap. The thought of the armoured car made me feel claustrophobic. Caught inside one of those tin cans by an enemy patrol, trying to get the lid off while 88 mm armour-piercing shells are pounding into it. Not an attractive prospect.

"When do I go?"

"Right now. Flight Sergeant Bailey has the team organized. The sooner you leave the better."

The trucks were packed and ready to go. One of them was loaded with the British metal fuel cans that were so notably inferior to the German equivalent, the "Jerry can". They leaked so badly that we had to take twice as much petrol as was needed to fly the aircraft back. The other truck carried tool kits, spares and a starter trolley. We were taking a fitter and a rigger, in case anything required to be repaired or if difficulty was encountered in getting the engine started. A corporal and an airman from the M.T. Section drove the vehicles. Flight Sergant Bailey, who headed the team, was in the regular Royal Air Force, what we used to call an "old sweat." He was about forty, spoke with a strong north country accent and was a born grumbler who had been seconded, obviously against his inclination, to help run one of the flights in No. 451 Squadron because of a shortage of Australian NCOs. As we drove through the evening he made no secret of his misgivings. He was a fitter, not a bloody soldier. He had a wife and two teenage children in England. He hadn't joined the air force back in 1922 to risk his neck behind enemy lines because some whippersnapper of a young pilot couldn't read his compass. He was so accustomed to blaming pilots for everything that went wrong that he quite ignored the fact that poor old Tommy had been chased by MEs.

I felt sympathy for him and at the same time saw how preposterous his attitude was. He had been a member of a military service for twenty years yet he was shocked that he should be put in danger. Danger was for pilots. That's what they joined up for. His view was that he was a technical expert and only the damned incompetence of the flying boys could ever have landed him in such a scrape as this. He talked non-stop about his wife and children who were living in married quarters for the duration of his overseas tour at some station near Liverpool. He really thought he might be going to his death or at least into captivity. I wasn't asked what I thought of the exploit we were engaged in. I was just doing my job that I'd joined up for. He was the one who had cause for complaint.

We arrived at the headquarters of the 11th Hussars when it was almost dark. It was a small tented camp, the unit transport and armoured cars widely dispersed around it. Flight Sergeant Bailey and the airmen were at once taken off by friendly soldiers to places of refreshment and I was directed to the officers mess. To my amazement it had several leather armchairs and a rack filled with periodicals. The rough unvarnished wooden table, standard equipment in the British services, had been covered with a white cloth. A steward in a white coat offered me a drink. It was a sharp contrast to the squalor of our own mess; clearly higher standards of comfort obtained here. It was the ghost of a regimental mess in England, the camouflaged canvas of the tent incongruously flapping where the gold-framed painting of famous battles should have been. I was alone for half an hour and had begun to enjoy an old **Tatler** when an officer came in.

"We're ready to go," he said. "I have sandwiches and coffee."

He didn't introduce himself, nor did he ask my name. He was not in a good humour. There were two armoured cars to escort us. I traveled in the leading car with the officer. Soon we were rolling off, raising a little dust storm behind us, towards the Libyan frontier.

From overhearing words between the captain and his gunners I understood that the car was of a new and untried type. It was a Humber and was equipped with two guns, one of them a small cannon and the other a heavy machine gun. The first impression was of four oversize wheels surmounted by an armoured turret, but the shape of the car was disguised, intentionally and otherwise, by numerous bulky objects attached to it. A row of stuffed haversacks lay on the stubby bonnet, bedrolls were strapped to each flank and some cans, perhaps containing petrol, oil and water were attached to every horizontal surface. The consequence was that its originally formidable and warlike shape was reduced to nonentity.

Inside the car it was like an oven. I opened the window on my side but the dust blew in and made me cough. I shut the window and sweated. It was far too uncomfortable to sleep. The captain was not good company. Wartime officers in the army were often not unlike their counterparts in the RAF, doing a job with no special style or pretensions. Regular officers in smart cavalry regiments were clearly different. This one could have come from Central Casting to play a war hero, straw blond hair, ice blue eyes and an expression on his face like James Bond in a very bad temper. His accent was what the Americans call "veddy veddy" British. Even this far from Saville Row his uniform was impeccable, the narrow trousers cut by a good tailor, the bush shirt built for him only. I had hoped for a companion who could make the time pass, someone like Hugh Davies, who could make getting knocked out of a burning tank sound hilarious. This fellow was serious and unsmiling throughout. He didn't see the humour of Tommy forced to land behind Rommel's lines. The Cherry Pickers, by God, had enough to do without the airmen complicating their problems. He wasn't nasty. Just grim, and, I must say, superior. No doubt about that. There was a strong whiff of Radziwill about him. He made me feel that flying was not a respectable profession.

I tried at first to engage him in conversation.

"You know exactly where to go?"

"Yes."

"How far beyond the wire?"

"Fifteen miles."

"Is the pilot in good shape?"

"Yes."

"Was it you who found him?"

"Yes."

"Do you patrol much behind enemy lines?"

"Of course."

"Did you hear his radio call?"

"No. I saw him go down. Recognized a Hurricane. When it got dark we penetrated and found him. Bloody fool got lost."

"Sorry to drag you back."

Grunt. He didn't want to talk. Everyone blamed Tommy, I thought. Wizard first, then the flight sergeant and now the only person who'd seen him since the incident.

The long night in the armoured car was a weird variation of fear as I'd known it. I did not relish being a passenger. I felt as helpless as I had as Molly's cover. Until the aircraft was found, I would have no function to perform. This stuffy, noisy armoured vehicle was so unfamiliar that I couldn't even plan what to do if a German patrol caught us. When I was in the air I had an ever changing series of plans to meet imagined dangers which comforted me and kept me busy. To have that first quick action on the tip of my mind, as it were, was a kind of security. Jogging along in the heavy car at a steady twenty-five mph, a lay figure and somewhat discouraged by the taciturn captain, I felt myself getting cold up the spine.

We drove all night and as we approached the frontier the captain became more and more cautious. I mustn't be ungrateful to this able officer. He always seemed to know exactly where he was. From time to time he stopped and ordered all engines in the convoy to be turned off. Then he would walk away and listen. I recognized in him, if not exactly a brother in arms, at least a fellow survivor.

It was still dark when we drove up to the wire. There was a wide gap and a rutted track made by many vehicles led through it. He stopped the convoy at this point and stood for ten minutes in silence. There was nothing going on that I could hear. A theatrical sliver of moon, low down on the horizon, scarcely affected the darkness of the night. Then we moved on, the engines of the cars sounding grossly loud. It was hard to believe that we could get through without some other figure - an enemy, listening like the captain - being alerted to our racket.

When dawn broke and the sun rose slowly above the rim of the desert, the captain relaxed.

"We've got some more sandwiches," he said.

"No, thanks."

He ate and drank coffee. The blue sky was empty. Too far south for Messerschmitts, I thought, and a passing communications plane would take us for friendly forces; we were safe enough from the air. The desert, rose coloured in the early light, showed no sign of life, human or animal.

Thomas' Hurricane appeared suddenly.

From a distance it seemed to be perched on a mound, though when we approached it was seen to be only on a slight rise in the ground where it had stopped its landing run. The flatness of the terrain exaggerated small contours to the eye.

Thomas was lying on his parachute underneath one of the wings. He rose to his feet as we drove towards him, waving excitedly. He was slightly overweight and looked like a farm boy, though I believe he had been brought up in the suburbs of Durban. I'm sure his untidy appearance had been responsible for the universal blame he'd received. If it had been Hudson, with his Australian warrior pin-up look who had landed in Libya out of fuel, he'd have been praised for evading the enemy and saving his craft. Tommy couldn't have been older than twenty and he was still flying as cover to more experienced pilots. On this occasion his never very impressive appearance was marred by cruel sunburn, acquired on the previous afternoon when he had been scanning the horizon for signs of rescue or capture. While the Hurricane was being refueled I told him the bad news.

"Wizard thought you might not be up to it," I said. "He gave me orders to fly it back."

Thomas waved his arms about in protest.

"I put the kite down, man. I should be allowed to fly it. It's not fair, man."

"I'm sorry, Tommy. You'll have a nice ride with the Cherry Picker. I hope you get more out of him than I did. He hardly said a word to me."

"That bastard saved my life," said Thomas, with more warmth than accuracy. But I took his point.

"Smithy told me you were bounced. How'd you get out here?"

He grinned, recovering his good spirits as he told the story of his escape from death.

"When I saw the MEs coming for us I just opened up and made off. I had no idea of my direction except that it was vaguely south, away from the coast. They took pot shots at me but none of them hit me. Then they sheered off. When I realized that I'd got away, I looked at my compass. I was flying due west. So I turned and flew back, keeping south to avoid trouble. But I overdid my detour. By the time I'd started worrying about my fuel I was almost down to nothing in the tanks. When the engine coughed I landed straight ahead."

"Did you know where you were?"

"I could see the wire as I glided down and I guessed I was pretty far south. I expected to be captured. I thought of walking in and giving myself up, rather than die of thirst. But after a couple of hours the armoured car turned up. I had my bloody hands up to surrender!"

MESSERSCHMITT ROULETTE

The refueling was done at speed, Flight Sergeant Bailey had no intention of remaining west of Maddalena a second longer than he had to and he got the airmen working on the aircraft like ants. Fortunately no damage had been done in the landing so repairs were not needed. I looked around for a safe path for take off. You can't land and take off anywhere you please in the Western Desert and rocks, clumps of shrub and soft patches are to be expected. Thomas' bit of desert was standard rough stuff, but the path he'd chosen proved lucky. Since the breeze was light in the early morning I didn't have to concern myself with taking off into the wind over questionable ground and perhaps bursting a tire. That would have been a catastrophe. Apart from the loss of an aircraft I would have to spend another day with the captain, so I decided to play it safe, to line up with the tracks Thomas had made on the sand and take off in the reverse direction.

There was no time for ceremony. I shook the captain's hand and neither of us spoke a word. I hiked Tommy's parachute into the cockpit and put on my own helmet, which I'd brought with me. The engine started with no trouble and I drove off hastily. The ground party was now in much more danger than I was and I didn't want to render them conspicuous. They had to creep back into Egypt in daylight, skirting Fort Maddalena. I climbed to 2000 feet, just to check whether our little convoy was clear of trouble. I stupidly hadn't discussed this with the captain before take off and I wondered what I'd do if an armoured column was heading in his direction, because I had no radio contact with him. Happily the surrounding desert looked empty.

I did not much like Captain "Veddy Veddy," but I respected his way of life, reconnoitering ahead of the army, in contact with the enemy on a day-to-day basis. It was a harder role than our own, if statistically less lethal. It was exhilarating to be in the air again and to see the airspeed indicator on my dashboard register 220 mph. I dived to just above the desert surface and headed south for ten minutes, to disassociate my lone Hurricane from the convoy if by chance it had been observed.

Back at L.G. 75 Wizard beamed at me for rescuing a serviceable aircraft. Thomas turned up the next day and was sent on leave for a week to cool off.

XI

COMBAT FATIGUE
(24 October - 5 November 1941)

The three senior RAF replacements - Jasper Brown, Willy Whitlock and Ken Dawlish - had all flown protracted tours with Nos. 6 or 208 Squadrons in the Wavell campaign which had ended with withdrawal to the Libyan frontier. After too brief a rest they were back in the firing line. Later on in the war - after the Americans came in - the supply of pilots improved and rest periods became longer, but in 1941 combat fatigue was either not fully understood or more likely ignored.

Jasper made an effort to make himself agreeable to the Australians and South Africans and was more or less instantaneously accepted by both groups. For reasons of his own he decided to consider himself as a sort of guest of the Squadron for the tail end of our tour of operations and he made no attempt to alter the balance of power. He continued to fly cheerfully until the end of the campaign, never quite belonging.

Whitlock and Dawlish were not up to Jasper's standard and certainly shouldn't have been sent into action without further rest. I judged them harshly at the time because they threatened my moral position vis-a-vis the colonials, but today I'd view them as battle weary. Willy was short and rather overweight, with a pasty face that resisted sunburn. He didn't look healthy and his characteristic expression was fearful, as if he'd recently seen a ghost. He had an ingratiating manner, however, and was a fascinating narrator of war stories, knowing the names of army units as well as the details of casualties. His central characters were dead pilots, always made vivid by a thumbnail sketch, who went out to do their duty at the behest of insensitive army authorities and got bounced. If you had time he would tell you tales of the overwhelming superiority of all things German - their tanks, their guns, their wonderful Messerschmitts and their jerry cans. This kind of talk was widespread enough at the time and every fresh defeat - in Greece, in Crete, in Cyrenaica - added to it. It is traditional to denigrate the performance of our army and its commanders and to inflate the qualities of the enemy and in some hands this could be amusing, but Willy had an axe to grind. His own terror seemed to motivate his accounts of the war and his personal despair filled out his judgments on German arms, making them seem invincible. I'd never encountered a man whose morale had so clearly cracked. He said he was suffering from some physical ailment and he was often across at the sick quarters when the daily sorties were being allotted.

MESSERSCHMITT ROULETTE

Ken Dawlish had a thin face with delicate features and he looked dashing in his fore-and-aft hat, the very image of an intrepid airman. By desert standards he was a natty dresser, wearing whipcord trousers and a Fair Isle jersey under his open battledress top. His appearance was marred by a pronounced twitch. When it occurred he looked as if someone had just struck him across the face. This was disconcerting to the onlooker but he seemed not to notice it. He chatted on and even smiled while both eyes were closed in the involuntary grimace. Unlike Willy he didn't refuse to fly sorties but he made every effort to avoid them. They were always together, telling each other and anyone else who would listen, stories of defeat and death. One only had to move within earshot to hear the tales of retreat and confusion in the previous campaign, the air black with enemy aircraft, our own planes destroyed on the ground, escape on the back of an army truck, kit lost, and of course the magnificence of German equipment in comparison with our inferior stuff. The fascination of their narratives drew most of the pilots into their orbit, much to my disgust. They would sit on the ground like boy scouts round a camp fire, listening to Willy and his twitchy friend. Everyone had time on his hands in those days. There must have been half a dozen extra pilots hanging around waiting to fly, cannon fodder for the big push, ready to believe anything Willy told them, and he was a past master at tailoring his obsessions to the vague fears of his audience.

I grew to hate them both. If you have to do a job that may result in your death, or in lesser evils like burning or incarceration in a POW camp for the remainder of your youth, it is not good to dwell on those who have gone before you into trouble. I listened to them once or twice and then steered clear. For this reason I was late in noticing what was happening to the pilots they influenced.

One day I saw Ray Hudson walking up to Willy's group. He had recently returned from Tobruk with Ed Kirkham, frustrated at having done no flying. He stood behind Hutley, who was seated on the ground like the rest. After a minute or two of listening intently he slapped him on the back.

"Let's get outa here," he said loudly.

Everyone looked up and Willy stopped talking, his mouth open. He looked like an embezzler with a policeman's hand on his shoulder. Hudson's remark was the standard imitation of a sheriff directing his posse in American cowboy films, but the contempt in his voice was obvious. Hutley got to his feet and they walked away together.

I was upset by this incident. For the previous three months the RAF pilots in the Squadron had been improving their image. Now the process was going into reverse. No sooner had we altered the picture of ourselves as effete poms when Whitlock and Dawlish, with a few fine artistic flourishes, were painting out our work as if it had never existed.

I knew I had to take some action when I overheard Hutley talking to Ron Achilles in the latrines. They were sitting down at the long bench performing their morning duties, leaning forward, not looking at one another. I was about to enter, hidden by the tall canvas wall.

"You flying today?" said Ron

"Nah! I'm going on sick parade with the poms."

Ron laughed.

It was difficult to get a word alone with Wizard, so I took the fairly unusual step of going to his office, a place I seldom visited. I walked past Bill Langslow and saluted.

"Sit down, Geoff," he said. "What's the grisly problem?" You look as if your baby has gone down the plug 'ole."

"Nearly has."

"I thought things were fairly quiet now."

"They are. But I'm worried about Whitlock and Dawlish. They act as if they're scared to death. They talk too much and none of it's encouraging. I don't think they should be around."

"They seem decent enough chaps," said Wizard, looking puzzled. "Doc told me that Whitlock has a touch of Gyppy tummy. But he'll soon be flying. Dawlish has a terrible twitch but so have I."

I laughed at Wizard's imitation of Dawlish's twitch.

"They're tired out. I wish Doc would invalid them out."

"Give them time," he said. "It's early days. I'm sure they'll settle down on the job. Let's wait and see."

I had no confidence that they'd settle down but I found myself unable to explain to Wizard the ramifications of the issue. How it affected himself. How Sid Cooper's medical category darkened the scene. How we couldn't afford to have these RAF pilots not flying. After a few minutes I left, feeling frustrated.

I blame myself for lack of resolution. I should have told him about Hutley's remark, but I was afraid he would take it personally. I couldn't talk to Carmichael because his attitude seemed to exclude reality. His pose was one of brisk, mindless cheerfulness and he was still acting out some peacetime fantasy of "doing a good job for the army." Doc Reid was still keeping him grounded, but I remembered his old-maidish preparations before a sortie, his map exquisitely folded, his message pad equipped with two pencils. "Always carry two pencils," I can her Molly say, "for one of them may drop." His reaction to my alarm would have been to enquire if any regulation had been infringed.

I tried to raise the matter with Doc Reid. We were both heading in to the mess tent for lunch and I managed to walk him off for a private chat.

"Willy may have some medical problem," he said, very serious and professional. "He says he feels crook. It's too early to be sure. He seems a decent fellow. Had a hard time of it in the Wavell campaign. I quite like him."

So Willy's been spinning Doc some yarns, I thought. He must have some charms I hadn't suspected.

"I just want them out of the way. I don't care how decent they are."

"You're a bit hard on them, Geoff. But I'll watch them carefully."

Once again I'd failed to spit it out. I wanted to say that we couldn't afford to protect these guys while Ray Hudson and Colin Robertson and Ed Kirkham flew their arses off. "I'm closer to this, Doc," I should have said, "it's a powder keg. The whole bloody squadron'll go up in smoke if it goes on much longer. Willy's the big danger. He's talented in the worst way. He talks too much."

But I didn't say it.

There was little operational excitement in the latter part of October. Routine reconnaissances of the frontier were made each day, but the Luftwaffe was not active. When there was too little to do I had difficulty keeping my problems in proportion. I may have spent some of the time in my bivouac reading Yeats, but reading led to thinking and thinking had to be avoided like the plague. Flying helped to ease the tension. I note from my log book that I managed to fly at least twice a day during this period.

In peacetime "hogging the flying" was considered the ultimate malpractice and I had often harboured evil thoughts about flight commanders who took unto themselves too large a share of the available flights. But there was no longer any general enthusiasm among the pilots for leaping into the air. I had to search around for someone to do an air test after a minor inspection. There was no queue to fly to Qasaba for spares. It was too far from Alexandria and had no laundry facilities or hot showers to soothe the hide of dirty flea-ridden desert pilots. But the longer flights to the Delta, where all our machines received their major overhauls, were hardly more popular. Flying for the sake of flying had been a creed of mine from my first solo in 1937 and I still had a wonder of it that protected me. Even before a dangerous sortie when fears crowd the mind, once the business of climbing into the cockpit had begun my apprehensions dissolved. Just as in a good marriage the experience of falling in love can be constantly renewed, so with flying my heart never lost its amazement at rising into the air and seeing the familiar earth from the point of view of a visiting angel. Masher Maslen seemed to be the only competitor I had for these flights. He was always hanging around hoping to get airborne and we quickly became friends and collaborators.

Maslen was a tall ungainly fellow with coarse straw-coloured hair. No matter what clothes he wore they never seemed to fit him. With his beak of a nose, thin lips and un-military shamble he was downright ugly, looking like an escaped inmate from one of Charles Dickens' orphanages. His nickname was ironical, "masher" being a Victoria term for a man-about-town. He was the son of a farmer in Essex and before joining the RAF he had been a junior clerk at Barclays Bank in London and a star batsman for their first eleven cricket team. In spite of his physical appearance his dexterity was remarkable and he was a natural pilot.

On 26 October, neither of us having a sortie to fly that day, Masher and I drove two Hurricanes to Qasaba for inspection and returned in the squadron Lysander, which had been at the base airfield for some reason. After twenty minutes of flight, just as we were passing Garawla, a strip with Blenheims of the South African Air Force dispersed around it, the engine began to make a knocking noise. I throttled back a bit. Instead of going away it got worse. Masher and I looked at one another. We were flying at 2000 feet, following the coastal road and had been enjoying the ocean from the grandstand view offered by the Lysander's cockpit. I turned back towards Garawla and while I was in the turn the motor choked noisily and stopped solid, the prop remaining in the coarse pitch position. When one flies so many hours looking through a rapidly rotating propeller nothing looks stranger than one which is stuck sideways, as it were, right in front of one's face, doing nothing.

I dropped the nose to maintain speed and knew at once that I was not going to make it to Garawla. The Lysander was a specialized craft. At speed it had a clean shape and a fairly flat glide, but as the speed dropped off the flaps and slots operated like an old four-masted ship shaking out sail. There was a wadi, a dry water course, perhaps half a mile from the Garawla strip and beyond that was a cleared space that looked good for a landing. I made for it. It had been a tented camp at some time and I could see the old tent patterns on the sand. I was successfully negotiating this wadi and preparing to slide off speed for the landing when I saw the telephone wires. They were slanting across my flight path and I was about to fly right through them. I heaved back on the stick to clear, which reduced my speed to 75 mph.

My engine was dead and I was in desperate need of power, practically stopped in mid air and about to flutter heavily to earth. I jammed the stick forward and dived, hoping to achieve sufficient speed to retain control and get my tail down for a landing.

The Lysander, sweet monster that it was, did not fail me. It was designed to maintain flight at low speeds and by God it stood the test.

I yanked back on the stick and hoped for the best. There was just enough bite on the elevators to raise the nose and sufficient speed to produce the ghost of a float. Immediately afterwards we made contact with the ground in quite a respectable landing. I could hear Masher in the next seat crowing.

A warrant officer fitter came out with a crane from Garawla and pulled the Lysander into his tech section. A big end had gone, he told me, and there would have to be an engine change. More trouble for the indefatigable Acker Kerr. I went with Masher to the officer's mess tent and had lunch, arranging for a Blenheim on an air test to deposit us back at L.G. 75.

While we were eating I gave Masher my thoughts on the state of the squadron. He was serious and supportive.

"I'll fly as much as you like," he said, looking up at me through a lock of straw hair.

"Il know you will, Masher," I answered. "But I've got to get rid of Whitlock and Dawlish. The boys won't stand for it."

MESSERSCHMITT ROULETTE

He laughed. Old Bill Langslow had an expression that everyone in the squadron had heard. Whenever the rights of his countrymen were at stake he would come out with it. "The boys won't stand for it." It carried a truth that really did separate the Australians from the rest of us. Englishmen, Irishmen, Scotsmen, Welshmen and both species of South Africans were on the whole disinclined to complain about conditions and weren't sensitive to slights. The Aussies were a little different. They were alert to any hint that they were traveling second class and they would get angry if they thought they were being put upon. Bill's phrase just about summed it up.

XII

HEAVY GUNNERS
(24 October - 5 November 1941)

On 26 October I flew another Tac/R of the frontier from Sollum to Maddalena, which still had its camp and its collection of vehicles that the armoured car captain had skirted so successfully. Ray Hudson covered me, an extraordinary event that both of us remembered afterwards as significant. We had been competing with one another for almost three months and even though we'd both wasted time in Tobruk, we led the field in sorties flown. To fly together was a poor use of pilot resources and it could only have happened because other pilots were not available. In a letter he wrote me in 1985 Ray wrote, "Of all my three operational tours this was the most exhausting and protracted. A lot of pilots were showing fatigue at this time and the fact that the two most experienced people teamed up to do a routine sortie proves that willing workers were already lacking."

Encouraged by the lull in enemy air activity 13 Corps staff began again to make requests for photographic sorties. On October 29th I flew a line overlap from Sidi Omar to Halfaya. The weather had broken up in the change of season and there was plenty of cloud about, which was good for escaping into but less satisfactory for taking photos. I'd become accustomed to flak and was only scared of Messerschmitts, so the clouds soothed me. I almost enjoyed this flight, knowing that there was always a friendly spot of moisture in suspension, formless and deceptive, that I could nip into if attacked. However, when Hugh Davies looked over them the next day there were patches on the prints. On 31st I flew it again, but Halfaya Pass was completely obscured. I had to finish the job on November 1st in fair weather, hating every minute of it.

Wizard had been asked to provide artillery reconnaissance for a forward regiment which had been shelling the Halfaya area at long range and the next few days were occupied in practice sessions with these gunners. A major and a captain drove to L.G. 75 on the morning of 2nd November and Hugh Davies tried to produce an atmosphere of ease and friendliness. It wasn't possible. Some officers of this regiment had been part of the British Expeditionary Force evacuated from Dunkirk the previous year and they had not forgiven the RAF. In the retreat of spring, 1941, the army had once again been disappointed by the lack of air support. It is only too easy for a man on

105

the ground to believe that his brother in the air is shirking, for air battles occur beyond his vision. A front line soldier wants to see bombers laying carpets of explosives in the path of this advance, and he want to see fighters perpetually circling overhead to keep the enemy's close support aircraft from attacking him. It was a dream that did not become a reality until three years later.

In 1941 our resources of aircraft and pilots had been stretched so thinly in an attempt to cover the series of defeats in the Mediterranean that being a disappointment to the army had become routine, but never comfortable. I, for one, was very prickly on the issue. I didn't want anyone to suggest that we were deliberately letting down the other services, although it was difficult to argue against the facts. Also, there was a basic misunderstanding in regard to how air power should be exerted. Airmen thought in terms of keeping their force in being and they resisted the commitment of total effort to passing emergencies. The soldier resented this attitude. After the withdrawal of our army to the wire, during which many units had been decimated by Stuka and Ju 88 attacks, there was a resurgence of bad feeling. They thought we were timid, if not cowardly, and we thought they were stupid.

In the special circumstances of Tobruk, when my single Hurricane had the appearance of a sacrificial offering to army demands for air support, I lived in an atmosphere of applause, like being a rock star for three weeks. It wasn't that way anymore. In spite of Hugh Davies' affability and his efforts to present No. 451 Squadron as wiling and able to help, there was no great warmth in our meeting with these 4.5 heavy gunners. The thought crossed my mind that the heavier the guns the lower the spirits. We made the arrangements with them sensibly enough, though in an atmosphere of unexpressed hostility. I flew two practice Arty R's and finally Hugh took me to see the guns firing and to meet the crews I'd be working with. They were very swift and workmanlike. The guns were deafening. I was given ear plugs but thought it would be an experience to hear at least one unmodified explosion. It was a mistake. For the rest of the day my ears rang and I found it difficult to hear what was said to me.

That evening in the bar Wizard asked me about the sortie.

"I think it'll be interesting," I said. "But you couldn't meet a set of more hostile pongos. Hugh Davies sang his siren song in vain. We couldn't get a smile out of them."

Wizard and I took off in open formation just before noon on 3 November, flying low to the target zone, calling the gunners on the radio as we approached them. From the height of 1500 feet, which I'd chosen because it kept us well below the heavy barrage, Halfaya was an impressive sight. The high plateau dropped steeply to the sea at this point and the coastal road was forced to wind tightly up a narrow defile in the escarpment. A small force could defend it here. It was another Thermopolae. To the south and west the situation was less favourable for defence because the slopes were less severe. It was there, on the edge of the escarpment and overlooking the desert plain, that the Germans had placed their heaviest guns.

I found it difficult at first to get my bearings. I'd flown over it in a panic with Molly. I'd cruised through its formidable barrage several times photographing it at 6000 feet. But I'd never really observed it. Blundering around its southern fringes, looking for the targets, I was caught in a cloud of light anti-aircraft fire.

As I flew clear of the explosions, a constipated voice, distorted by static, cracked over the airwaves.

"Have you identified the target area?"

"No, I haven't. Stand by," I yelled.

"Tell 'em to fire at number one," said Wizard quietly. "That might give you an indication."

This was the voice of experience and I didn't hesitate.

"Target number one, fire!" I said.

Our 4.5s were firing at their extreme range and were expected to be inaccurate. I also knew there would be a respectable time interval between the order to fire and the fall of shot. I gained a little height and looked anxiously towards Halfaya. The ground rose gently towards the escarpment, obscured a little by the dissipating remnants of the German light flak.

Suddenly there was an impressive explosion just below the ridge. It mushroomed, pink tinged from its impact on the red rock.

"See that?" said Wizard.

"Roger."

I not only saw the shot, I could also see the three massive enemy gun emplacements. They were farther up the hill than I had estimated, their long barrels sticking aggressively out of heavily sandbagged positions.

The first round had been wild, however useful in showing up the targets. It was 800 yards short and 600 yards left of its mark.

"Add 1600, right 1200," I shouted, eager to begin.

We were in business at last, I thought. In high figures, too. What a contrast to the small but accurate 25 Pounders at Tobruk! Wizard could be trusted to look out for interference from Messerschmitts. I could now go ahead and finish the job quickly.

Once I had identified the target area it was relatively easy to avoid the worst of the light flak and still observe the fall of shot. After a couple of corrections the rounds were getting close and the gunners moved me to the next target. As Blue Nelson had remarked, once you've straddled, mathematics would do the rest.

Thirty minutes later they had registered a direct hit on No 2 and the other targets were neatly bracketed. From time to time Wizard had cut in to say that the sky was clear of enemy fighters. I always pressed my speak button to say thanks, and I meant it. They were golden assurances, exactly what I needed to keep my mind on the job.

The shoot ended on a sour note. The third target had been closely bracketed and I was looking forward to seeing its destruction in the next couple of salvos. But the gunners dismissed me abruptly, without explanation or thanks.

"Exercise completed. Return to base."

Exercise, my arse! Flying over Halfaya and dodging flak was more than a bloody exercise. Unfeeling so-and-sos. No imagination. Rude, too, I thought.

"Roger," I replied, turning steeply away from my contemplation of the targets towards the harsh outline of the coast.

We flew back to L.G. 75 in silence.

I crossed the cliffs, giving Halfaya a wide berth and returned low over the sea, feeling frustrated and angry.

When I'd switched off my engine, I walked across to Wizard's Hurricane and waited for him to disentangle himself from the cockpit. He descended like an old man. In mock ill humour he cursed the whims and follies of aeroplane designers who took no account of the human beings who would have to get in and out of them.

"Every conceivable temptation to slip and fall to earth," he concluded. "Every spike, every sharp projection cunningly angled to tear the flesh and ruin clothing. Look at my side pockets! Torn to shreds!"

We walked towards the flight tent, humping our parachutes.

"What did you think of the shoot?" I asked.

"It was a satisfactory shoot, as shoots go," he replied. "Nothing to write home about. But our friends on the ground didn't really appreciate our good offices, did they? You sometimes find a clutch of pongos like that. No milk of human kindness. We risk our arses and they don't even say thank you."

"That's what I was thinking myself," I said. When they cut me off after the last target I —"

Wizard wagged his head and put on his long suffering face.

"It's the human condition," he said. "I expect pongos have their problems too."

When I heard that the Gloucestershire Hussars, a regiment my brother Peter drove a tank for, had arrived in the Middle East, I at once went to Hugh Davies who knew all about our 13 and 30 Corps dispositions.

"General Norrie is assembling 30 Corps for the big push at this moment," he said, emphasizing "big push" and grinning wickedly at me from his chair. "The Gloucesters arrived in Egypt on 24 October and they'll be coming up this way soon. I'll see if I can get the movement details."

He came up with precise dates and times the next day. The regiment had been having some trouble re-equipping and their arrival in the front line had been delayed. They would be passing five miles south of Matruh on 12 November.

HEAVY GUNNERS

On that day Wizard lent me a truck and a driver and we set off early in the morning, reaching the spot around 9 A.M. We sat there until 2 P.M. watching the transports making their way slowly west, nose to tail, eating their own dust. This was the 22nd Armoured Brigade moving into position. I couldn't help thinking what a wonderful strafing target they would have made for a squadron of MEs.

The column was mostly composed of support vehicles, but every now and then a tank unit would go by, grinding up the desert surface into a fine powder with their tracks and blowing it up in clouds behind them. The trucks following them would stick in the soft patches the tanks had churned up, halting the column while men rushed out with boards to put against the back wheels. The progress was intolerably slow and I wondered why it was necessary for them to follow one after the other when the wide desert was available there, like a sea on either side.

There was an empty crate in the back of the vehicle and I sat on the top of it, peering through the screen of dust to spot the regimental insignia. Every half hour I would stop a leading vehicle and ask about the Gloucesters. They always reported cheerfully that the Gloucesters were just coming up behind. Finally they came through, a line of British Crusader tanks. I had to do some frantic shouting to the crews sitting on top of the tanks, my voice lost in the snarl of powerful engines and the ironmongery noise of rotating tracks. When I located him, Peter was driving and had to be relieved.

We couldn't hold up the procession. After embracing we got into the squadron pickup and followed the tanks from one side for a mile or two. He looked very tough and soldierly in his black beret. And very young. He possessed one of those olive skins that don't wrinkle and his neat features had been tanned by the Egyptian sun to an even tone, making him look like a soldier in a recruiting poster, too good to be true. Pete was to have the toughest of wars, for he was knocked out of several tanks in the coming campaign and again during the battle of Alam Halfa and the disastrous retreat to El Alamein which followed. He was commissioned in the infantry and fought through Italy, ending up street fighting in Athens to prevent the attempted Communist takeover in 1945. I hadn't seen him since 1938 when he was still at school. Looking into each other's familiar faces we must both have wondered if it was to be for the last time.

I wrote that night to my parents, giving them the good news of our reunion. When my cousin, Brian Orpin, an officer in the artillery, joined the 8th Army in 1942, all the men in our immediate family of military age were in the Middle East.

MESSERSCHMITT ROULETTE

XIII

WILLY

One morning I was looking for a pilot to fly to Fuqa for spares. I walked through the scattered bivouacs but could see no one around. This was unusual. The rites of shaving and ablution were performed at random hours and it was normal to see one or two people so occupied, folding blankets or tidying up. As I approached the mess tent, I saw Willy with at least ten pilots sitting in a circle round him. Corporal Coffee, rising to the occasion, had supplied an urn of tea and was handing out steaming cups. He grinned cheerfully at me.

"Want a mug?" he called out.

"No, thanks, Len."

Willy was in full swing, his colourless visage shining with the intensity of his narrative. He didn't actually have a twitch but every thirty seconds he would close both eyes in a mini-spasm.

"In the first push, when Barce was captured, they found some casks of plonk in a cave behind the town."

"What's plonk?" asked an English voice.

"Red wine. Chianti, I think. Pretty coarse stuff. The Italian troops were issued it with their rations. Well, it wasn't long before the Aussie 6th Division got hold of it, and you know what they're like for booze. And they hadn't had a drink for months."

"Too right!"

"One bright outfit walked off with a full barrel," said Willy. "Took it back to their own lines."

"Goodo for them," said Hutley. "We could do with some plonk here."

"The trouble was," Willy went on, "the men drank it in pints, like beer. When the dawn came, they found the entire section lying unconscious round the cask. Two of them died before the doctor could get to them."

"Jeez!"

"After that the commanding officer ordered the remaining barrels to be destroyed."

I tapped Walford on the shoulder and walked him away to the flight tent. That was a good story, I thought. I wonder what else he's telling them. He's a sweet singer, all right, but watch out when he parks by your city gates.

I could sympathize in part with the interest they took in his yarns. The 6th Division was an enigma and no Aussie was immune to the fascination of

111

its legend. They'd whipped the Italians easily in the Wavell campaign and they had a fine military reputation, but they were the bad boys of the Western Desert. If one can believe the anecdotes, they behaved like Roman legionnaires crossed with a Tartar horde. They fought like fiends, drank like Scotsmen and looted like mercenaries. Whether the tales were true or not, they made an interesting contrast with the 9th Division, which fought as bravely and whose members behaved like gentlemen. The rivalry between the two divisions seemed to reflect tensions in the Australian population between the descendants of convicts and those of peaceable immigrants. It was as if all the Ned Kellys had joined the 6th Divy and the paying passengers the 9th.

A day or so later I heard Willy again. It was impossible to avoid him because he gathered all the spare pilots in the unit. He was the only entertainment provided, so he had full houses for morning and afternoon performances.

"The Italian C.R. 42 is a super biplane," he was saying. "Much faster than the Hawker Fury and just as manoeuverable. Our Lysanders were sitting ducks to them. No one attacked by one ever got away, but luckily the Eyeties weren't too keen to engage us. Now, when the Jerry air force arrived on the scene it was a different situation. Two of our boys were shot down near Agedabia during the first few days the Messerschmitts were out. One managed to bail out but he was so badly burned that he died before they could get him to hospital."

"How fast is that ME 109?" asked Watson. He was the youngest of the new RAF replacements, a round faced boy with curiously flat cheeks that made him look like an owl. I didn't like the question, nor the frightened way he asked it. He was sitting on the ground close to Willy, gazing up into his stricken face.

"You've seen the way they streak across the sky. They can outclimb and outdive us. In a terminal velocity dive they're as steady as a rock, while our bloody wings are coming off. We're hardly better off with these clapped out Hurricanes than 6 Squadron was flying Lizzies."

I walked away full of disgust. What he said was not even true, for we were lucky to have Hurricanes. They were sound aircraft and to complain because a front line fighter could outfly you was simple nonsense. We didn't have to do battle with the Messerschmitts. Our job was to avoid them. Willy was what I'd always known he was. A coward. A bad influence. He was spreading his hopelessness through the squadron, displaying his psychic wounds like a Madras beggar. I couldn't let him go unchallenged. I walked back to where Willy was addressing his audience. He was off on a description of a Lysander disaster from the previous campaign.

"His engine was gone but he managed to land," he said, glancing round at the seated figures. When he was telling his stories his usually sad countenance seemed to light up from within, giving him a ghastly animation.

WILLY

"The co-pilot was lucky. He leapt out while the kite was still on its landing run. It was still running when the MEs strafed it. Blew it up with Jimmy inside. When the fire died down we tried to get him out. My God, he was a terrible sight. His goggles had melted into his skull."

At this my rage bubbled over. I shouted at him, waving my arms.

"Shut up, Willy!"

They all looked up at me, roused from their dream of burned flesh.

"You talk a lot of bullshit. You don't make anyone's job easier by moaning and groaning about dead men. Shut up, for Christ's sake!"

I started to walk away and then turned back.

"And I'll tell you another thing, Willy," I shouted. "It'll take a fucking good Jerry to shoot me down!"

I stamped off, my face flushed, embarrassed at losing my temper. There had been supportive laughter and some cheers for the boast that had burst from me uncensored.

I wasn't too happy about my performance. Boasting couldn't counteract whining. But I'd made up my mind. We could no longer drag this pathetic soothsayer through the campaign setting up his little school for cowards wherever we camped. I had to provoke a crisis. Willy must be forced to fly.

It was a fair distance to Wizard's office but I wasn't in a hurry, so I strolled across. I needed time to think. A tented camp in the Western Desert had very little shape. This one sprawled and bunched in places, mostly to the south of the airstrip. I thought of it as having corners. There was Wizard's corner, with his clump of square, camouflaged headquarters tents. Beyond it was the sick quarters, Doc Reid's bell tent standing on its own, and farther out was the photographic section with its mobile dark room and inside its rack of dripping plates. Unwilling to be reminded of the sorties I feared most, I didn't often visit the photographers. In another corner were the signallers, the cypher office and the storekeepers, all Aussies. The engineers were close to the sergeant's mess tents, prudently adjacent to the Aussie technical NCOs. The individual bivouacs were pitched in the area of the mess tents, blocking entry of vehicles except from one direction. Walking trails ran through them, like lanes in rural England and for somewhat similar historical reasons of property and territorial rights.

In such flat terrain you only had to be on your feet to see all the dispersed aircraft. The Hurricanes sat up alertly, the triangular fairings on their cylindrical legs giving them from the side a falsely robust look, like a woman's slim calf can sometimes be magnified when she crosses one leg over the other. As I passed each plane I could see inside the fairings the shiny metal oleo legs of the undercarriage, looking like a display of prosthetic limbs in a medical store. The single Lysander stood tall and bulky, with its high angled wing and heavy struts.

Wizard was standing outside the cluster of tents talking to Bill Langslow who, as usual, had a fur felt on his head as a mark both of his office and his personal identity. While threading my way through the camp I had composed an elaborate speech, but I suddenly decided to make it short. I had already complained about Willy's behaviour so I would say no more on that score.

"Willy Whitlock is down to fly a sortie," I said. "I thought you ought to know."

"OK. I've got word from Stan Reid that he's fit. Go ahead."

"Right."

I saluted and walked away. A short interview. Wizard could see that I was worked up over the issue and, in his political way, he was keeping clear.

An hour later, after lunch, I told Willy I wanted to see him at the flight tent. He was senior to me but had put himself in this position of being ordered about by a junior officer. He stood before me sagging like a punch-drunk boxer, his pot belly tight against his belt buckle. It looked as if his belt was holding him up and that without its support he'd have spilled out on the ground. I felt no sympathy for him, nothing but irritation.

"You're going to fly as cover to Edmondson on a Tac/R tomorrow." I said. "You've not flown on ops since you came to the squadron. If you don't want to fly this one, we'll walk straight over to Wizard and have it out with him."

"No, I'll fly."

"Do you need a practice flight? You haven't flown for some time."

"No. I'll be all right."

I suddenly felt a wave of sympathy for him. He looked as if I'd given him the death sentence. His face had gone whiter than ever and he seemed to be trembling.

"That's fine, then. Cheer up. Edmondson'll look after you. He doesn't take unnecessary risks."

"Yes."

He stumped away and I saw Dawlish, who had been doing an air test, walk up to him. They went off together, talking earnestly.

I hoped this was going to be the end of the affair. I'd keep Willy busy in the air and cut down on his speechifying and I'd tell Charles to be particularly careful not to frighten him. When he returned from the sortie I was going to warn him again not to tell any more subversive stories. I had a discourse prepared for him. "You tell a good yarn, Willy," I would say, "but it's not healthy for young pilots to look on the black side. Be a nice fellow and keep that stuff to yourself. When we get out of the desert you can write a book."

At eleven o'clock the next day I watched Charles and Willy take off. I was so obsessed with him that I wanted to satisfy myself that he'd actually got airborne. I wanted to see his wheels coming up, watch him go into a weave behind Charles' tail and head for the frontier. What happened was shocking. They took off, as we usually did, in open formation, as it avoided flying through the leading aircraft's dust, but halfway down the strip Willy's Hurricane fell back. It lost speed and veered to starboard on a turn so abrupt that the port oleo leg collapsed and the port wing dug into the sand, sending up a billow of dust and making a crumpling noise as the wing folded. The fire truck and breakdown crew hurried across.

I stood there feeling sick. He had deliberately been allotted the best aircraft to reduce the chance of his finding something wrong with it. A burst tire would have been a legitimate cause for such an accident, but he had crashed purposely rather than go on a sortie, taking one of our precious kites with him. It was a fake accident, quite neatly executed. Willy had throttled back to a safe speed before putting on full right rudder and wrecking the plane.

I was at the army liaison section and, without bothering to ask permission, I took their staff car and roared across to Wizard's HQ. Since early November we had all been instructed to wear our side arms and I had a heavy service revolver attached to a webbing belt around my waist. I braked in a cloud of dust and ran inside. Wizard rose up from behind his desk, looking startled.

"Christ! What's the matter?"

"That bastard Whitlock has crashed on take-off," I raved. "Put his bloody wing in. He couldn't refuse a sortie so he broke one of our aeroplanes."

I dragged my pistol out of its stiff holster.

"You'd better get rid of that bugger, Wizard. If I see his face again I'll kill him. I'll shoot him like a dog!"

He walked round the side of the desk and put his arm on my shoulder.

"Geoff, put that gun away. Stay here with Bill. I'll tell him to pack his bags."

I didn't, in fact, hang around in Wizard's office. He drove off at high speed in his vehicle and I drove the army staff car back to the A.L.O. section and walked back to the flight tent. I had no wish to look towards the airfield, to see that stricken Hurricane and the melancholy traffic of technical vehicles preparing to tow it away. I tried to calm down, but whenever I thought of Whitlock I could only think of killing him. I hoped Wizard was keeping his promise. He'd better keep it, I muttered to myself. He'd better make sure I don't see Willy again.

Charles landed back, topped up with fuel and flew off again with Masher. Thank God for such as Masher and Edmondson. I stayed in the flight tent till tea time, grinding my teeth, then I walked up to the mess.

Wizard came in, took off his felt and sat beside me on the bench.

"He's gone. We had to pick up some spares from Qasaba. I've sent him back with the truck and told him to report to the postings branch in Cairo."

"Thank Christ! I never want to see him again."

I don't know what happened to Willy when he arrived at Middle East Headquarters. I imagine Wizard and Doc Reid cooked up something charitable to say about him. I ceased to think of him. A mountain was suddenly removed from my path and I had too much to occupy me in the days ahead. Dawlish disappeared quietly from the squadron a few days later.

MESSERSCHMITT ROULETTE

My irrational behaviour can be partially explained by the serious shortage of operational aircraft in the Middle East. To avoid having to fight convoys through the Mediterranean, which since the Italians entered the war had become a hostile lake, aeroplanes were shipped to the port of Takoradi on the Gold Coast (now Ghana) and flown across the African continent. I'd met ferry pilots who'd done the trip many times - 3700 miles to Abu Seuir in Egypt, via Lagos, Kano, Marduguri, Fort Lamy and Khartoum. The route was so punishing that ten percent of the planes never completed the journey. When they had been overhauled, squadron pilots would collect them from the maintenance depots in Egypt. To destroy such a precious article as a new Hurricane Mark I, after such heroic efforts had been made to bring it to us, was obscene.

Did I do the right thing by forcing the issue? Probably not. But Willy was clearly a psychological threat to me and I moved to save myself as much as anyone else. I'm not proud of my homicidal anger, my hatred of another's weakness, but real life doesn't provide a training ground for its crises. They always take us by surprise, inevitably revealing our faults of character. However, Willy would have done serious damage if he'd been permitted to go forward with us into the impending battle, adding his imaginative and deadly voice to the shame he'd already brought on the RAF by his reluctance to fly. Once he was out of the way the nastier insinuations that the poms weren't pulling their weight died down, though I don't think the squadron was ever completely healthy again.

Strangely enough, my boast that it would take a good Jerry to shoot me down was repeated with glee and gained me more respect than derision. The timing had been right. The lull was almost over. The balloon was about to go up.

XIV

THE LUFTWAFFE RE-EMERGES
(9 - 16 November, 1941)

At the beginning of November two experienced Australian flight lieutenants, who had joined the squadron a week or two earlier and had been getting their hands in on Hurricanes at Qasaba, began to fly sorties as cover to other pilots. K.H. Springbett I did not get to know at all. He seemed to fade into the background as soon as he arrived and I can't recall speaking to him. This was partly because Alan Ferguson, who came with him, was such an impressive personality. I could feel the molecules of the squadron rearrange themselves into a more beneficent and sensible pattern as soon as he turned up. He was a tall, lean fellow with a sandy moustache and one of those long faces common in the eastern counties of England and Scotland where the Scandinavian settlements have left their mark.

Alan at once, and almost officially, made friends with the RAF officers in the squadron. He was like an Australian ambassador, representing his nation by diplomacy and courtesy, rather in the same way that Murray Gardiner had handled himself in his role as the senior South African. If he had been with us from the start, he might have controlled the aggressiveness which did so much to threaten Wizard's authority. As it was, he relieved a lot of my anxieties by his presence and by his overt support. He was funny, too, never taking disaster seriously and setting a tone of useful cynicism.

Other late Australian arrivals were Ken Watts, Wally Gale, Morgan Bartlett and Ray Goldberg, all sergeant pilots. Ken Watts was a good-looking blond hunk with a friendly smile. There is a photograph of him brushing his teeth in front of his tent which shows the Australian physique in its quintessential form. He came too late to show his qualities in the Western Desert, but his distinguished war record is noted in Appendix A.

Ray Goldberg looked about fourteen years of age, with a fuzz on his upper lip which did not quite belong to the cherubic innocence of his face. He was also slightly overweight, which added to his schoolboy look and contrasted with the Pentathlon physiques of the other Aussies. But Ray was a good soldier and went on to distinguish himself in ground attack operations and shipping interdiction.

On 9 November I had flown an extensive Tac/R, lasting an hour and a half, of the northern section, Sidi Omar-Sidi Azeiz. I had seen no tanks but the numbers of vehicles moving over the desert tracks had greatly increased, indicating Rommel's preparations for an advance. On the 11th I completed the second of the artillery observation sorties with the 4.5s at targets around Halfaya. There was no interference from fighters; in fact, for a week or so we had been flying over the frontier area as if the Luftwaffe did not exist. On 12 November Whalley and Thomas were sent out on a routine recce and both of them were shot down, the first powerful signal to us that the Luftwaffe had come out in force.[1] Enemy fighters remained a constant threat until the end of December, by which time the military situation had greatly altered.

Thomas had graduated as a lead pilot since his forced landing near Maddalena. I was sorry to see him go; but it was Whalley's death that hit me forcibly. He was too young, too unaggressive, too frightened. Seeing him embark on adventures for which he was so ill fitted worried me. He had been shaky and unhappy from the beginning but he hadn't cracked. He was the latest sacrificial victim to set against the shame of those who had mysterious oil pressure drops. In real terms he was the squadron hero, for he wasn't cut out for violent action, yet he persisted white about the gills to the end.

At ten o'clock on the morning of 15 November all the available officers were assembled in the mess tent for a talk by General Godwin-Austen, the recently arrived commander of 13 Corps, who had flown in by Lysander. The weather was beginning to turn cool and the change of season caught most of us unprepared. My own winter uniforms were still en route from India in a tin trunk bound for Aboukir. But the squadron stores had laid in a supply of standard army khaki battledress and all of us - Australians, South Africans and British - were issued with these ugly, ill fitting garments and you could only distinguish us by our hats, dark blue for the RAAF, khaki for the SAAF and light blue for the RAF. Fur felts were mostly abandoned, though the Adjutant continued to wear his. With our unpressed trousers, scruffy pullovers and dusty flying boots we looked like a collection of tramps. The General's appearance was in sharpest contrast. He had probably flown straight from GHQ Cairo. His belt, buttons and boots gleamed, his uniform seemed brand new and scarlet tabs burned brightly on his lapels. He told us that there was to be a battle shortly but he gave no details except to say that it was the intention to destroy Rommel's armour and relieve Tobruk, which we already knew.

"I'm sure you chaps are eager to move forward and get into the fray," he said. "The army relies greatly on the information you give us. You have a very important role to play. Good luck and good cheer in the days ahead."

His speech was designed for a fresh, untried infantry unit just arrived in the desert from the rain-soaked training grounds of England and we didn't like it. We were dirty, smelly and had been in the fray for months. Whether the army moved forwards, backwards or sideways our job was the same.

---

1. **12 November, 1941. PO Whalley and Lt. Thomas failed to return from a Tac/R mission." *Fighters Over the Desert*, page 60.**

THE LUFTWAFFE RE-EMERGES

Armies spend most of their days preparing to fight and living in comparative safety behind the lines. The soldier thinks in terms of the clash of arms, great victories like Blenheim or Waterloo. Air forces meet the enemy on a routine basis and our psychology is different. We abominate pep talks because every day is somewhat similar. Crisis is normal. Instead of stiffening the sinews for a decisive encounter, we "sweat out" a tour. Decorations are awarded not so much for individual acts of courage as for length of time on the job.

The General seemed to have come from another, brighter world. I remember standing there with the others, a disheveled warrior whose life wasn't worth much. I was conscious of our miserable appearance and the insane dedication of our existence. Benedictines in their monasteries did not have to be as pure and unattached as we did and their lives were soft and safe in comparison. The spruce Godwin-Austen and his equally perfect staff officer - a young man of my own age who was holding the General's "British warm" overcoat and briefcase - were an abomination in my sight. I walked away with "Blue" Thyer, the Aussie cypher officer, a heavy balding man with pale blue eyes and eyebrows so fair they looked white. Because of his job he knew everything that was going on and I always enjoyed talking to him.

"What did you think of the General?" I asked.

"No offence meant," he replied, "but that's a prize example of a super-pom! And the bastard was dressed for a light opera."

An hour later, as I was working on something in the flight tent, Hugh Davies came in with a request for a recce west of Gambut along the Via Balbia to Tobruk involving a penetration of about thirty-five miles beyond the wire. General Morshead was apparently worried that a force of tanks which had been observed in the area was getting ready to attack his perimeter.

I was in a foul mood and instantly up in arms.

"For Christ's sake, Hugh," I shouted at him, "We're not starting that nonsense up again. Particularly now the bloody Jerries are out looking for trouble. Don't tell me Wizard agreed to this one."

Hugh looked genuinely grieved and I was sorry for being angry.

"Wizard didn't see the request," he said. "He flew off with Godwin-Austen to a staff meeting. Do you want me to turn it down on your authority? I'm sure Wizard will back you."

"No. I guess I'll have to do it. The problem is how!"

I couldn't ask anyone else to do the mission, and I didn't want to force Wizard to fight an issue for me on the first day of the new general's tenure. My snap judgment was that an anti-air force staff officer at 13 Corps had slipped us a fast one on the principle that the fly boys were too darned careful of their skins. Horrocks had departed from his job as B.G.S. to command a brigade and had been replaced by Brigadier Harding, an extremely efficient, kindly little man, who carried on the policy of listening to what we had to say before making demands. I knew him and had been personally briefed by him on a few occasions. It could have been a straightforward error, a product of the panic and confusion of staff members on the eve of battle.

My anger was justified. No recces had been carried out in the immediate vicinity of the Luftwaffe airfields since Wizard's reconnaissance "sweep" in late September. I ran through the bivouacs looking for Masher, cursing under my breath. I tried to get a mental picture of the air situation. Every sortie in recent days had encountered fighters. They were over the frontier forts and I was being asked to fly past Gambut, for God's sake!

Wait a minute! We had fighters, too.

A wing of Hurricanes and Tomahawks (the American P-40) had begun to operate from Landing Ground 110, about fifteen miles to the east of us and I had seen the sweeps going out, flying high along the coast in the direction of Bardia and Sollum. A fighter sweep is an impressive sight. Twelve to twenty-four aircraft in loose formation, moving fast and weaving. It had not occurred to me that they had much connection with us. They were the glamorous fighter types, an object of envy. They occupied a different sphere.

But did they?

Since September 15th, when Rommel had chanced his mini-push with an entire tank division, the lull in army activity had been matched by a similar lack of challenge in the air, but this had now changed. It suddenly struck me that it was our own fighters that had brought about the change. The Luftwaffe had been saving itself for an all-out effort in support of Rommel's next move, but they couldn't ignore the aggressive RAF sweeps over their own lines.

Why had we been so slow to realize what was up?

We belonged to the same nation, the same service even. We flew over the same ground, but they could have been Russians for all that we knew of their operations. Being such amateurs at war, we had to learn everything from scratch, but we didn't have the luxury of being able to try, try, try again. The first time might so easily be the last time. The Luftwaffe was out, but why was it out? My guess was that it was responding to the fighter wing, not to our puny little reconnaissance penetrations. We'd never be certain how Whalley and Thomas were shot down but it appeared most likely that, totally unaware of our fighter movements, they blundered out behind a sweep. I could just see them dutifully flying from one designated recce point to another right under an air battle. As the Messerschmitts looked down they must have seen Whalley and Thomas, offering themselves for destruction. I told Masher my thoughts on all of this, then we flew over to L.G. 110. I was determined to use the sweeps to my advantage, rather than be betrayed by them.

L.G. 110 was a flying circus, nothing like the thinly dispersed aircraft and desultory activity of a reconnaissance outfit. I landed and was given a place to park in a dispersal area where eight new Hurricanes were sitting, desert camouflaged on top of their wings but underneath sky blue. As I climbed down from my cockpit a trio of them took off and climbed away in tight formation, pulling away from the earth at a tremendous angle. A jeep picked me up and dropped me at the operations centre.

The operations centre was a large marquee crowded with pilots in flying overalls. Around the canvas walls were office tables with clerks sitting at them. There were numerous blackboards with situation maps pinned to them or covered with tactical diagrams. Apparently a briefing had just been completed and this concourse of people was the aftermath of it.

The fighter boys were variously dressed but they had style. Some wore the high black flying boots over blue slacks. Their overalls were new and many of them had silk scarves round their necks, giving them a casual and dashing air. In shameful contrast I was wearing my winter garb, dictated only by the need to keep warm in the chilly weather. It consisted of the once shiny inner lining of an old flying suit which I also used to sleep in. It had the additional disadvantage of not distinguishing me by rank. I began to wish that I'd dressed more formally before setting out on this enterprise.

I approached one gilded youth, his round service hat perched on the back of a mop of fair curls.

"I'm a reconnaissance pilot," I began.

"Bad luck!" We both laughed.

"Thanks."

"Anything we can do?"

"I need to know when your sweeps are going out."

"Ask Wing Commander Cross. He runs everything around here."

He pointed to an older man who was surrounded by a group of pilots. He was wearing a faded RAF blue jacket over khaki drill trousers. The jacket buttons were open to reveal a knitted pullover of the kind women make for their menfolk, beginning to unravel at the bottom. He had wavy hair, a prominent nose and a trim moustache. Bearing in mind the distorting perspective of my own years, he may have been no more than thirty.

Ten minutes passed before he had finished giving out orders and dealing with individual problems. He seemed immensely efficient and sure of himself. When we were alone, I gave him the little speech I'd prepared, carefully stripped of redundancies.

"I know you're busy, sir," I said, "but I need to know about the sweeps. I'm a recce pilot from 451 Squadron and I have to fly west of Gambut. Do you have anything going out that way that I could use?"

I had braced myself for a quarrel if he had attempted to dismiss me, and I was ready to take Godwin-Austen's name in vain and demand that his interests be served. I was going to claim that he'd sent me to L.G. 110 personally to obtain assistance in carrying out this important sortie. The bullshit, however, wasn't required. He shuffled through some papers he had with him and gave me a brief smile.

"We don't go that far, of course. At two o'clock we have one flying just beyond Halfaya and then turning south. I could route them to take you as far as Bardia."

"That would be wonderful. I'd be miles below, of course, but it would take the heat off me completely. And when they swing south they'll fetch all the trouble with them."

"All right. I'll speak to Fred Rosier.[2] Come over here and we'll fix it up."

Masher had stayed with our aircraft and when I arrived back at the dispersal I explained the whole thing and we exulted together. I let the wing take off before we taxied out. It wasn't going to be difficult to keep them in view. No point in flying directly under them, close to the Halfaya and Bardia defences. That was for military thinkers of Molly's class. We aimed for the coast and got down low over the water a mile out from the shore, edging further out to sea as the swarm gained height, heading west. They seemed to fill the sky with dynamic activity. Masher and I didn't speak until we were off Bardia and the fighters were beginning a wide sweep to the south, away from us. The army request was to check movement on the Bardia-Tobruk road.

"I'm going in now, Masher."

"Roger."

I opened up my throttle and started weaving, crossed the paved road and stayed south, following it. Five miles inland I could see a gaggle of MEs at four or five thousand feet, climbing rapidly in an eastern direction. They would not worry us.

Southeast of Gambut something was moving and I could see it from miles away. It is impossible to hide a large military force in the desert. Tanks tear up the surface and make dust clouds which differ in density and size from those of wheeled vehicles. I knew it was an armoured column, so I climbed to 500 feet and skirted the congregation of tanks and trucks. The tanks were moving southeast, away from Tobruk. This was surely the force that had worried Morshead, and it wasn't threatening him.

I moved closer to count. Fifty tanks and twice that number of transports plus a few tractors pulling the long barreled dual purpose 88 mm guns. Looking back I could see the dust of more aircraft taking off from Gambut. The planes made streaks of less dense clouds, quite unlike tanks. If they follow me, I thought, I'll take refuge in Tobruk. It was a good feeling knowing exactly where to go to disappear like magic.

We dived to ground level and edged towards the sea. Didn't want to run over Sidi Resegh airfield which I knew was stacked with Luftwaffe aircraft.

I pressed my R/T button.

"Think we've gone far enough, Masher?"

"I'd give it a few more miles."

Masher wasn't letting me off. I was feeling uncomfortable now and decidedly put upon. All these bloody airfields. Messerschmitts buzzing around. It was crazy.

---

2. **Wing Commander F.E. Rosier, DSO, DFC**

Westland Wapitis of 27 Squadron, RAF over the Northwestern Frontier of India (now Pakistan) in 1938.

The Hawker Audax, a variant of the Fury, was considerable improvement over the Wapiti but still obsolete by the start of WW II.

Note: All photos are from author's collection unless otherwise credited.

Pilot Officers Billy Bowden (left) and Geoffrey Morley-Mower in their Northwestern Frontier open cockpit winter outfits, January 1939.

In December 1940, prior to transfer from India to Egypt, Geoffrey Morley-Mower began training in this early model Bristol Blenheim.

A Short Sunderland flying boat of the type that carried the author from Karachi to Alexandria.

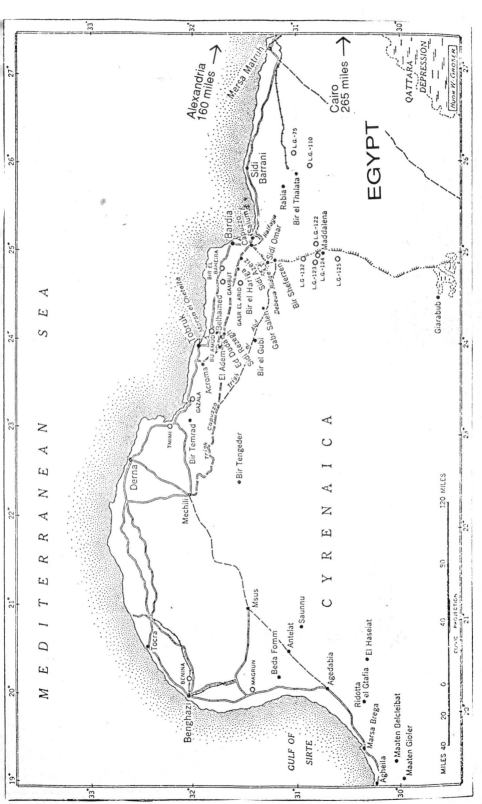

Map derived from John Herington's *Air War Against Germany and Italy*, Canberra, Australian War Memorial, 1954

Above:
Not even modest comforts were available in the Western Desert. Shown here in the Fall of 1941 are (l. to r.) : Unknown, Micky Miller, Peter Campbell, Paddy Hutley and Kevin Springbett.,

Below:
Ken Watts displays the Australian physique outside his tent, November 1941.

'The Wire,'' marking the frontier between Egypt and Libya, is viewed from an armored car of the 11th Hussars.

Fort Capuzzo, 1941, on the Egyptian-Libyan frontier.

Geoff Morley-Mower up in Hurricane Z 4641. There is no explanation for the name "Olive II" as pilots were not assigned their own planes. (Jerry Scutts)

The Westland Lysander was used extensively in the Desert War.

Sollum, Egypt from the Mediterranean. (Chris Shores)

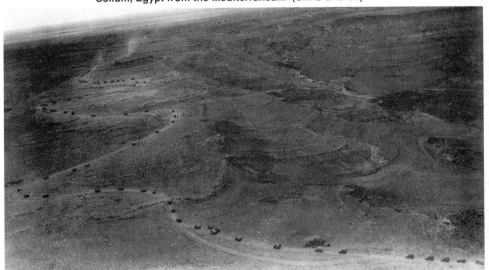

A motorized convoy snakes its way through Halfaya Pass. (Chris Shores)

Bardia, overlooking the Mediterranean Sea (Chris Shores)

A wrecked Henschel 126 of the type downed by Ray Hudson

A German truck convoy dives off the coast road as strafing fighters tear into the column. (Chris Shores)

Sidi Aziez, January 1942, a chat in front of the 451 Sq. command tent involves Adjutant Bill Langslow, (left) Sqd. Ldr. Wizard Williams (in dress uniform to meet Gen. Trenchard), and Doc Reid.

"Masher" Maslen, DFC, one of 451 Squadron's youngest, survived his service in the Western Desert but was killed in action in Italy on a subsequent tour of combat.

Brigadier B.G. Horrocks (later Lieutenant General) of 13 Corps.

Alan Ferguson, DFC and bar, in sheepskin to keep out the cold, served briefly as CO of 451 Squadron in 1942, then assumed command of another Hurricane unit, 450 Sq., was shot down and seriously burned on his second tour of combat in North Africa.

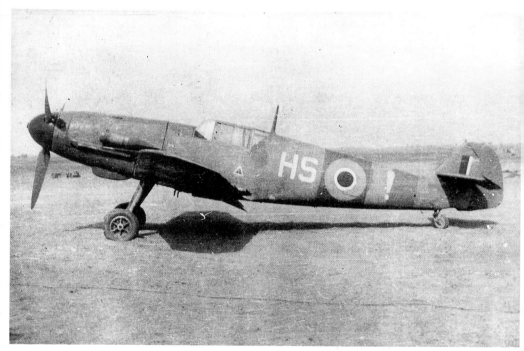

A Messerschmitt Bf 109-F captured by the Allies and placed in flying condition. The F Model was some 80 mph faster than the Hurricane Mark I in level flight at maximum speed.

The author flew this 451 Sq. Hurricane into besieged Tobruk where it was housed in this camouflaged hangar near the sea.

The battered town square of Tobruk.

General Leslie Morshead (with cane), commander of the besieged Australian contingent at Tobruk, shares a moment with staff officers. The officer in long trousers is RAF liaison Wing Commander Eric Black.

The Junkers Ju. 87B Stuka dive bomber was widely employed in North Africa.
This one carries Italian markings and served with 101 Group. (Chris Shores)

Arabs pass a German Messerschmitt Bf 110 of III/ZG 26 at a Libyan landing ground. (Chris Shores)

A British entertainment contingent in Egypt included Norman Hackforth (beside the driver), and on the rear sear (l. to r.) , Marilyn Chambers, "Fluffy", and Hugh French. French was cousin to the Morley-Mowers.

The Morley-Mower brothers (l. to r.) , Peter, Ken and Geoff, meet in Cairo briefly in early 1942.

Hans-Joachim Marseille (left) and wingman Reinar Pottgen of I/JG 27. Marseille scored 151 victories in North Africa (158 overall). On September 30, 1942 the "Star of Africa" fell prey to mechanical failure. His cockpit filled with smoke, the German ace attempted to parachute but struck the tail and fell to his death. (Chris Shores)

A damaged Messerschmitt Bf 109-F of the I/JG 27 abandoned at Gambut, December 1941.

German Ju. 87 Stukas returning to their base in Libya.

A tail damaged Fiat G. 50 shown at a landing ground near Gambut, Libya, in November 1941. This aircraft was from Sq. 352 of 20 Group, Regia Aeronautica. (F.F. Smith)

Pilots of 451 Squadron hamming it up. (l. to r.) Geoff Morley-Mower, Ed Kirkham, Ron Achilles, Paddy Hutley, and Colin Robertson.

Ray Goldberg, clip board still on his leg, briefs the A.L.O. after a recce flight, December 1941, in 451 Squadron's # Z4771. (Jerry Scutts)

A captured Italian Fiat CR 42 CN fighter, unit unknown. F.F. Smith)

A drinking contest with Australian beer at Sidi Azeiz eases the chore of digging a squadron shelter. Officers (l. to r.) are: Ray Hudson, Doc Reid, Geoff Morley-Mower and Micky Miller.

The ravaging effects of desert operations are apparent on this Hurricane of 451 Sq. (F.F. Smith)

One of the best Italian
fighters was the
Macchi MC. 202, its
profile sometimes
causing mis-identifi-
cation as a Bf 109.
This aircraft was from
Sq. 97, of 9 Group.
(Chris Shores)

The wreckage of war machines littered the landscape across northern Egypt and Libya. Top: A Curtiss Tomahawk crashlanded in the desert. (Chris Shores) Center: The crew of a British Crusader tank observes a burning German Mark IV near Sidi Resegh. Bottom: Members of 451 Sq. pose atop a German Heinkel 111 bomber. (Jack Florey)

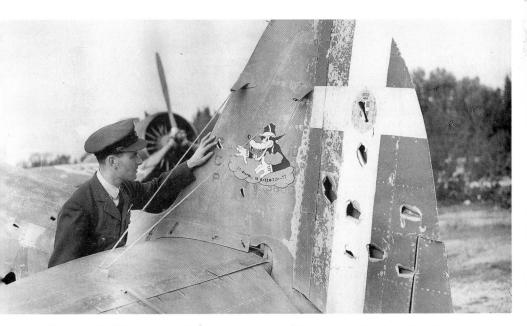

Top: An Me 110 and other German aircraft are scattered about Gambut after its capture. Also abandoned at Gambut (center) is a British Hurricane, captured by the Germans and recaptured by the advancing Desert Rats. Bottom: The tail of an Italian Breda Ba. 65 bears the marks of an encounter with a British fighter. (Chris Shores)

Aussies of 451 Sq. at their desert bivouac.

Below:
November rains pond on the desert hardpan at 451's landing ground.

Below:
(Left) The grave of RAF Cpl. Tom Farr, killed by machine gun fire near Sidi Azeiz on 27 Nov 1941 when an advance party ran into German forces. (Jack Florey)

Three of the RAF enlisted men seconded to 451 Sq., (l. to r.) Don Spinner, Alex Kelley and Jack Florey, all members of the Signals Section. (Jack Florey)

Officers and Sergeant Pilots of 451 Sq. RAAF, November 1941: Top row standing: (l. to r.) Dave Strachan, Bill Buckland, Ron Achilles, Pete Campbell, Harry Rowlands. Middle row: Jim London, Colin Robertson, Stan Reid, Kevin Springbett, Temple Haddon, Alan Ferguson, Acker Kerr, Ken Watts, Blue Thyer, Morgan Bartlett, Ray Goldberg. Pilot known only as "Mac;, Bill Langslow, Evans. Front row, sitting: Micky Miller, Ray Hudson, Ed Kirkham, Paddy Hutley, Murray Gardiner, Sq. Ldr. R.D. Williams, Geoff Morley-Mower, Chris Miller, Hugh Walford, Charlie Edmondson.

Geoffrey Morley-Mower, Cairo, 1941.

EXTRACT FROM LONDON GAZETTE DATED 7 APRIL 1942

The King has been graciously pleased to approve the following awards in recognition of gallantry and devotion to duty in the execution of air operations:

Distinguished Flying Cross

Flight Lieutenant Geoffrey Francis MORLEY-MOWER (40557), No 451 Squadron

This officer has carried out 56 operational flights involving 110 hours flying. His sorties have included tactical, photographic and artillery reconnaissances and flights as protecting cover to other pilots. His artillery reconnaissances have frequently been highly praised by the army formations with which he was co-operating. In particular, his reconnaissances immediately preceeding the fall of Bardia were outstandingly good. Flight Lieutenant Morley-Mower has shown complete disregard of his personal safety, and his unfailing keenness, enthusiasm and cheerfulness have set an excellent example.

THE LUFTWAFFE RE-EMERGES

I shot up to 1000 feet and there was the etched line of the perimeter and Tobruk harbour beyond it.

No sign of blown sand churned up by a hundred heavy metal tracks making for the fortress. Mission completed!

"That's it," I said to Masher as we dived for the coast and the safety of the blue sea.

When I reported to Hugh Davies, he was very excited. Anything to do with tanks animated him. He jumped up from his canvas chair and strode to the situation map.

"Well," he said grimly, "they're not threatening Tobruk, that's one good thing. But you can be sure they're not just milling around, either. I must get this off to Corps."

When I saw him later he had more information on the origin of the request.

"It came from Harding, all right," he said, "but he had no chance to talk it over with Wizard. The fact is Tobruk is mighty nervous. They were screaming for a recce."

I understood their anxiety. When I had been in Tobruk the big talk among the staff was the break out. When the next push came, they said, the engineers would clear a narrow passage through the minefield, then the "I" tanks, followed by the infantry, would drive out to attack the enemy's rear. Clearing the minefield, however, was dangerous. It rendered the entire defence system vulnerable to German panzers which could punch through the hole made for them and capture the fortress.

That night I told Wizard and Murray Gardiner about the fighter sweeps and their significance to us. They were interested, but not dramatically so. Murray's face always seemed to have a smile of disbelief on it. He was five years older and looked down on me a little from the great height of his own maturity. I couldn't tell what he was thinking. Had he understood me? Did he not realize that fighter sweeps were life and death to us?

Wizard was too occupied with higher matters. 13 Corps headquarters was about to move to the area of Sheferzen and No. 451 had to move lock, stock and barrel to L.G. 132, closer to the wire. He soon began to talk administration, humorously grumpy, with Doc Reid.

MESSERSCHMITT ROULETTE

XV

INTO BATTLE
(17-20 November, 1941)

The connection I had discovered between the fighter operations and our recce sorties was valid for only two weeks. As the air war progressed our fighters gradually achieved superiority and once again everything changed. But air superiority never fully applies to reconnaissance. The necessity to infiltrate enemy lines and to outfly the fighters remained, and being low down we were always at some risk from the ground and easy meat for any Messerschmitt squadron that sighted us from above. A badly planned sortie, no matter how the air battle was going, could kill you.

I assumed at the time that Masher and I were the only bright boys to make use of the fighter sweeps, but I was wrong. As I learned later Ray Hudson was on to the same game and had landed at L.G. 110 a number of times but admitted that most of his cobbers were too fatalistic to be interested. I should have talked to him about it but the pilots were very polarized in November, 1941. It was like three small squadrons engaged in a single task and occasionally co-operating if one of the sections was short of pilots. Talking to Murray was easy and his calmness soothed me, but Ray was a walking tornado and I avoided him, knowing that he'd end up criticizing Wizard's handling of things, the Willy Whitlock and Dawlish affair, and a catalogue of errors that fell short of his notions of how the unit should be managed. Apart from rivalry he had nothing against me personally, but I was touchy as hell about the RAF and knew we'd finish in a quarrel.

I paid a few more visits to L.G. 110, feeding my hero worship of Wing Commander Cross and Fred Rosier and studying their routines. Rosier had a little boy face and a shy smile and was always amusing and courteous. He had no big gestures, understated everything and would have laughed at the image I had of him as a charismatic leader of men. I yearned to fly a Hurricane beside him into battle and cursed my luck in being a messenger boy for the army.

Hugh Davies was relieved of his duties and went back to his tank regiment. Two A.L.O.s, Tony Bridges a British gunner and Jim London of the Australian army, replaced him. On 17 November 13 Corps headquarters moved to the area of Sheferzen close to the frontier wire. It was a day of almost continuous rain and the desert seemed to have turned into a series of shallow lakes. In accordance with my policy to fly whenever I had a legal excuse to do so, I managed to get airborne for an air test of a Hurricane. Cloud was at 800 feet and the visibility wasn't very good but I saw plenty of movement on the ground as units inched forward into position for the great push. I felt sorry for them, struggling through slush and sheets of water at a snail's pace in the pouring rain. There were many stranded lorries, their crews gathered round the buried wheels. I passed over long columns, held up by one stationary vehicle. My brother Peter was down there somewhere, driving his Crusader tank towards the enemy.

On November 18th the long awaited British advance began and the Squadron moved forward to L.G. 132 in the wake of 30 Corps whose armour had penetrated the wire early that morning. The infantry units of 13 Corps were also on the move, the New Zealanders going along the line of the coastal highway and the 4th Indian Division moving some way to the south of them.

Organized messing was suspended and we were issued with personal rations of bully beef and biscuits. Apart from cups of tea, an ingrained ritual which would take more than a major attack to dislocate, this was all we had to sustain us for a few days. Flying people aren't used to such interruption of their comforts and we grumbled loudly.

The advance party, a caravan of trucks led by Micky Carmichael, had left on the 17th to set up the necessary organization on L.G. 132. On the 18th I flew a long sortie and was briefed to land at 132 on completion. It was still raining and a thick blanket of cloud, ragged at its lower edge, hung at 1800 feet above the ground. Underneath it the light was feeble. The desert floor was dark and sodden and pools of water reflected the heavy blue-grey clouds overhead. It was as if the weather had changed in response to the prospect of battle. Fighters were probably grounded on both sides for I saw no other aircraft.

The more experienced pilots were taking out the new boys as covers. I had Ian Porter with me. He'd been trained in Rhodesia under constant blue skies and I think this was the first rainy day he'd flown on.

"It looks really shitty," he remarked apprehensively.

"Be grateful for cloud cover," I told him. "And the more it pisses down the safer we are from ground fire. Gunners get lazy in the rain."

Because of the atrocious conditions, and my expectation of an uneventful trip, I was talkative over the R/T, pointing out objects on the ground like a tour guide. Wizard had asked me to look at Sheferzen for a sign of 13 Corps headquarters, which were temporarily out of wireless touch, so the first thing I did was to head south down the wire and check up on their position. A few days previously there had been a tiny garrison of Italian troops. Now there were over five hundred assorted transports in the area, all British. It took me several minutes to find the caravan-like vehicles and to satisfy myself that 13 Corps was there. I counted three staff cars parked nearby, several trucks, three "I" tanks, and two armoured cars.

Then we flew north, following the Trigh El Abd to the area of Gabr Saleh. I had been told by the A.L.O. that I was on a tank search and I recorded it as such in my log book, but the only tanks I saw were our own. There was some refueling going on. Large conglomerations of vehicles, all stationary, making ideal targets for the Luftwaffe if the weather hadn't been so bad. Further west I counted forty Crusader tanks on the move and numerous accompanying transport.

"Those are ours," I said. "You can recognize them by their long shape and short guns."

It could have been Peter's regiment, I thought. 22nd Armoured Brigade, probably.

We swung north into the empty desert, seeing nothing until we passed over a pair of armoured cars sloshing down a track, recognizing them by their curiously blurred outlines.

"Armoured cars," I said, being instructional.

"Roger."

"Almost certainly ours."

I could have sworn they were Humbers of the 11th Hussars, but I didn't want to say so out loud over the airwaves. To this day I don't know whether the enemy listened to our transmissions, or whether they could have gained anything useful by doing so.

At Fort Capuzzo we ran into anti-aircraft fire for the first time. Italian tracers coming up in globules, making elegant parabolas in the gloom. I skirted gingerly, counting a pretty large collection of tents and vehicles. It was clear that 13 Corps infantry were moving ahead more slowly in the northern sector and that the Italian infantry was still in its original position.

I landed back full of the extraordinary sight I'd just seen; an army moving west, like units of a fleet sailing into the emptiness of the ocean. As soon as I'd given my report to the A.L.O. I walked over to the mess for a cup of tea. A hundred yards away I knew something bad had happened. All the South Africans, with the exception of Murray Gardiner, were standing outside the tent, surrounded by a mixed group of Australian and RAF pilots. Half the Squadron was there. This was most unusual at three o'clock in the afternoon, but whenever there was a crisis pilots would trail in from their bivouacs like moose at the prospect of spring pastures. There was no need for a public address system. The word would be passed, or a general movement would be perceived and in a minute a crowd would gather. Someone had been shot down, I thought. How many is it now? Readett, Rowlands, Hutley, Molly, Graeme-Evans, Whalley, Thomas and the three 33 Squadron boys. Eleven in all. I prayed it wasn't Masher.

On the outskirts of the congregation I saw Jasper Brown.

"What's up, Jasper?"

"Bill Andrews was shot down this morning. He was covering Smithy." They were both South Africans.

"Couldn't have been 109s. Too much cloud cover."

"Ack ack."

"That's strange."

Jasper grimaced.

"Cloud was pretty low this morning. These greenhorns must have wandered over the top of something. Capuzzo's heavily defended."

"Capuzzo? They must have done the sortie before me."

I moved closer and listened to Smithy's story.

"We got a bit of flak over Capuzzo," he was saying. "We were only at five hundred feet. They fairly plastered us. We both seemed OK, though. Then as I was crossing the wire I looked back and Bill had disappeared. He didn't say a word to me. Perhaps he blew up. I feel really rotten about it."

All of us felt rotten about it and murmured in sympathy. The discussion went on obsessively. Small arms fire? Engine trouble? Why didn't he say anything on the R/T? I drifted off.

There was gloom and doom in the air when the squadron was together again for the evening meal. It was cold bully beef once more and hard biscuits that threatened to break your teeth. Murray Gardiner sat at the table without saying a word, letting the speculation go by him. His air of humorous detachment from the trials of this mortal life seemed unaltered by the tragedy. He presided over his minions like a father over his children or a professor with his students. The discussion was all of Bill Andrews. Smithy was in a complaining mood. He was a friendly person at normal times, like many big men. He was taller than Pat Byers but he had the same muscularity. His white-gold hair was cut very short, making his head look naked and enormous. He glanced round at the company, his face showing both embarrassment and determination.

"We've lost Tommy and now Bill," he said slowly.

I knew exactly what he was going to say and I felt sensitive on the issue. Equality in sacrifice between the national groups was a constant theme of the squadron grumblers and the numbers were on the tip of my tongue. Three Aussies had been shot down but two had survived. Four RAF pilots had been killed. Two South Africans. I led with my aces.

"We've lost Pat Byers, Molly Malone, Graeme-Evans and young Whalley," I said.

"Yiss, man, but you've got more pilots than we have."

Murray's patience with this unphilosophical chatter finally broke. He smiled broadly but dangerously round the company. Weight of personality is a difficult thing to define but it is easy enough to recognize it in action. When he chose to exert himself he looked bigger, handsomer and cleverer than anyone else present. He didn't have the raw power of Doc Reid but his manner was more distinguished. One didn't wish to be ridiculed by this man.

"Ah will not listen," he said, "to such unutterable bullshit."

He spoke slowly and deliberately, his South African speech pattern perceptibly more emphatic, his consonants clicking liquidly in the silence.

INTO BATTLE

What he said was not remarkable, but the way he said it was. Everyone shut up after that.

The sharp crack of a Bofors anti-aircraft gun situated a hundred yards from my bivouac woke me on the morning of the 19th of November. I scrambled out of my tent, pulling my clothes on and sticking my bare feet into desert boots. It was just after dawn, everything white and grey under the cloud cover. Four Messerschmitts scudded across the airfield very fast, looking like toy aeroplanes, their engines making a high pitched snarl. In a second the other seven Bofors of the airfield defences were barking away, their gun muzzles flashing streaks of flame in the semi-darkness. The MEs wheeled to port and descended in a rough line astern formation to strafe our widely dispersed Hurricanes. On all sides men struggled to their feet and began to run for cover. A pile of stones about four feet high had been left near my tent by the team of workers who had cleared the landing ground. A dozen pilots had already run towards it, throwing themselves on their faces, the late arrivals landing on top of the others, their rear ends sticking well above the level of the cairn.

I didn't fancy a cannon shell through my backside so I stood still, ready to run in any direction if I was unlucky enough to be in line with one of their targets. In comparison with the eight machine guns of the Hurricanes the Messerschmitts were lightly armed and not especially suitable for strafing. Their cannons were of heavier calibre but they only carried three of them. The crackle of gunfire sounded as the leading aircraft opened up early in its dive, scattering its shells over a wide area. Since I was not in the line of fire I could watch it like a spectator at an air show. First the crack and whistle of the guns, followed by spurts of dust tracking across the surface, the shells striking with a high pinging shriek and ending with a low sob as they rebounded into the air. The ME climbed away in a steep turn without apparently having hit anything.

The second ME, coming from a slightly different angle, fired a long burst which kicked up a line of dust between two parked Hurricanes but did no damage. The Bofors guns banged away at him as he climbed, the shells falling behind his tail. The next two came in together on parallel tracks, very fast. As soon as the leading one opened up there was an explosion and a sheet of flame as he hit a Hurricane about fifty yards from where I stood. It was sitting birdlike one moment and the next enveloped in flame. The illumination was blinding. Meanwhile the first attacker had returned and had lined up with his target, heading straight for me.

I ran at right angles to his approach path, past the little mound of stones and the heaped bodies. The crack and ping of striking missiles was very close and I cursed my untied desert boots which flopped uncomfortably as I galumphed along. There was a bang and a sheet of flame behind me. The noise of aircraft, Bofors shells and the sob of spent rounds. Another

Hurricane had been hit and something on the far side of the strip was burning vigorously.

Suddenly it was over.

One of the Bofors crews shot a few ineffectual rounds after the departing Messerschmitts which disappeared rapidly in the poor light. As I walked towards my bivouac bodies were disentangling themselves from the heap that had collected behind the pile of stones. No one was hurt.[1]

"Poor shooting," said Hudson, dusting himself off. Being nimble, he'd been the first to take cover and had suffered the weight of several bodies on top of him. The fires were still raging but it seemed a small result for such an impressive outlay. They'd chosen a perfect time to attack and with a little more determination they could have wiped out our grounded Squadron to its last precious Hurricane.

We saw Wizard's staff car touring the camp. Eventually he drove up to where we were standing. The M.O. was with him and two medical orderlies sat in the back seat clasping first aid kits. They looked a little formal for the time of day and gave the impression of having been on duty all night waiting for an attack.

Wizard pushed his head out of the car window.

"No casualties so far. One of the Hurricanes they hit was unserviceable. An MT lorry went up. The Hun was a bit tentative this morning."

He waved his hand and moved off.[2]

When I walked to the mess about 5 P.M for the evening meal the much lamented Bill Andrews was already back with the Squadron. He had spent the day and a half since he'd been shot down walking and thumbing lifts in the direction of L.G. 132. Luckily there was plenty of friendly traffic following the wire. He looked tired and dirty. Hutley, who had been shot down in September, was enthroned as expert witness beside Bill.

"Man, with me everything happened so bloody quickly," Bill was saying. "My engine must have been hit, though I didn't hear a strike. It got rough and started smoking badly. I wanted to land straight ahead but I was afraid one of the petrol tanks might blow up on me, so I throttled back and began to get out but the smoke died down and I decided to land wheels up. I'd seen the line of the wire just before I was hit, so I knew it was only a question of walking in that direction and hope the Jerries didn't pick me up. After I'd tramped an hour I saw a procession of trucks coming my way. I was pretty

---

1. II/JG 27 managed to get four Bf 109s into the air and these strafed L.G. 132 twenty miles north of Maddalena damaging three of 451's Hurricanes." *Fighters Over the Desert*, page 64 [It occurs to me that the attack was probably led by Lt. Marseille, re-visiting 451 Squadron, but this time not in peace.]

2. Charles Edmondson records that there were, in fact, three persons injured in the strafing, one being Major, later Major-General McArthur-Onslow, whose hand was hit by a shell fragment. Charles met him long after the war was over and was shown the scarred hand.]

sure they were ours so I took off my battledress top and waved it. They were army signals people, making for Maddalena." [3]

Murray Gardiner loomed in the tent opening, interrupting the story. There was a wry smile on his classic visage.

"Hey, young Bill," he said, "so you decided not to emigrate to foreign parts after all."

There was considerable anxiety about what Rommel's reaction would be to 30 Corps' thrust west of the wire. It was predicted that he would have to respond to the threat to his supply lines and to the likely breakout of the Tobruk garrison, although the emptiness of the desert offered him an infinity of choices. Everyone expected Rommel to do the unexpected. There was an enormous population of soft-skinned vehicles containing ammunition, fuel, technical support, food and every other necessity of war, spread over the are and totally vulnerable to armoured attack. Before the campaign began the 8th Army had craftily positioned two supply dumps in enemy territory south east of Gabr Saleh and El Gubi respectively. They were heavily camouflaged and watched over by the Guards Brigade, but if Rommel had discovered them it would have halted 30 Corps' advance. Major Jasper Maskelyne, a scion of the famous illusionists, Maskelyne and Devant, whose show my parents used to take us to see each year when we were children, was in charge of their concealment. He didn't succeed in making the dumps disappear, as he might have done on the stage of the Palladium, but he did a marvelous job of disguising them.

Military historians have given partial credit to our aggressive fighter sweeps for keeping German and Italian reconnaissance aircraft out of the area, though I can't grasp the logic of that view. Nearly all fighter operations were to the north, between the coastal road and the Trigh Capuzzo. There was nothing to stop the Axis recce boys from approaching sneakily from the south as we did, or from penetrating low down, or from avoiding the fighters by the simple procedure of running away.

On November 20 the 4th Armoured Brigade assaulted the Italian Ariete Division which was entrenched at El Gubi about forty miles south of Tobruk. That section of the battle was being covered by No. 208 Squadron, the reconnaissance unit which had been resting for a few months and had recently begun to work for 30 Corps. Our area of interest was north of theirs - Fort Capuzzo, Sidi Azeiz and the broad track of the Trigh Capuzzo westward to a point just short of Tobruk. I flew a dawn sortie on that day. A week or so earlier this had been the suicide run, but on the third day of battle it was anybody's guess what I would find and I was keyed up at the prospect. Our fighters would not be up so early, nor, I hoped, would theirs. It was still quite

3. *Fighters Over The Desert* reports that Allied losses were light on 18 Nov. "Lt. Andrew of 451 Squadron was shot down while on a Tac/R mission, but he returned safely on foot the next day." (page 63)

dark under the cloud cover when we took off and there wasn't a glimmer on the surface of the desert, the nearest city being Alexandria, two hundred miles to the east. My navigation lights were on so that Ron Achilles, who'd volunteered to guard my tail, could see me. Although he was one of the original Aussies I didn't know him well and this was to be the only sortie we flew together. I think the prospect of a very early flight intrigued him.

I could just see the ground when we crossed the wire and headed north. The Italian camps at Capuzzo and Sidi Azeiz were still in place, firing their characteristic display of colourful ack-ack at us as we gingerly skirted them. No great change there; however, west of Sidi Azeiz we came across forty German tanks, spread out and followed by assorted support vehicles. They were driving hard toward El Adem, looking formidable, their long gun muzzles poking aggressively out of squat hulls.

The cloud was solid at 4000 feet giving us plenty of protection from fighters as we flew west, keeping the Trigh Capuzzo on our left and the coastal highway on our right. In the distance I could see the unmistakable outline of a parked Stuka, sitting on what was clearly an abandoned field, the bombers having removed themselves from the path or our advancing forces. If an unserviceable Stuka had to be left behind, I argued, they would surely try to retrieve it, so I swooped down and strafed it, hearing the putter of my guns and feeling the mild vibration from the wings as I pressed the button. The Stuka lurched sideways and ignited. Very satisfactory. A primitive joy, like popping balloons or trampling an elaborate sandcastle before leaving the tide to do its work.

Then we ran into a second airfield, crowded with Messerschmitts looking skinny and low, their fish shapes pressed to the ground. I felt an extra tautness at the sight of them, so helpless on the ground, so formidable in the air. There were eight of them, well dispersed. A Fieseler Storch, the tiny German communications craft which ferried staff officers around and sometimes spotted for artillery sat outside a large marquee that might have been a headquarters. I was about to climb towards the safety of the cloud when three 109s in line astern formation appeared from nowhere, 2000 feet above us.

"Fighters," I shouted to warn Achilles and that was the last I saw of him. I dived, automatically opening my throttle and selecting maximum revs, weaving slightly to keep the Messerschmitts in view, hoping they hadn't seen us.

No such luck! The leader peeled off and headed down towards me like a hawk after a hare. By this time I'd reached ground level and pulled into a steep defensive turn. The situation had been in my dreams for months. I had some advantages. The Hurricane had a lower wing loading than the Messerschmitt, and this meant it could fly in a tighter circle without stalling the wings and crashing to the ground. In order to shoot me down an attacker would have to fly inside my track to aim a deflection shot that would hit me.

If I flew well, that was technically impossible. Also the ME pilot would be worried about hitting the ground while concentrating on his gun sight. The disadvantages were that there were three of them and they could take pot shots at me from above until I ran out of fuel and then I'd have to make a run for our own lines. They were much faster and I'd make an easy target. All these thoughts were present as I forced the stick back towards my stomach, feeling the pressure on my body as the desert scrub flashed past my wingtip.

I held my head back, resisting the pull of gravity, watching the leading Messerschmitt creeping up behind me. He was a little higher than I was, his wingtips vertical to the ground, too far away for a shot. Trying to fly the perfect maximum steep turn at the lowest possible height, I was too busy to feel fear. Fear came at breakfast time before a tough sortie or in the middle of the night before a photographic trip.

I tightened up my turn a bit and felt a slight judder through the airframe. Was that the beginning of a high speed stall? I eased off the turn a little. It could have been an updraft of air or my imagination. Tighten up again, damn you! Suddenly there was a flash of cannon fire, brilliant against the overcast, the shells kicking up dust outside my path and behind my tail.

He broke off the attack, zooming upward and out of sight. I waited for the second one. He came in slower and closer to the ground, holding his fire. This was what I feared most, that one of them might get inside me momentarily and blast my tail off. Two small encampments of German or Italian soldiers were in my path and I had to make minor adjustments of height to avoid them. As I looked back all I could see over the top of my head was this dark, fish-shaped miniature German fighter.

Getting closer.

Closer.

I was madly tempted to do something, to straighten out and turn the other way, anything to break up the pattern. No! No! No! Lead us not into temptation! As soon as I leveled out he'd get me. I'd be a perfect sitter, big in his sights with no deflection for a second or two as I changed direction and his cannons would rake my fuel tanks and fry me like Pat Byers. Except that I was less than fifty feet from terra firma and my exit from this life would be blessedly instantaneous.

What about putting down some flap? Twenty degrees of flap would reduce the stalling speed and allow me to tighten up my turn still further. I was just going to act on this inspiration and my left hand was feeling for the flap lever when the Messerschmitt pilot fired. A real fireworks display this time, the shells striking the the earth beneath me and bouncing over a wide area.

I took my eye off his aircraft and when I looked back he'd disappeared.

One moment he was there, trying to shoot me down, the next instant he was gone. As I continued on my circular path I saw a line of minor explosions and sheets of flame quite close to one of the army camps. It was the Messerschmitt. He must have done a textbook high speed stall at a hundred feet and flipped in. I remember dog fighting with Batts Barthold in a couple of Audaxes high over Amritsar and its glittering temples. Exactly the same thing had happened to me. I'd yanked the stick back too far in order to keep a steady bead on him and suddenly stalled out. There was no warning at all. The aircraft just snapped on its back, dropped like a stone and began to spin down vertically. No problem recovering from an altitude of 10,000 feet, though Batts pulled my leg about it. But at a hundred feet it was sudden death for the German in a wild skid of dust, flame and assorted aircraft parts. Body parts, too, I imagined. Poor bugger! He should have practiced high speed stalls and got used to the little warning signs. Probably a wartime entry with fifty hours on type, still all fingers and thumbs with the mighty Messerschmitt.[4]

I searched for number three but couldn't see him. Then, glancing upwards, I saw both of them high above me, obviously leaving the scene. I was drenched with sweat and my glasses had steamed up at the tops of the lenses. I wiped them roughly with my fingers as I climbed to the safety of the cloud and set course for base.

When I returned Ron had already landed, having escaped without further incident. I handed in my report to Jim London, who wrote it all down. I told him I'd been attacked but he didn't react with much interest, his mind being on broader issues.

"We're expecting a big showdown near Sidi Resegh," he said gravely. "I'm surprised the Jerries are still hanging on to the airfield you saw."

"Maybe you've got it all wrong," I replied, a bit miffed at his lack of interest in my dice with death.

In spite of the weather there was plenty of enemy air activity that day. Several hours later Ray Hudson and Pete Campbell were in the Sidi Azeiz area. Ray descended to identify some trucks on the ground, while Pete kept his height under the cloud cover. Ray saw turbans and knew they must be part of the Indian Division. They were stationary, probably brewing tea. A few miles away a German tank formation was advancing meaningfully towards them. Ray dropped a message to warn them. When he looked around for Pete he saw him being pursued by four 109s. They all disappeared together in the cloud and haze and Ray fled the scene at low level. He returned to L.g. 132 "with a teacup of fuel," as he said. Pete didn't get back till the next day. He had escaped the 109s by entering cloud, headed south, got lost and ran out of gas beside some South Africans who were driving American Stuart tanks. They put him up for the night. At dawn they filled his Hurricane with what they had - 87 octane M.T. petrol - and by some miracle he got the engine

---

4. I have described this incident throughout as I experienced it. I never had a doubt that the planes which attacked me were Messerschmitts. However, it has been pointed out that Italian Macchi 202s were always being mistaken for MEs, and I was not at the time aware of the existence of Macchi 202s. The attempt to shoot me down so close to the ground and the delight in maneuvering seems more Italian than German.

started on his internal batteries. It spluttered and banged, but he staggered home.

That evening I walked across to Doc Reid's tent. It was easy to find in the darkness as his oil lamp was the only light to be seen. When my glasses had misted up that morning it had reminded me of the dirty little secret I kept from the world. Back in 1937 I had entered the RAF by a trick. As a boy my eyesight had always been mildly defective and at the age of eleven I needed glasses to read words on the classroom blackboards. When I decided to join the air force I consulted our family physician on how to temporarily sharpen my visual acuity enough to pass the medical board. He didn't think I could pull the wool over the eyes of trained medical staff and strongly advised me not to try. But I persisted. He ran through a list of noxious drugs that one usually only comes across in murder mysteries, eventually choosing strychnine, as far as I remember, and handing me a small quantity of white powder in a paper spill. He warned me that it would affect the heart and was not to be taken until the examination was over. I was lucky to have my heart and blood pressure checked first, so I ran for the lavatories and took my powder. My eyesight test was completed satisfactorily fifteen minutes later. It was extraordinarily perfunctory. I was simply lined up in front of a board with rows of letters, decreasing in size from top to bottom.

"Stand behind this line," said the doctor. He was wearing a white coat over his RAF uniform. "Put your hand over your left eye and read off the lowest line you can see clearly."

He looked down at the papers on his desk. It was so easy to cheat. I could use both eyes by simply opening my fingers slightly, and the white powder had given me gimlet vision. I read off the bottom line proudly.

Directly I entered flying training I ran into trouble. I couldn't wear my glasses and dual instruction became a fitting punishment for my arrogance in trying to outflank the regulations. At the circuit height of 1000 feet the windsock and signals square were a blur, so I had no idea what direction to land in. My instructors were baffled. If other aircraft were on the circuit, I could follow them in to land and had no problem, but otherwise I was lost on those square featureless grass airfields and was judged a halfwit. In the end I fudged my way through the courses, happy when I could fly solo with my glasses on, seeing the earth below me etched in the blessed detail of normal sight. In my log book the Chief Flying Instructor wrote, "Lacks concentration," and that was the nearest anyone got to the truth.

Doc Reid was highly amused to hear my story of deception.

"You had a nerve to think you could fool an Air Ministry medical board," he said. "If I'd been there I'd have caught you out."

"I fiddled two annual medicals in India by memorizing the chart."

He laughed.

"You should have been a cat burglar! Well, we'll get you some goggles. I'll read the A.M.O. tomorrow, give you a test and get the thing going."

I walked back to my bivvy in the dark, glad to be rid of a secret I no longer needed to keep. The goggles, however, didn't turn up until the campaign was over. [5]

5. The final chapter carries an account of my post-war struggles to retain my flying category.

XVI

THE NOVEMBER HANDICAP
(21-26 November, 1941)

On 21 November I got up early and flew across to the fighter wing in a Lysander to make arrangements to use the fighter sweep for a recce around noon that day. I figured that the Luftwaffe would be all over the place, taking advantage of an improvement in the weather. In the middle of the day there'd be no chance of sneaking in and sneaking out as in my previous dawn sortie. One of the flight commanders briefed me and afterwards I pumped him on fighter operations. He couldn't have been more than five foot five in height, a ball of energy, his hair brushed straight back from his forehead and plastered down.

"What's the 109 really like?" I asked. "I mean, when you come against it on equal terms. I've nearly been shot down by the buggers, but they always dived on me with a speed advantage. I'd like to know how you cope with them."

"The 109 can outclimb us, outdive us and it beats the hell out of us in level flight," he said. "They've got a better aeroplane." [1]

"So I gathered."

"But we're more maneuverable. We can turn inside 'em any day of the week. So basically what we do is fly off and challenge them to fight. They don't like that because if they're forced to stand and fight we have that slight advantage in maneuverability. Their advantage is that they can always break it off if they feel like it, which we can't do. Sometimes they'll mix it, but often they climb above us and try to pick off targets in a single dive. It's not very effective but stragglers do get shot down that way."

---

1. In *Fighter Over the Desert*, Wing Commander G.C. Keefer, DSO and Bar, DFC and Bar, observes, "I cannot think of one occasion when we encountered 109s and were above them. They were invariably on top of us every time we met. They seemed to be faster, had a better climb and much better altitude performance. Notwithstanding all this, the old "Hurri" provided some considerable comfort in its ruggedness and maneuverability. I certainly had the feeling that with this ruggedness and maneuverability no one could get me as long as I could see him coming. (page 226)

On the other side, Oberst Friedrich Korner, a pilot in I/JG 27, says , "The Bf109F was an excellent aircraft, and I flew it with enthusiasm. It was superior in operational height to the Hurricane, Curtiss and Spitfire. Our tactics were the results of its performance: dive from height, out of the sun, climb, renewed attack - no dogfight if possible. The MG 151 cannon was very good, and mostly I did not need to use the machine guns in the fuselage. (page 229)

"Just one attack?"

"Yes. Then they disengage. We can't follow them down because they can outdive us by a mile."

"Would you rather have 109s than your Hurricanes?"

"I suppose so." he smiled. "We'd rather have Spitfires, of course."

Spitfires were the front line British fighters of 1941. They were operating with increasing credit over England but they hadn't yet reached the Middle East.

The fighters took me as far as Gambut. The skies were almost clear of cloud and low down over the sea. I watched their progress with satisfaction; a dynamic weaving swarm of Hurricanes, asking for trouble and drawing all hostile attention to itself. Passing back over the coast east of the Resegh airfields, it was obvious that the scene had changed from the day before. The Messerschmitt squadrons were gone and the outline of the airfield they had occupied was scarcely discernible. It was now a battleground. Random explosions dotted the landscape and tanks and trucks that had been set ablaze poured out black smoke. There was little movement to attract the eye and there was no way to see who was winning or what the pattern of the engagement was. I contented myself with pinpointing and identifying British Crusader tanks, German panzer Mark IIs with the long 50 mm gun, some 88 mm anti-tank guns and British, German and Italian trucks. Tony Bridges had asked me to look for the New Zealand Division which was thought to be advancing towards the Resegh area and I flew back towards Gambut looking for them without success, eventually returning to the battlefield. I watched the gun flashes and the smoke for a few minutes, hoping to find something coherent to report, but it was an indecipherable mess. I'd have been more usefully employed running over the scene with a camera and handing the problem over to the photographic interpretation teams. It was an illustration of the limits of visual reconnaissance. I took the desert route back to L.G. 132, feeling very frustrated.

When I landed back at L.G. 132 it was to hear that Smith and another South African had been bounced by some Messerschmitts. Smithy had been the unlucky one they'd followed and it was presumed that he'd been shot down. [2]

November 22nd was one of my few non-flying days. The squadron was due to move forward to a new landing ground which had been prepared by the Royal Engineers close to the little fort on the wire called Libyan Omar. Micky Carmichael, whose head wound had not healed, again got the job of leading the advance party, consisting of three trucks and fifteen men.

---

2. **"21st November, 1941 .. . . 451 Squadron lost Lt. Smith, who crashed in flames on a Tac/R mission."** *Fighters Over the Desert*, page 65.

THE NOVEMBER HANDICAP

On 23 November I flew another sortie over the Resegh airfield. It was, in fact, the critical day of battle, though I didn't know it. The New Zealanders had made their way along the coastal road and up the escarpment to Resegh, and in the conflict that followed they suffered their worst casualties of the war. The Gloucesters lost most of their tanks. My brother Peter rode off the field lying on the top of one of the few remaining serviceable tanks, with half a dozen other survivors clinging to the turret.

When I flew overhead in the early afternoon of that day the confusion worried me more than the carnage. Explosions, burning vehicles and clouds of dust set off by tank tracks obscured the area. A reconnaissance pilot is good at counting and identifying objects on the ground when they are on the move. He can say, that is an infantry formation because there are many trucks, some anti-tank guns and a few "I" tanks. These are armoured cars, notice the blurred shapes and the comparative sprightliness of their advance. This is a panzer unit, moving slowly and dustily with its supporting soft-skinned vehicles trailing behind it. At Sidi Resegh, however, everything was static and I could discern no units. I started off counting tanks but realized that it was impossible to distinguish a serviceable tank with its crew intact from one that had been stopped by gunfire. If it was not on its side or obviously burned out it might look operational, yet the men inside it could be dead.

There were over a hundred German tanks, but half of them may have been out of commission. There seemed to be twice that number of Crusaders and Stuarts, most of them obviously disabled. Half a dozen canvas-topped lorries had red crosses painted on them. German? British? There were men on the ground, too. New Zealanders or Italians? There must have been much captured equipment which could not tell its story from the air. Nothing announced to me that a victory had been won or who had won it. The troops down there were too busy to notice me, much less to fire at me.

"This is all useless information," I said to Tony Bridges, as I handed in my report. Nothing but numbers."

On the same day, the 23rd, Edmondson and Ferguson were sent to Sidi Azeiz, where Micky Carmichael was attempting to operate an advanced L.G.[3] He had been foiled by enemy forces at his designated location but had found refuge with the New Zealanders. The following account is from Charles Edmondson's notes.

---

3. John Herington, *Air War Against Germany and Italy, 1939-1943,* page 205, has this to say:
"At Sidi Azeiz the advanced party of No. 451 Squadron was taken into the armed camp established by the 5th New Zealand Brigade, the pilots sleeping by their machines. The expected attack came early on the morning of the 27th and part of the Australian maintenance party was overrun and captured, but the four Hurricanes took off in the dark without any kind of flarepath in an attempt to observe and report progress to the New Zealand troops."
The date seems to be wrong in this account and I have no evidence for the four aeroplanes at Sidi Azeiz. Such lack of caution does not sound like Wizard Williams.

Flying in, we could see that Sidi Azeiz was surrounded by the enemy, and everyone I spoke to within the perimeter assumed that it would be overrun that night. We spent a good part of the day sitting on the cabin of a truck watching the German and Italian columns which were always on the move and skirmishes which broke out when they ventured too close - grandstand view, no admission charge!

We flew one sortie to Sidi Resegh and were bounced by 109s coming back, but there was plenty of cloud cover and we managed to return safely. In the evening, Micky gave us messages to drop on 13 Corps H.Q., but for some unexplained reason he refused to refuel our aeroplanes. We took off anyway and landed back at base right out of gas. My prop stopped soon after landing. My most vivid memory, however, is of taking off from Sidi Azeiz over the myriad campfires of the enemy forces surrounding it."

13 Corps was out of touch with the squadron and there was no word from Carmichael that night. On 24th, Wizard drove up in his staff car, looking more harassed than usual under the wide brim of his Aussie hat.

"I must find out what's happened to Micky, and I've got to contact Corps. We sent four of our aircraft to Azeiz this morning, and all they got was hostile fire. Would you fly cover for me?"

We approached Sidi Azeiz at 1000 feet and Wizard spotted the landing ground without difficulty. I saw some vehicles on the ground which I at first assumed to be Micky's, but there were too many of them. I began to count out of habit - five, ten, twenty, forty. Hey! Where did he get all this transport from? At that instant the ack-ack came curving up at us. Wizard turned sharply away out of range and a very Welsh voice broke the R/T silence.

"I can't believe that's Micky trying to shoot us down!"

"Italians," I replied.

"I'm going to drop a message on corps headquarters."

Wizard headed down the wire towards Fort Maddalene where No. 13 Corps was temporarily parked. Judging by the proximity of enemy troops it seemed altogether too far forward for comfort. But stories of generals and their headquarters staffs being captured because they followed the front line troops too closely are common enough. The armies, I thought derisively, spend their time "building up", and when they are ready to go they lose their minds. It was very stupid of us to send an advance party over the wire. We should have waited until the New Zealanders had won their battle and the Germans and Italians had removed themselves. But no doubt Major Hurst, the focus of so much military wisdom, "knew" the bloody place was secure.

There was a landing ground about a half a mile from No. 13 Corps headquarters vehicles, with a couple of communications aircraft parked on it. After circling meditatively, Wizard came through on the R/T.

"I'd better land here and talk to Harding directly. You go home."

In the evening, Wizard, who'd spent most of the day at Sheferzen, gave us his account of the battle.

"Well," he said, "we're not moving forward in the wake of our victorious army just yet."

He took the pipe from his mouth and made a vainglorious gesture. Everyone laughed. He often spoke in shorthand these days. We knew his comedic routines and were prepared to explode with mirth at his account of the vanity of human aspirations.

"Nobody really knows what's happening, least of all our neat little staff officers at Corps. They're looking a wee bit ruffled. I saw one or two hairs out of place today. Their situation maps seem to have been rearranged overnight by Harpo Marx. One of their A.L.O.s was captured on his way to join Micky's advance party and he had all his secret codes with him. He probably didn't have time to destroy them. Anyway, they're assuming our signals can now be read by the enemy. The cipher boys are busy lashing up a secure means of communication. Micky's disappeared from the face of the earth. Major Hurst, our resident expert on disaster, believes they've been snatched by the column that's now sitting on our airfield at Libyan Omar. I'd rather accept that than think old Micky got lost."

More laughter.

"They all tell me that 30 Corps has won its battle at Sidi Resegh. Which probably means they haven't. And there's a good deal of what they call 'random movement,' so watch out for what happens next."

"Hard cheese on Micky and his boys," said Doc Reid, who was inclined to use out of date British expressions from his years doing surgery in London.

"They're in the bag," said Wizard, nodding his head sadly. [4]

That night I went to bed early, since I had been up before dawn. The discomforts of our migratory existence had begun to irritate and the desert sore on my right ankle was playing up. The messes were still packed for the move forward and it was cold bully beef once more for dinner.

There was a lot of noise that night. Distant gunfire. Then closer and more alarming sounds. The profoundest sleep couldn't shut out those threatening whines and crumps. A machine gun chattered somewhere far away. I wondered if the whole camp was awake. I waited to hear voices but heard none.

---

4. "On 23rd November, when the headquarters of XIII Corps moved forward to Bir el Hariga, the advanced party of No. 451 set out for Gasr el Arid. Unfortunately the enemy was still active between Marsa el Cheteita and Gambut, and the army liaison officer with all his codes was capatured, though the main party delayed by a puncture had meanwhile fallen in with the New Zealand troops and was safely diverted to Sidi Azeiz." John Herington, *The Air War Against Germany and Italy, 1939-1943*, Page 202.

I stuck my head out of the tent flap and looked around. No lights to be seen. No men running. Clearly no panic. From the direction of the latrines a figure approached. It was Ray Hudson.

"Someone's having fun over there," I said, pointing to the west.

"The New Zealanders are not far off," he replied. "They've probably clashed with some of the Eyetie infantry I saw today. Noisy bastards!"

"Did they wake you up?"

"No. I'm ready to sleep through the crack of doom. Those hard biscuits they've been serving us must have worms in 'em. They've given me the squitters."

He walked on and was soon lost to sight in the darkness.

There can't be a major battle in this sector, I reasoned. It's all happening thirty miles to the west. My watch said after midnight. Nobody fights at this hour, for Christ's sake! I lay down again and maneuvered my hip into its depression, hoping to ignore the urgent bangs and cracks.

Suddenly the noises ceased, as if an over loud radio had been abruptly switched off. There was perfect silence. The wind had dropped and even the sound of flapping canvas could no longer be heard. I drifted off, relieved that I hadn't been obliged to shift from my comfortable bivouac.

It was some hours later that I was awakened by someone beating on the tent above my head.

"The Jerry tanks are on our airfield!"

It was an Australian voice shouting in my ear. As the confusion of sleep cleared I heard the noise of his boots scratching the stony surface as he ran away. I didn't doubt the truth of his message for an instant. I scrambled into my clothes and ran towards the flight tent.

Sure enough, in the growing light twenty tanks could be seen, unevenly dispersed on the western end of the strip. They were less than a thousand yards away. The whole camp was in a fever of activity. Men were rushing in all directions loaded with their few possessions. Trucks, overcrowded with bodies, were already departing in clouds of dust. Only the tanks were still and silent. It was as if they were waiting for orders before they swiveled their guns and began to destroy our Hurricanes and then us.

At the flight one of the technical sergeants was allocating aircraft to pilots as they ran in. His own truck was ticking over, filled with men and equipment and ready to go. I saw Robertson and Achilles making off at speed towards the aircraft, parachutes slung over their shoulders banging noisily as they jogged. They both carried a parachute bag with their belonging in it.

"Is there a kite for me?"

"I sent the serviceable ones off first, sir."

The N.C.O., a tall, lean Aussie, looked embarrassed at having nothing respectable for me to fly. I'd been sleeping like a log and had arrived very late on the scene. I was ready to fly anything.

"What about an unserviceable one?"

"Take "J." The undercarriage was being worked on."

He pointed out a Hurricane that was standing on its own between me and the tanks. I ran.

When I reached the aircraft several ground crews, dragging a starter trolley, were making hurriedly towards it. Hurricanes were already taking off and the noise level was high. I looked towards the tanks, expecting any moment to see the flash of their guns, but they sat there, heavy and inert, ignoring the pandemonium their presence had created.

I swung up to the cockpit, threw the parachute on to the bucket seat, and vaulted in. I decided against fastening my parachute. It would have taken thirty seconds to arrange and secure the straps. Too long. I sat uncomfortably on top of the tangle of straps and buckles and stuffed the parachute bag between my knees. It interfered a bit with the free movement of the stick. The engine fired and I waved away the chocks. Before I could get the aircraft rolling the crew was aboard its truck and it was beginning to move off. I closed the cockpit hatch and took off in the dust cloud of two Hurricanes ahead of me. The wind was light and we were all taking off away from the tanks.

Once in the air I felt perfectly safe. The relief was exhilarating. I looked down at the strip and saw that nearly all our vehicles had departed. The tents were still standing, and one lone Hurricane that couldn't be flown. The German tanks sat there looking solid. They had not fired at the aircraft taking off, nor at the fleeing trucks. It was as if all the men inside them were dead.

I was grossly uncomfortable at first but by shifting my buttocks around and arranging the parachute buckles to lie between my thighs, eventually I settled down. I did not secure the straps. There seemed no point in it. The aircraft I was flying had manual locks in its undercarriage. When a check is being made of the hydraulic system, the riggers insert robust locking devices to prevent the wheels collapsing while they are working. There was no way I could get the wheels up, so I had to fly slowly. As a matter of fact I worried a little about how fast I was permitted to go without straining the frail oleo legs. I decided that 160 mph was maximum.

All the other aircraft had departed, but I was reluctant to leave. No flak was coming up at me. I thought I would fly around a bit and see what I could see. I began counting. Eighteen tanks on the edge of the airfield. A mile to the west were twelve more and a collection of soft-skinned vehicles. A few miles to the north was an even larger group of trucks and a half a dozen tanks. It was getting quite light by this time and I was a magnificent target at 1000 feet with my undercart down, motoring along at 140 miles an hour. Mysteriously, there was no reaction from the ground. This had been a cheap sortie for me. No tactical problem of entry or exit. All good Germans sleeping soundly. Days of hard fighting, followed by a long trek eastwards, must have so tired the tank crews that even the noise of our takeoffs had not disturbed them.

Peter tells the story of a night in the desert after a day of fighting. His regiment was in laager and the crews were lying on the ground beside their tanks. The night was pitch black with a low cloud cover and no moon. Around midnight a German armoured car unit approached on reconnaissance. Everyone in the regiment could hear it as it gradually got closer. Every fifteen minutes or so it stopped for five minutes, listening. Nobody moved. Eventually it came so close - perhaps fifty yards from the nearest tank - that Pete heard the officer get out of his car. He heard him cough and the scratch of his boots on the ground. An order was given in German and they moved off. Why did the Gloucesters' crews not react? Tired out, said Pete. It had been one of those days. So it must have been for the tank crews of the 5th Panzer Regiment as they slept beside their machines on the morning of 25 November, while No. 451 Squadron, Royal Australian Air Force, was taking off to fight another day.

Looking to the east I saw one of the memorable sights of my life; a modern army in headlong retreat. As far as the eye could see the desert was streaked with individual dust trails, as thousands of trucks, driven by soldiers whose units had been disorganized and stampeded, made their way from the Egyptian frontier to safety. The sun was just rising above the horizon and the lines of dust from all those racing wheels were tinged with pink, trailing like exotic feathers against the dark, plum-coloured sand. It was what came to be known as "The November Handicap," named ironically after the annual horse race.

I was so excited by all this movement that the implication of national defeat did not occur to me. The desert looked beautiful in the dawn, decorated by the retreating army; the parallel patterns of dust rising from the wheels of so many vehicles, all taking their private tracks to safety, made it look like an abstract painting. I no longer thought of the big issues, like the outcome of the war or the domination of Europe by Nazis. I was just a reconnaissance pilot with some timely and accurate information to report, like a journalist with a scoop.

I knew that 13 Corps HQ was only fifteen miles south of L.G. 132, so I headed in that direction, hoping to find the bulky headquarters vehicles and drop an appropriate message, but there was such a melee of crisscrossing traffic that I soon gave up the idea as hopeless. Running across L.G. 122, a strip east of Maddalena, I decided to land and enquire.

The strip itself was an extraordinary sight. There must have been over a hundred and fifty aircraft stacked around it, some of them wingtip to wingtip. Dispersal had been abandoned in the confusion of withdrawal, making it the best Luftwaffe target I ever saw. There were Blenheims, Lysanders, many Hurricanes and half a dozen Tomahawks. Apparently there had been an emptying out of the forward airfields to the north in the wake of the sudden German advance and someone in authority had designated L.G. 122 to be a safe refuge.

XVII

A HURRICANE WITHOUT PRICE
(26-27 NOVEMBER, 1941)

I landed and was waved to a dispersal stacked with Hurricanes, most of them belonging to fighter squadrons. I walked up and down the lines looking for No. 451 Squadron markings and hoping to see a friendly face, but found no one I recognized and no squadron aeroplanes. Afterwards I learned that Wizard had ordered our pilots to land at L.G. 75, further to the rear. The order had missed me because by the time I lurched over to the flight tent the getaway operation was in its final phase and no one thought to inform me of Wizard's instructions.

I spoke to a boyish looking pilot who was sitting on his parachute under the wing of his freshly painted machine which contrasted sharply with my own beat up unserviceable model. It had probably arrived a month before, undergone its operational checks and then been camouflaged for the Middle East. On its nose was neatly inscribed "P.O. L.G. Price." Some squadrons encouraged the allocation of aeroplanes to individual pilots and they were permitted to put their names on them. Some marked their victories, as I had once dreamed of doing, with a row of swastikas. Nothing so glamorous was possible for us. We won no victories and had no heroes. "P.O." stood for Pilot Officer, the lowest commissioned rank in the air force.

"Is this your kite?" I asked.

"Yes, sir."

You don't address flight lieutenants as sir. Scorn began to supplant envy in my mind. Red cheeked and tubby, he was probably just out from England where he'd called all his instructors sir. He couldn't have been more than nineteen. I was only four years older, yet I felt in a different category of human being.

"Have you seen any army liaison people around?" I asked.

"Yes, sir. Major Havelock is in the tent just over there."

He pointed to a cluster of tents fifty yards away. A dusty, desert-camouflaged staff car stood outside one of them.

"The one by the staff car," he said.

"Thanks."

Conscious of my importance as a bearer of very precise and up-to-date bad news, I walked over to what turned out to be an A.L.O. section, with several army officers and their clerks employed in it. The tent flaps were tied open and I could see them working away inside.

145

I spoke to a major who was standing in front of the tent, formally dressed in winter khaki and service cap, with a leather belt and the leather sling diagonally across his chest called a "Sam Brown."

"I've just done a recce," I said. "Our squadron woke up this morning to find Jerry tanks actually parked on our strip."

I took out my map.

"There are eighteen tanks there and some more here."

"Christ," he said, "Save this for the General."

"What do you mean?"

"General Cunningham has his HQ a mile from here. Get in my car and we'll go to see him."

This was better than I had imagined it. I would have settled for a debriefing by Brigadier Harding of 13 Corps. I'd have been flattered by an interview with General Godwin-Austen. But Cunningham! He was the Commander of the Eighth Army. I knew that he flew around in a Blenheim. One of the Blenheims I'd seen parked on the landing field must have been his.

A few minutes of driving along a well-worn track from the airfield brought us to a typical clutch of mobile HQ caravans. Major Havelock ushered me up the steps into the command vehicle, which had a table, some folding chairs and a big situation map. After a minute General Cunningham appeared. He was a tall, lean man in his mid fifties. As a matter of fact he looked like the elder brother of the Aussie sergeant who had allocated me Hurricane "J" an hour or so before. A fur felt would have suited his angular face well. He was unshaven and dressed in khaki drill slacks, a brown pullover covering his pyjama top. I had the distinct impression that they had just wakened him.

I told him my story, giving figures and pointing out locations on his situation map. He was obviously worried, but he did not fail to smile bleakly at his tragic messenger.

"This is very valuable. But it's already slightly out-of-date information. This was about six o'clock?"

"Yes, sir."

"I'd like you to fly right back there and report on the situation as it is now. It may have greatly altered. I want you to fly around the whole area and try to get a picture of it."

"My aircraft is unserviceable and I don't know where my squadron is."

"Borrow one!"

He said these last two words with great authority. Obviously, I thought, the Army Commander could have any aeroplane he wanted and I had already decided on that nice new Hurricane with L.G. Price's name on it.

When we got back to the strip I asked the major to stand by while I wangled the aircraft from Price. It wasn't going to be easy. I wanted to sound very reasonable at first and to get tough later on if necessary. It certainly goes against the grain to give one's aeroplane away to a pilot from another squadron, and Price would probably think he was committing a military crime by doing so. A more experienced officer would find it easier to accept. I knew this schoolboy was going to act as if his teeth were being pulled.

He arose from his parachute and stood apprehensively as we approached him. He wasn't actually standing formally to attention, as he might have done on a parade ground, but his posture was rigid, both subservient and defiant.

"Price," I said, "is you squadron commander here?"

"No, sir."

"Your flight commander?"

"No, sir. I don't know where they've got to. I'm waiting for orders. Major Havelock says he . . . " He looked at the major, who looked at me.

"I'm afraid I have the authority to fly your aircraft on a special sortie for General Cunningham. You know he's commanding the Eighth Army?"

"Yes, sir. But I can't let you have it without my CO's permission. He'd kill me."

Havelock stepped forward and put his hand on Price's shoulder.

"There's no time for that, old boy," he said. "This is an emergency."

Price was visibly weakening. He looked at his beautiful Hurricane and back to me.

"Will it be all right, sir?" he said, pleadingly.

"Sure, Price," I said, "it's the right thing to do."

I took off just after 9 A.M. I didn't arrange for another pilot to cover me. I think it was my sense of the occasion. The British forces seemed to have suffered a catastrophic defeat and my own squadron was scattered. This flight wasn't like any other. Another reason was my growing belief that a cover didn't make all that difference. I would search the skies unremittingly on my own behalf.

I had neither eaten nor drunk anything since the previous evening, yet although hungry and thirsty, excitement took over. Reconnaissance has little glamour, admittedly, but a personal sortie for the army commander is as close as a recce pilot is likely to get to it. I knew it was a critical day and I was determined to make the best reconnaissance of my career.

It worried me that I didn't know what the air situation was; however, I assumed that most of our own fighter forces were scattered and were also trying to re-form on other overloaded airfields fifty miles to the rear. The Luftwaffe, I thought, might be all over the battlefield, so I kept low throughout the flight, mostly below 400 feet, only once rising to 2000 feet to get a better view and then down again. Actually, I needn't have bothered. The advance of the New Zealanders along the coast towards Tobruk had persuaded the Luftwaffe to clear out all its forward operational squadrons to safer positions and the inevitable disorganization reduced German fighter activity for that day. It was typical of desert warfare that one of our infantry divisions should be advancing successfully in one sector, while enemy tanks were counter-attacking by punching a hole right through our centre.

As soon as I was airborne I could see the same scenes of widespread retreat that I saw earlier. However, at L.G. 132 things were a little different. The two groups of tanks near the airfield had joined forces and were now fanned out, driving in a direction more north than east. A large formation of trucks and some 88 mm guns were following them some miles behind.

I kept low and skirted the columns. I saw no other aircraft and concentrated on making a detailed situation map of the area. There were a number of smaller groups of enemy vehicles, some stationary, some moving. I wasn't able to avoid flying directly overhead some of the transports, and whenever I did I would see the same reaction. Men would throw themselves from their trucks and run. One or two would aim a weapon and fire upwards at me. I saw the occasional mounted machine gun firing in my direction as I passed overhead. I was expecting the familiar white puffs from German light anti-aircraft batteries, but received none. Perhaps it was because they were on the move. Flying low and fast, I didn't feel at all threatened by the small arms fire.

I flew ten miles north and saw nothing significant, so I turned west, climbing to give myself a broader view of the situation. I had been almost forty minutes in the area by this time and had done what I though was a good job. Diving down to my safe height again I saw a perfect target. Five of the German support vehicles were lined up, one behind the other, heading north. My front gun button was on "fire" so all I had to do was to draw a bead, press, and rake through the trucks as I flattened out of my shallow dive. They exploded satisfactorily. I didn't see anyone jump out. I watched the conflagration for a few seconds, then I turned away and headed for home.

I was feeling good as I approached L.G. 132 and considered putting on one of my aerobatic performances at low level. It seemed a more appropriate occasion than Tobruk and unlikely to be misinterpreted. But something stopped me. I did not really think I had been hit by any of the bullets that had been aimed at me but I had, after all, been flying for a long time over hostile forces and within range of their fire. I decided it would be prudent not to put any extra strain on the aircraft.

After landing I was waved into the same dispersal. Most of the transient planes had departed, but there were still a number of Hurricanes on the ground and several Blenheims. I switched off and began to unstrap. Price was standing there with a proprietary grin, glad to see his very own Hurricane safely back.

I slid the hood to the rear and stood up in the cockpit. Just as I swung my right leg out and was feeling for the first foothold faired into the side of the fuselage, I saw the figures running towards me. With my helmet on I couldn't hear the shouting. By the time I'd reached the ground and had slung the parachute over my shoulder, there were twenty people staring at the airframe and talking excitedly.

When I looked I saw that it had been punctured by hundreds of bullets. The worst area was from behind the cockpit to the tail section. While I was flying I'd been conscious of my wing tanks and I thought of that as I went to inspect the wings. The tanks were untouched but there were over fifty bullet holes, all outboard of the tanks toward the tips.

Most of the spectators were concentrating on the tail section, which had been substantially destroyed. The crowd had swelled to include numerous airmen and a technical flight lieutenant. He told the curious to stand back and, tearing the damaged fabric with his hands, began to inspect the interior. There were so many heads in the way that I could see nothing. Pilot Officer Price was standing apart with tears running down his cheeks. He was not sobbing, but the tears were clearly visible and his face was working.

I felt a mixture of sympathy and contempt for him. After all it was only a bloody aeroplane. Lost in a good cause.

"I'm sorry about your kite," It said, putting my arm around his shoulder. "It can't be helped."

It was the time for saying really bland things like that. I remember an occasion when I was about five years of age. Trying to help my mother, I had picked up an overloaded tray and had tripped on a stair rod, scattering coffee and cigarette ash over the wall. My mother had been sweet about it, saying such comforting nothings. I found myself imitating her tone of voice.

"It really can't be helped. You weren't to blame."

But he was not to be so easily consoled.

"I only joined the squadron last month," he said. "I've flown two bloody sorties. Now my kite's gone."

He was genuinely moved, like a child is moved, seeing a mere setback as something tragic and irremediable. The Hurricane was his pride and joy. He 'd persuaded the rigger to paint his name on it; a silly thing to do in the first place. Then perhaps, someone in the photographic section had taken a picture of it, with himself in the cockpit looking boyish and warlike. He'd mailed a copy to his parents, so that they could see the "P.O. L.G. Price." on the nose and feel proud. Then this fool from another squadron had come along, pulling rank on him and had got it filled with bullet holes. Half of me bled for him; the other half wanted to kick his rear end. I turned away and looked at my map, hoping that my scribbles were decipherable.

All this had taken only seconds. Havelock was eager to drive me away to General Cunningham and was shadowing me closely, trying to get my attention.

I dropped my parachute under the wing of the aircraft. Map in hand I followed him to his car.

The General was properly dressed now with red tabs on his battledress jacket. He did not smile, but listened me out. I thought he looked very tired, his face grey and worn. Havelock and another staff officer made notes. It was soon over. He thanked me and said it was very useful information.[1]

Back at the aircraft, the technical officer gave me a guided tour of Price's Hurricane. The damage was even worse than I had thought. He pointed to the wings.

"You can see these holes here," he said. "they're through the main spar. That makes it a write off for a start. We'll be able to cannibalize a few items and then tow it to one side and put at match to it. You were lucky not to have your fuel tanks pierced."

"I knew I was being shot at," I said, "but I had no idea I was being hit. There's no way you can tell with the noise of the engine."

"Come and see the tail."

He led me down the fuselage, followed by an admiring group of pilots. The outer skin had now been cut away to reveal the control wires of the rudder and elevator. "

"Do you see those wires?" he said.

He looked up at me, grinning, ready to enjoy the expression on my face when I saw the damage.

"The elevators might have held a bit longer, but look here at your rudder controls. This one has only a few strands left."

I stared at the shredded wires. The port rudder control was the worst. It was hanging on by a hair. If I'd attempted a roll off the top as I swept over the airfield, the strain would have been enough to break it off completely. Could I have landed safely without a rudder? I began to struggle with that thought. I could have used coarse aileron and flapped the limp rudder from side to side. Hair-raising! No. I suppose the likelihood would have been loss of control and a crash. I'd had a lucky escape.

Price had disappeared and I didn't seek out any other members of his fighter squadron or attempt to send a message to his CO to apologize for pranging one of his Hurricanes. An all-ranks mess had been set up and while I was eating wolfishly at a meal of bull beef fritters and a glutinous mess of canned bacon I was approached by a clerk from the signals section who told me that No. 451 Squadron was assembling at L.G. 75. I returned to my unserviceable Hurricane, which still had its manual locks in place, but I decided not to raise the subject lest the zeal of engineers delayed me. I had enough fuel for the short journey. By three o'clock in the afternoon I was tooling sedately eastward to join my mates near Sidi Barrani.

It was a day of scattered cloud which cast a pattern of purple shadows on the barren landscape. As I neared the coast my heart warmed to see the little broken fishing village, the frill of surf on the narrow beaches. I loved it. It was home.

1. *General Cunningham was relieved of his command on 25 November, 1941. (Winston S. Churchill, *The Grand Alliance*, Houghton Mifflin, Cambridge, 1950, p. 569) [I suspect that while General Cunningham was having his interviews with me he already knew the bad news.]

A HURRICANE WITHOUT PRICE

Looking down at the field I saw to my surprise that the squadron was almost intact. I counted eleven Hurricanes. The unit Lysander had also made it back safely. I could identify some of the sections by their shapes; the M.T. Section with its cluster of assorted vehicles; the bulky caravans of the photographers; the big mess tents. All over the camp canvas was laid out on the ground, ready to be erected.

I flew round and round the circuit, slumped in the cockpit, half asleep with quiet pleasure, relief and, I must admit, a bit of triumph on my own account. It looked to me as if the other pilots had flown obediently to our former base and missed a lot of fun. Whereas I, the late rising dimwit, had stumbled into the thick of things.

General Cunningham, I thought to myself. What a scoop! Personal sortie for the Army Commander! Stone the crows, they'll say. I wasn't going to blurt it out the first time I hit the bar tent. I'd let them worm it out of me.

Let's face it, a downtrodden reconnaissance pilot doesn't have many such moments.

MESSERSCHMITT ROULETTE

IIX

ROMMEL RUNS US RAGGED
(27 November, 1941)

As soon as I'd landed I discovered that other recces had been done. This slightly took the edge off my little adventure. Ray Hudson, for instance, had cased the area and filed a report. Masher had distinguished himself, in his usually cool way, by thinking of the danger the tanks presented to troops on the ground. He told me about it as we were staking out our newly acquired bivouacs.

"I must've woken up about four o'clock. It was pitch dark, but I could hear grinding noises. You can't mistake tank tracks. Terrible racket. Everything had been quiet for hours, but now there was this unmistakable sound. It soon stopped, but I was too worried to go to sleep again. I dressed and walked to the mess. Some other officers had collected and we talked about it. Then Wizard arrived with the Adj. By this time a glimmer of light was beginning to come from the east, but we didn't spot the tanks on the western edge of the strip till forty minutes later. Then all hell broke loose."

He gave me one of his twisted grins.

"I was the first aircraft off the deck and I did a little recce seeing more or less what you saw. Then I thought I'd warn the New Zealanders."

"Ray told me they were nearby."

"Yes. About ten miles to the north of us. 5th N.Z. Brigade. They were marked on Jim London's situation map. I thought I'd warn them. So I flew round and round, fairly low down, making a hell of a noise. Not a sign of life could I raise. There was no use in dropping a message and have no one pick it up, so I climbed up and dive bombed the buggers, roaring across their heads at a hundred feet. That finally did it. They thought they were being attacked and the whole unit scrambled out into the open air."

"How can you drop a message," I asked, "without a message bag and lead weights?"

"I wrote on my message pad, THIRTY GERMAN TANKS TEN MILES SOUTH, and then threw it out, board, straps and all!"

It was amazing how quickly the Squadron managed to reassemble and begin its task again. We'd lost all our bivouacs and personal kit and most of the squadron documents, but by 26 November the technical sections were operating normally and the mess tents were up. The Aussie ground crews had been elated by the events of the November Handicap, the contact with enemy tanks, the excitement of retreat, and their spirits went up a notch or two as a result. Wizard was making gravedigger jokes at the army's expense. Several sorties had already been flown. Micky Carmichael and his advance party had not been heard of and it was assumed that they were prisoners of war.

The panic caused by Rommel's sudden thrust had stampeded the soft-skinned, non-fighting echelons and disrupted communications. Some drivers of trucks, it was uncharitably rumoured, didn't take their feet off the accelerator pedals till they reached Cairo. We soon found out what had happened. The move of 13 Corps along the coastal road had gone according to plan and the New Zealand Division and the 4th Indian Division successfully pinned down the mainly German garrisons that manned the frontier defences. In a lucky move the forward headquarters of the Afrika Korps was surprised near Bardia and captured. By the 24th General Freyberg's New Zealanders had reached the Sidi Resegh airfield and Tobruk's garrison had begun to fight its way out against determined opposition by German infantry. At that point Rommel concentrated both of his panzer divisions to assault Sidi Resegh; and despite some extraordinary heroism by Brigadier Jock Campbell, a man of legend in the desert and a tank leader of the first order, the British troops were thrust off the ridge. General Norrie, commander of 30 Corps, having lost two-thirds of his tanks, ordered a withdrawal twenty miles south to regroup.

I met Jock Campbell's aide, a much decorated young captain, about six months afterwards in a bar in Beirut. We both remembered Sidi Resegh but from very different perspectives, and had a memorable evening discussing the battles fought there. He described to me the Brigadier's habit of driving around under fire in his staff car, seemingly oblivious of his personal danger. There is no such thing as a standard hero. A hero does what has to be done and in this case it was to show himself unarmoured to the enemy, while the troops he led looked on from behind several inches of steel plate. Nelson was killed carrying out a similar performance at the Battle of Trafalgar. Such defiance of the ordinary laws of caution on the part of a commander gives him considerable authority and at Resegh he certainly needed it. The Panzer IIIs and IVs were armed with such superior guns that they could pick off a British tank before its two-pounder was in range. Most of our tanks were being put out of action before they had fired a shot. This made commanding officers of armoured regiments understandably reluctant to advance. On one occasion Jock sent his A.D.C. to give a personal message to a tank colonel.

"Tell him to advance one thousand yards," said the Brigadier. "He'll object, I suppose. If he does, get out your pistol. Let him see it. Then say that if he doesn't obey the order at once you have my instructions to shoot him."

The aide did exactly as he was told. The colonel, who had stuck his head and shoulders out of the top of his tank for the interview, looked amazed and popped back inside again. Within thirty seconds the regiment was grinding forward once more.

ROMMEL RUNS US RAGGED

Rommel, the great opportunist, as soon as he had won his tank battle, gathered his remaining armour for the knockout blow. On the evening of the 24th he had set out down the Trigh El Abd towards Bir Sheferzen and, incidentally, towards the quietly sleeping members of No. 451 Squadron. It was one of his characteristic gambles and it almost paid off. Winston Churchill admiringly compared this "dash to the wire" with "Jeb" Stuart's ride round McClellan's army in the American Civil War, but in spite of its disruptive effect it failed. In my second sortie in Price's new Hurricane, I had observed the northward movement of Rommel's tank columns and subsequent reconnaissance kept them in view. All that day our bombers attacked them, protected by our fighters which by that time had achieved air superiority over the frontier area. On the 26th the Axis columns took refuge in Bardia and the next day made their way back via Gambut to Sidi Resegh, which had been recaptured by the New Zealanders. On arrival at the battleground the 21st Panzer Division had only forty-three serviceable tanks left. The 15th Panzer, with twenty tanks was still enroute from the frontier.

Much has been made of Rommel's willingness to live rough on campaign, sleeping in the back of a truck on a pile of blankets, drinking from a water bottle and opening tins of food. He prided himself on keeping up with the spearhead, but on more than one occasion this led to problems because he was out of touch with the progress of the battle and his staff were out of touch with him. The dramatic thrust he called "Midsummer Night's Dream" of 14/15th September achieved very little and was costly in tanks. The "dash to the wire" suffered a similar fate at the hands of our bombers. Finally he underestimated the crucial importance of Sidi Resegh. When he exerted his full force for the second time, he had insufficient armour to clinch the battle.

On the 27th, the day that Rommel returned to his El Adem headquarters and the second battle of Sidi Resegh was about to take place, we were once again out of touch with 13 Corps through Wizard was aware of Godwin-Austen's intentions. He had stuck a worried face into my bivouac about 8 AM and proposed a mission. I was only just awake, lying uncomfortably on the hard ground, smoking the first of many "C to C"s and coughing well. Smoking relieved the first ten minutes of consciousness, when hips, chest and elbows felt as if they'd been dealt a glancing blow by a truck.

"Godwin-Austen is moving his headquarters to Tobruk," Wizard said.

"Better him than me," I replied. "He'll run into trouble before he gets there. Hasn't he been reading our recce reports? It's a shambles up there."

"He's chancing it. As a matter of fact he's half way there. They've been driving all night. Look, you know what their caravans are like, don't you?"

"Of course."

"I have a message that's got to reach him before he gets to Tobruk. Do you think you could find him and do a drop?"

"What do I drop it in? I'd like it to be fairly heavily weighted."

"What has to go will fit in a canvas pay bag, and Bill Thyer says he'll steady it down with lead pellets. They should be close to Sidi Resegh in an hour or so."

"Christ!"

I dressed hastily and rushed through my breakfast. Since I had to be in the operational areas to drop the message on Godwin-Austen, I took one of the routine recces of the Resegh battle. Wizard had already detailed Ian Porter to cover me. We flew west about three miles out to sea, crossing the coast at Gambut. We were at 1000 feet, a bad height for both fighters and small arms fire, but I had to make sure we wouldn't miss the caravans. Bearing in mind that German tank units were in the immediate vicinity, it seemed almost crazy for the general to be taking this route and I half expected to see his little convoy burning merrily on the ground or halted by artillery fire from the escarpment a few miles to the south. In the event we soon spotted the two big command vehicles, escorted by a couple of armoured cars and followed by some staff cars and trucks. They trundled along with a dust cloud trailing behind them, the only fast moving things in the red, exhausted landscape. From the height of the escarpment the German panzers and field guns looked down. If they had known that 13 Corps H.Q. and its commander were in easy range they would surely have opened up on them, but the rather insignificant train of wheeled transports was not identified as British. At a distance they could have passed for ammunition lorries or ambulances enroute to the scene of action.

I swooped over the leading car. It must have been making twenty-five miles an hour, a good speed for a desert track. The vehicles were close together, eating each other's dust. No friendly hand waved at me. The armoured car did not stop. I tried again. I split-arsed over the command caravan, making what I hoped was a hell of a noise. Still they wouldn't stop. Clearly they had identified me as a friendly Hurricane and were not concerned at my presence. Equally clearly they were in a hurry, driving through no-man's-land and overlooked by the hostile, shell-pocked ridge. Eventually I had to fly across their path of advance waggling my wings violently. They halted and I dropped the package. Hurricanes are not designed to drop messages and I felt vulnerable, with my hood slid open, twenty degrees of flap and at a speed of 120 miles an hour. It was like being in a Wapiti again, dropping mail on Tochi forts, except that I didn't have an air gunner to throw the mail clear for me. Bill Thyer hadn't put enough weight in it and I knew it would be taken by the slipstream. I flung the bag down as violently as I could with my left arm. It glanced off the tailplane and hit the earth fifty feet from the front car. Two men got out and waved, running to where the bag had dropped.

I didn't wait to see more. I closed the hood, raised the flaps and built up speed. Sidi Resegh was only minutes away to the north, a tragic sight, an illustration of the horror and waste of war. I noticed a damaged Italian C.R. 42 fighter, left behind on the airfield when it was evacuated, standing incongruously among the ruined tanks. I had never seen so many tanks concentrated in one small area, nearly all of them wrecked. Some were burned out, others sat skewed, tilted, with tracks off or showing gaping holes. Turrets had been blown away, revealing the dark interiors. There were several trucks with red crosses on them moving slowly at the eastern fringes of the conflict. The rusty tones and hard, eroded outlines of the escarpment gave the sad scene its own beauty. There was a big sky, a veil of high cirrus cloud cut down the light enough for gun flashes to be seen on the ground. The burning vehicles emitted well defined columns of black smoke which spiraled upwards in the still air, counterpointing the arid landscape. The sea, dark and glassy, shimmered massively to the north.

The battlefield was well beyond the reach of our fighters and I had no idea what the Luftwaffe was doing after its withdrawal from the forward airfields. El Adem was close and probably still active. I felt I had to keep my speed up, both to dodge the small arms fire and to give us a better getaway if Messerschmitts appeared. I slashed low over the escarpment trying to make sense of the general picture. There were many troops on the ground, lying down beside trucks or scampering after one another in ragged lines. I assumed they were New Zealanders resisting dislodgement from the high plateau. There were explosions and fires but I could see no pattern. Our Crusaders and Honeys and the long-barreled German panzers were scattered in random fashion over the escarpment and below it. A snap interpretation of what was happening was impossible.

Jim London had asked me to have a look at El Adem to make sure the Jerries were still in occupation. I approached carefully, satisfying myself that there were no aircraft parked by the big hangar. As soon as I flew overhead, however, I ran into a cluster of typical white puffs. I didn't know it then, but Rommel's headquarters was still there. Later on that evening he would fly back from Gambut in a Fieseler Storch to try to engineer the downfall of the Eighth Army with what was left of his armour. I was just about to leave when Porter's voice crackled over the R/T.

"MEs to port. Same height."

"Make for Tobruk," I replied.

Two 109s were flying towards us from the west. I suppose they had intended to land at El Adem and the anti-aircraft shells thrown up at us had alerted them to possible victims. Head-on, they made slim, deadly silhouettes.

I dived and opened my throttle.

It was difficult to gauge how far away they were, but I judged their chances of catching us before we crossed the Tobruk perimeter as not very good. It was only five miles and we were already going in the right direction.

It was going to be a horse race, though.

MESSERSCHMITT ROULETTE

My Hurricane didn't seem to be a swift one. Porter slid past me and was soon well ahead. He'd probably pushed his throttle "through the gate." You could get extra power for a short period this way, but it strained the engine. I wasn't sure our elderly Hurricanes could survive such treatment.

Meanwhile the leading ME was closing fast and beginning to get within range. If I stayed on course I would give him an easy no-deflection shot at me. I couldn't risk that, so I ripped into a steep turn to the left. His pursuit had given him excess speed. He couldn't stay behind me in the turn and broke off without firing. This enabled me to nudge towards Tobruk, which looked tantalizingly close. But then the second fighter moved in, forcing me to wind up again in my evasive turn. I was being manoeuvred like a hare with a couple of greyhounds in pursuit. A friend of mine at school, Jack Jones, owned a greyhound and some weekends we took it to a course with a local farmers' hunt. Once the hare was sprung from the tall grass, the dogs would be unleashed, heading it off as it dashed for the safety of the hedgerows. If the dogs could keep it in the centre of the field, turning it until it was exhausted they would win. It was an exact analogy to my situation, because my Hurricane was as manoeuvrable as a hare and the Messerschmitts were as swift as greyhounds. I remember the sudden flurry of fur as the hare was tripped and seized. I had no intention of leaving my scut on the North African sands.

I tightened my turn, thought about putting down a smidgeon of flap to hold off a high speed stall, decided not. The ME began firing but his burst went wide, kicking up dust behind my tail.

When he broke away I tried to straighten out and make another dash for the perimeter, but his companion was too close behind him. They were determined to head me off into open country. I thought of weaving violently in a direct line towards the defence system, chancing that their cannons would miss me. The only trouble with that play was that every weave concludes in a scary moment of straight and level flight before a weave in the other direction is initiated. Whenever I struggled with this problem the answer always came out the same.

Stay in the turn while you're being attacked.

Don't relax

Don't try anything fancy.

As each attack was broken off I managed to make a little ground, but it was slow going. As I scorched around, the blurred scrub a few feet from my wingtip, I could see Ian Porter's Hurricane gaining height over safe territory. I was glad he had made no attempt to rescue me. This was no occasion for heroics.

I don't know how long they kept me twisting and turning, a mile or so from Tobruk. It was probably not more than five minutes, though it felt an eternity. Eventually I found myself flying over the enemy siege guns, their sandbag castles looking gigantic from my low elevation. Knots of German soldiers watched us as we roared round.

My trial came to an end when a slight hiatus between attacks enabled me to make a dart across the well-defined perimeter. When I looked back the Messerschmitts were in loose formation, heading for El Adem. Climbing over the harbour, I suddenly felt tired, like an exhausted swimmer. I wanted to lie out on a white beach, drained and dizzy, letting myself recover slowly and deliciously. I had to shake my head violently to jog myself awake, to make myself remember where I was.

I circled slowly. A slow, wide turn.

Porter had joined me and was weaving just a little too energetically behind my tail, waiting for something to happen. I expect he wanted to head on home. Probably thought I'd gone daft. But he didn't press his buzzer and say anything. If he had I might have been as deaf and silent as Molly had been, though for different reasons.

I cleaned my glasses with a dirty handkerchief I kept in my top pocket. Then I searched the sky for trouble, trying to keep up my interest through waves of sleep that made me see double.

There was no danger out to sea. As soon as I'd recovered I'd head downward, cross the jagged coast, get down low over the placid water. Just be careful not to plunge in.

In my log book I have written: "Tac/R Sidi Resegh-El Adem. Dropped message on Godwin-Austen. Chased out by two MEs." Time in the air was one hour and forty minutes.

It was during this period that I realized that our fighters had won a decisive victory over the Luftwaffe. As I've said, air superiority is a term to be distrusted if you're a reconnaissance pilot. A flight of Messerschmitts on the prowl, or even a couple of them innocently commuting between airfields can be a nasty problem for one who has penetrated deeply into enemy territory and has no height or speed advantage. But from this period on we certainly had less and less interference from German fighters.

The victory was hard to understand, because the 109-F was so clearly a better plane. In fact, the Germans retained their advantage in technology to the end of the war, always producing more and better fighters than we could, though the Spitfire lobby might dissent from that judgment.

Did the British have a genius for air warfare?

Were our pilots more adventurous and resourceful than the Germans?

Probably not. But many of us must have been convinced that it was so. I think I believed it myself. The Battle of Britain had been a tremendous boost to national morale and it had made instant heroes of our fighter boys. The fighter wing I knew in the desert fought under serious technological disadvantages but their morale was enviably high. They seemed to think they possessed an innate superiority to the Luftwaffe and some of this feeling rubbed off on to us.

While all these clashes of arms were taking place, Alan Ferguson was enjoying the first of his many wartime adventures. He had flown a reconnaissance sortie on 26 November acting as cover to Charles Edmondson. South of Tobruk they were assailed by Messerschmitts eager to kill these low level, slow moving Hurricanes. They broke in different directions, and the pack followed Ferguson, who reported to me in a letter dated December 1988, "I suddenly found myself floating to earth in a parachute."

A German panzer unit picked him up and for three days he traveled around with them, guarded by a middle-aged corporal. They treated him with exemplary kindness. Their medical officer gave him a thorough post bail-out medical inspection and pulled two of his teeth that had become loose. But Fergie was not in a mood to go gently into a P.O.W. camp. He woke the corporal in the middle of the third night and asked permission to leave the truck on a call of nature. He returned carrying a rock, with which he "clobbered the dear old fellow", hopped off the back of the truck and disappeared into the night. By this time the tanks were in the Tobruk area, and after some anxious hours trying to identify friend from foe, he found refuge with our own troops. By December 4th he was back with the squadron and volunteering for every sortie going.

IX

SIDI RESEGH
(November 28-31, 1941)

When the Tobruk garrison broke out successfully and linked up with the New Zealanders, Godwin-Austen sent a witty telegram to Winston Churchill: "Corridor to Tobruk clear and secure. Tobruk is as relieved as I am." But his message was premature. The New Zealand brigades had captured Sidi Resegh, but they had not fully married up with the Tobruk force, which remained in an exposed position outside the perimeter.

My knowledge of the tactical situation was incomplete, though I necessarily had to be informed of our own troop dispositions so I was party to the anxieties of the General and his staff, handed down at second hand through A.L.O.s. I knew that the New Zealanders were hard pressed and running out of ammunition. Their call for help was answered on the night of the 28th, when a convoy of over 250 trucks set out from Fort Maddalena and drove forty miles in the dark, weaving past the Italian Ariete Division and the armour of 21st Panzer Division without being detected. It brought them much needed food and water as well as munitions. This was the kind of operation that desert warfare allowed and which so often lent it an air of dash and brilliance. When I heard about it I was reminded of the 11th Hussars whose role it was to escort convoys through enemy held territory. I could imagine my snooty captain, skillful in night exploits, sourly doing a very professional job.

Rommel was determined to destroy the New Zealanders in the open ground outside Tobruk and to deny them refuge within the fortress. On the 29th he ordered both his tank divisions to the attack. 21 Panzer approached Belhamed from the east. 15 Panzer attacked El Duda from the south west. Little progress was made against Belhamed, but at El Duda, where the 1st Essex and the 2/13 Australian battalions were holding out, they gained a foothold. However, they were thrown off the ridge in the middle of the night by Australian infantry supported by eleven "I" tanks. On 30th November Rommel overruled his staff's request for a postponement in order to regroup and pressed on with the attacks. His instinct was right. El Duda was overrun after a battle lasting less than two hours and the 6th N.Z. Brigade was destroyed, 600 prisoners being taken.

Once the Luftwaffe had withdrawn their fighters and bombers from the forward airfields, the Tobruk main airfield was repaired and opened up again. On the 31st I flew a sortie with Jesus Evans over Resegh and was briefed to land at Tobruk, reporting to 13 Corps directly.

MESSERSCHMITT ROULETTE

When I passed over El Duda, sporadic anti-aircraft fire told me that the Germans were still in possession although most of the trucks I saw seemed to be British. Even without the slight difference in shape one could sometimes tell them from the air because German camouflage was darker and greener than ours.

There were groups of men standing around and a good deal of nose-to-tail traffic moving to the west round the Axis Highway, a paved road that the Italians had constructed to bypass beleaguered Tobruk. British and German transport was all mixed up on this road but I was fairly certain that the drivers were German and that they carried German troops. They were making the most glorious front gun target. There was no anti-aircraft fire and I knew I could blow up fifty trucks without endangering myself or my cover. I had begun my dive and already had previsions of the chaos my guns would make of that section of the road, when another, stronger image superseded it. It was of Peter, sitting uncomfortably on the floor of a closed and crowded truck, staring unhappily across the dust-laden half-light at his comrades in captivity. I broke away and flew aimlessly for a while, examining my conscience. I decided it was unlikely that Peter was down there, but New Zealand infantrymen almost certainly were. I thanked God I hadn't fired and flicked my gun button to the "Off" position.

The Resegh area was looking its usual tragic mess, like a city garbage dump, smoking and torn, awaiting the arrival of earth-moving tractors to cover the outraged landscape. I was glad I couldn't see the blood from the air, though the escarpment with its reddish brown rock looked as if it had been soaked in it. I tried not to think of the men down there - since there was no way I could distinguish friend from foe in most cases - and I resorted to making a detailed map of the battlefield. It was a small circuit and I flew round and round, altering my height constantly and weaving to lessen the chance of being hit by stray small arms fire. I saw some fighters ten miles to the south, milling around. I thought they were ours. If they had been MEs I could have made it to Tobruk before they nailed me, so I continued counting and marking exact positions on my map. Molly, I thought, would have been proud of me. The fighters drifted away south and I forgot about them.

At Tobruk I was met by Major Havelock, whom I had last seen at L.G. 132 on the day of the "November Handicap" and it was he who debriefed me.

Back at the aircraft, one of the airmen on duty grinned and waved at me. He was the fitter from the concealed hangar. More retribution, I thought, for my slow roll over Tobruk. He gazed at me with admiration.

"Hallo, sir," he shouted, "have you shot down any more Jerries?"

"Not today," I replied, "I'm too busy on reconnaissance."

"Good luck, sir."

"Thanks," I said, twisting uncomfortably and cursing under my breath.

SIDI RESEGH

After lunch Havelock had another sortie for us to do. Godwin-Austen was anxious to know the fate of the New Zealanders. We took off in the early afternoon to look again at the El Duda battlefield. I knew the sortie was useless. Godwin-Austen might have imagined that one could tell New Zealanders from the air by their Boy Scout hats, but we knew that men on the ground, hiding from aircraft for good reason, were virtually impossible to identify. I was bright enough to tell German tanks by their long gun barrels and I knew Italians shot at you with red and white fireworks; but there the list of my certainties ended. There was such a mess outside Tobruk I could only fly overhead and weep ignorantly for both sides.

For forty minutes I crisscrossed the area, marking scenes of carnage, counting traffic, now reduced to a trickle, on the by-pass, noting the altered positions of men on the ground. Back at base I handed in my findings to Jim Leaky, who was to transmit the report to Tobruk. I'm sure General Godwin-Austen was none the wiser. Photographic sorties would have been a far better solution at this point in the campaign, and I am at a loss to explain why we were sent out on visual reconnaissance.

During the first half of December I flew thirteen sorties in as many days, about double the accepted rate. When flights were being allotted, pilots were not to be found. When discovered, they complained that they had flown the day before or felt that they'd been flying too much. Some did not feel well. They would not refuse a sortie, but it required a heart of stone to force a man to fly who said he was off-colour and looked it. The whole squadron was dead tired. Some of the Australians had been flying since early July and the strain was beginning to tell on them. Ray Hudson remembers giving pep talks to one whose morale was becoming questionable.

I wasn't doing so well myself. I remember how my mother used to behave when she was beginning to feel ill. She would become overactive in anticipation of her collapse. It was somewhat the same with me. I couldn't relax. I wanted to finish the campaign and go home and I flew compulsively, just as my mother would clean and scrub before retiring to bed with the 'flu. I was beginning to lose my nerve and was pressing to retain it.

In the air I was seldom frightened, but in the intervals between flights I was increasingly nervous and irritable. It was less upsetting to fly than to hang around and do nothing. When I couldn't find a pilot, or if someone who had been detailed was looking hangdog, I'd go myself. My policy of trying to fly more than anyone else had become slightly unhinged.

On December 1st I flew another sortie over Sidi Resegh, this time with Masher. We landed at Tobruk and gave our report. Nobody knew what Rommel was going to do next. Tobruk was now more vulnerable than ever and it was still under attack by enemy artillery outside the perimeter, though "Bardia Bill" was silent, for obvious reasons. The A.L.O.s had gloomy faces and worried me by asking for information on the New Zealanders that I couldn't supply from a cursory observation from the air. "Crusader" had not gone according to plan. Rommel still had some tanks left and the campaign was in the balance.

December 3rd was a rainy day of low clouds and gusty winds. I had to dress inside my tiny bivvy, an awkward procedure for a largish person in such a restricted space. I was running out of socks and my feet itched as they always did when I couldn't change into clean ones each day. Then I got soaked while walking across to the mess for breakfast. I sat at the bare table in the dim light of the heavily camouflaged tent, shivering with cold and impatient for hot tea.

Masher came in with Tony Bridges, who had a canvas briefcase under his arm. It was the badge of his office, containing maps, signal pads, air photographs and sometimes a clip of signals requesting sorties.

"Filthy day for the race," he said, slumping down on the bench beside me.

"Any requests?" I asked.

"Is it flyable?"

"It's a poor day for flying but a great day for a recce," I said. "Visibility is good and lots of cloud cover."

"They think Rommel's going to do something soon. He's pushed us off Sidi Resegh and is poised to strike at another tender spot. He's pounding away at Tobruk and may decide that's the big issue. He may attack the South African Division, which is just south of Tobruk. Or he may make another dash towards the wire. The General wants a recce for tanks that may be moving east."

"I'll go with you," said Masher, looking sideways at me, damp, yellow hair falling over his forehead. Unshaven, he looked like an out-of-work miner or one of the young derelicts who slept under the arches of London's bridges.

"Thanks," I said. "The fighter boys'll be grounded. We should have the place to ourselves."

There wasn't much rain. The desert was dark red, water glinted in the ruts left by trucks and tanks. The sea looked dull and angry, grey water with scattered white horses, like the English Channel I remembered when my father used to drive the family to Brighton during Christmas holidays. I flew along the line of coastal traffic between Bardia and Tobruk, zigzagging across the paved Via Balbia and the sandy Trigh Capuzzo. All the troops on the ground seemed to be ours and those which weren't moving west were stationary. Not far from Tobruk, however, I saw the unmistakable outlines of German tanks. There were fifty of them at Zaafran, a ridge east of the perimeter, and they were heading just south of east to cut the Trigh Capuzzo. Safe under the cloud cover, I watched them for a while as they made slow progress, tailed by their support vehicles.

"That's interesting," I said to Masher.

"Looks as if Rommel's heading east again."

"Maybe."

Just north of them, following a path parallel to the coastal road, were forty more tanks, also pressing ominously eastwards. I tried to estimate how long it would take the two columns to reach our infantrymen on the outskirts of Bardia and Sidi Azeiz. At ten mph, perhaps four and half hours with no stops. The thought of warning them flashed through my mind, to be at once rejected. Too many troops to warn. Too many options open to the tank columns. I decided to return at once and let the General know that his gloomy prediction had been fulfilled.

Near Sidi Azeiz I saw a biplane circling one of our units, getting a little flak. Part of the 4th Indian Division, I suspected. I yelled to Masher.

"Is that a C.R. 42?"

"Yes!"

O the unholy joy of seeing this outmoded Italian fighter. I suppose it must have been on reconnaissance, because C.R. 42s were no longer front line fighter aircraft. Murray Gardiner, who had fought against them in the East African campaign, had some hair-raising stories of the speed and manoeuvrability of these beautiful machines, which were the last and finest of the biplane era.

I had the advantage of speed - an intoxicating thought to one who had been operating Hurricane Is against Messerschmitts - and I had wild hopes of at last shooting down an enemy aircraft. I fined the pitch of the propeller and pushed my throttle wide open. I was approaching the biplane rapidly when the pilot saw us, turning steeply in our direction. For a second I thought he was going to stay and fight. My mind was full of probably erroneous tactical notions. I was faster but somehow I had to get inside him to shoot him down. He could out-turn me, but I could always disengage if he threatened to get a bead on me. If I missed him, Masher would get him. Matters were rapidly coming to a head when he began a steep climb and disappeared into the cloud. I had to make a violent movement of the stick to prevent myself from joining him in the murk.

Tony Bridges was very excited to hear that the tanks were taking an easterly path.

"I'll get this information out quickly. The New Zealanders are on the coast and the Indians are to the south of them. Those tanks are on a collision course with them."

"Is that good or bad?" I asked.

"Who knows?"

MESSERSCHMITT ROULETTE

XX

ROMMEL WITHDRAWS
(4 to 18 December 1941)

The next day the weather cleared and other pilots were sent to follow the progress of Rommel's tank column. My attention was diverted to another sector. Jim London, who was a gunner himself, asked me to do an Arty/R with the Tobruk gunners. He was a gentle Aussie, like the adjutant, Bill Langslow. No wild colonial boy. His long, lined face was usually solemn, but he had the most charming and apologetic of smiles. Being in his forties, he treated pilots with paternal admiration, like sons who had outpaced the achievements of their fathers. We talked it over in the air liaison section.

"This is the problem," he said, gravely.

I think he'd been a schoolmaster in peacetime and was inclined to overuse the word "problem," as if everything could be solved by logic or mathematics.

"You remember Tobruk had to clear a minefield to let its forces out?"

"I remember," I replied. "They were talking about nothing else when I was staying there."

"Well, it's the weakest spot on the perimeter now and they have a problem guarding it. Jerry and Eyetie guns are building up in the vicinity and Godwin-Austen's not happy about its security. He thinks they might be preparing the way for an assault with tanks and infantry. Now . . . "

He paused and gazed at me benignly, professor to pupil.

"Now . . . the Poles have a counter-battery thing going with some Italian siege guns and the General thinks it would be an excellent move if we helped them to deter the opposition a bit."

"Fine."

"Wizard told me to lay on a sortie."

"I'd be glad to do it myself. I know the area. And I've met the Polish gunners."

"Goodo! I'll signal that we'd like someone who can speak English well. Polish English can be strange at times."

We were still working on the signal when Alan Ferguson ran in, breathing hard. He'd let his moustaches grow and they drooped like a Chinaman's. His face looked narrower than ever. I wondered if my face had changed. The fragment of mirror I shaved with was too small to tell me.

"Caught you," he gasped. "I just heard there was a counter-battery needed at Tobruk. Have you got any volunteers yet?"

"No. Want to come?"

"Sign me on. Believe it or not, I'm a trained army co-op pilot. It doesn't get me much credit with this bunch of amateurs, but I've done this sort of work in Australia."

"And with distinction," I said, getting into his mood. It was safer to joke with Fergie or he'd pull your leg right off.

"Exactly."

"And with devastating results to concrete targets in the Great Sandy Desert."

"And I want to do it."

"I'll cover for you," I said.

In the afternoon we flew to Tobruk. It was relaxing for me to act as Fergie's cover. He was an experienced pilot and a cautious fellow to boot. We took the trouble free sea route to the area and I didn't have nausea gazing at tragic battlefields that no recce pilot could interpret.

The enemy guns were dispersed and camouflaged but we found them quickly enough. Fergie was very slick and swung from target to target expeditiously. I kept my eye on El Adem and points west for signs of enemy fighters, but none came to disturb the peacetime atmosphere of this sortie. It might have been the Great Sandy Desert if it weren't for a little ack ack of the Italian variety. The Poles made satisfactory hits on the enemy gun emplacements.

On completion the English voice we had listened to throughout changed to a foreign one. It was probably the Polish commanding officer.

"K'we are much grateful to k'you for goot work."

Fergie responded with unaccustomed formality and in deliberate tones.

"Four Five One Squadron, Royal Australian Air Force, was pleased to oblige you. Good luck, sir!"

When we landed at base I kidded him about it.

"You were a bit stiff and starchy, Fergie," I said. "I thought at first you were going to add something about coming to the assistance of a gallant and noble ally. It sounded like a political statement."

Fergie put his hand on his heart and raised his eyes to the heavens.

"I did it for Australia," he said.

I hadn't forgotten the drama of Rommel's wandering tank columns and at our debriefing I asked Jim London how things were going.

"They ran into the 5th Indian Brigade and the 5th New Zealand Brigade as we expected," he said. "But they got a hot reception and lost a few tanks. Then the Blenheims bombed them. Gave 'em a real pounding. The latest word is that they've turned back and are making for Gambut." [1]

---

1. "On 3rd December Rommel sent two strong patrols towards the Egyptian frontier, one along the coast road and one along the Trigh Capuzzo. Maximum effort was put into attacking these thrusts, which were driven back by air and ground forces with heavy losses." *Fighters Over the Desert*, page 72

ROMMEL WITHDRAWS

"That's the first time," I said to Jim, "I've ever done a recce and it's all worked out like clockwork. The Kiwis and the Indians were ready for them, which they wouldn't have been if we hadn't alerted them. And then the bombers were called in. There's a satisfaction in that. We actually did some good. The army never thanks us, though."

"Yes, we do," said Jim, gently. "We're always thanking you."

"You're not the army. You're one of us."

Rommel was the idol of the armies on both sides, though there was something masochistic about our admiration for him, because he hit us hard. Part of the universal acclaim which made him a military hero was well deserved.

Most historians give him full marks as a general and as a man. He was, apparently, a loving husband and father, and eventually an opponent of Hitler. He was certainly a virile commander and was master of the new role of tanks in warfare. But it has to be admitted that the German tanks were superior in every way and that this made a difference.

Our commanders seemed lumpish and slow in comparison to Rommel, but it is impossible to show fire and imagination if you are outgunned. The British strategy had to be boring. We had only one advantage, a numerical superiority in tanks, and our only hope was to wear him down. A British tank captain, like "Jock" Campbell, was restricted to attrition and exemplary deeds of heroism; whereas Rommel had the freedom to demonstrate tactical brilliance. If he'd been sending Crusaders, and Stuarts into battle, he would never have been called "The Desert Fox."

On the morning of 4 December German tanks made an all out attack on our positions at El Duda, the ridge south of Sidi Resegh, once again threatening Tobruk. I flew a late Tac/R of the area, the afternoon sun adding to my difficulties in separating friend and foe. The fighting had died down and the escarpment was populated by even more trackless and burned out tanks and smoking motor transport.

On the 5th Rommel had his last fling. He gathered the remaining armour of the Afrika Korps and struck at El Gubi, twenty miles south of Tobruk on the Trigh El Abd. It was a smart move because we had extensive dumps of ammunition, petrol and food there. The 11th Indian Brigade which was guarding the area was overrun, but the dumps they were protecting remained undiscovered. Another strike for Jasper Maskelyne and the London Palladium!

On the morning of the 6th a force of Blenheims struck Rommel's column and destroyed more of his tanks and support vehicles. Both reconnaissance squadrons - No. 208 RAF and No. 451 RAAF - were out watching the fun. Masher Maslen and Ian Porter, flying a mid-morning sortie to check up on the situation at El Gubi, were bounced by a squadron of 109s. Masher, as he put it, "ran in the right direction," south into the desert wastes.

Ian headed east toward our own lines but was pursued and shot down. As it turned out, Ian was the last squadron casualty of the campaign.

By the 7th of December Rommel knew that he had no alternative but to withdraw to the Gazala line. On that day the heavy artillery and the Italian infantry formations retreated from the Tobruk perimeter. It was the climax of the campaign, though we did not know it. Rommel was still much respected and his retreat never became a rout. The withdrawal was a fighting one and British units were often overrun as they advanced.

By 5th December all the operational airacraft of No. 451 Squadron had moved to the Tobruk main airfield and L.G. 75 was deserted, except for technical staff carrying out routine repairs and inspections.

I think it must have been the night of December 7th that we heard about the Japanese attack on Pearl Harbor, but it may have been the 8th. I remember that Sid Cooper gave me the news as we met, walking towards the bar tent. Wizard, Doc Reid and Murray were sitting down in the available chairs. Nearly all the other officers were there, standing or sitting on the bare ground. Visibility was dim in the light of two small oil lamps.

"Australia's going to be in the front line," said Doc, authoritatively. "I wouldn't be surprised if the 6th and 9th Divvies get recalled. There's going to be a helluva dust-up in the Pacific."

"How could the Japs have been such tunts as to attack the States?" said Wizard. He had a look of suppressed mirth on his face. Joy's grape had burst upon his palate fine but not quite reached his outer being. "They're going to lose their balls along with their breeches."

They have a reputation for being short-sighted," said Murray, mischievously, making a myopic Japanese face.

"I wouldn't mind if we ended up in Singapore," said Wizard. "I'd welcome a gin sling after all this Aussie beer."

The talk went on cheerfully and, after a few more drinks all round, jubilantly. I felt solemn and grateful rather than excited. We'd been getting some assistance from the USA, of course. There were Tomahawk squadrons in the desert, RAF Transport Command was flying the Douglas Dakota, and some of our armoured units used an American tank. But for over a year the major anxiety was that we would lose the war and have to face a long resistance to Nazism at home. Some old American destroyers and what munitions could be carried across the Atlantic by our own merchant shipping could never have been enough to save us. There'll always be an England, said the patriotic song; but what kind of England?

I had often thought morbidly about the possible aftermath of defeat. After they hanged Winston Churchill, after the Duke of Windsor had been brought back to supplant his brother, Adolf Hitler's portrait would stare down at our children from classroom walls and Fascism would be taught officially to the innocents. The Nazi boys I'd met on summer holidays at Berchtesgarten would have overcome their romanticism about daggers in stockings and would be wearing pinstripe suits, appropriate for ruling a subject people, their thin lips ordering torture and execution for the resistance fighter.

Brother Ken was wryly looking forward to being a blower up of power stations. He was cut out for that sort of thing. I knew I wasn't alert enough or sophisticated enough to be a good conspirator. My incompetence would discover me to the enemy and I would end up like Guy Fawkes - the prototype of shortsighted Catholic heroes - being racked a foot longer in the Tower of London. Whenever I thought of being shot down by a Messerschmitt, I comforted myself with the reflection that at least I would never be flogged to force me to betray my comrades. Yet I could foresee that the day Britain surrendered I would be automatically metamorphosed; one moment a recce pilot, fighting a clean war in the skies, the next an inept foot soldier in the British resistance forces. Until December, 1941, this had been a real issue, but when the news of Pearl Harbor came through all those trepidations were over. With the USA on our side we were bound to win; it was only a matter of time. The day to day terrors remained the same. Personal survival was still in doubt. But the cheerful thought - that the Nazis would not prevail - was a daily comfort for the rest of the war.

Once Tobruk was, in truth, relieved we were given our marching orders. On December 9th the whole squadron moved to the main Tobruk airfield. Three more Aussie pilots joined us a day later, accompanied by the exotic figure of Capitaine Foch, grandson of the Marshal Foch who had commanded the French armies in the Great War of 1914-1918. He was in the dark blue uniform of the Free French Air Force and his elegance made a dramatic contrast to the sartorial uncouthness of most squadron pilots. He was tall and good-looking in a long-faced way under his pillbox kepi. He had been attached to us to learn something about reconnaissance before joining a Free French unit. I took him out on one sortie as cover but failed to record his name in my log book.[2]

I have remarked earlier that my own winter wear was a torn inner lining of an old two-piece flying suit. It was fastened by a large safety pin where the zipper had failed to function, making me look like a disreputable version of the Michelin man. Masher's gift for scruffiness put him in a class by himself. He wore a dirty, white, roll-necked pullover that was too long even for his long body. It had lost all its elasticity and hung down at the same level as the skirts of a Twenties flapper. If an attractive girl had turned up in the Western Desert to make us conscious of our scarecrow appearance, we'd have rushed off to our bivouacs to find more presentable clothing. There was, in fact, one woman in Tobruk that December, an American journalist. She was quite handsome, but too middle-aged to provide the necessary incentive for reform. She interviewed me in the mess one evening but my only recollection of our meeting is of my anxiety about her bathroom needs. Would

2. **Capitaine J. Bertout-Foch, grandson of Marshal Foch.**

they cordon off our latrines and stand guard until she was finished? I shuddered at the idea of this neat creature - she wore a quasi-military uniform with a khaki skirt and flesh-coloured silk stockings - entering our squalid and smelly bogs.

As the Afrika Korps retreated our sorties became longer. On the 12th I flew a Tac/R to Mechili, one hour and fifty minutes. It was the first time I had flown the Trigh Capuzzo west of El Adem, past Segnali, deep into the desert. Mechili was forty miles south of the coast and ninety miles from Tobruk. I took Masher with me as cover. This was not our beaten track; it was deep into enemy held territory and I wanted his support. Beyond the immediate battle area the track to Mechili was not crowded. I made notes on movement, but it was an anti-climax to go so far for so little.

Directly we landed back, another sortie was requested and we went out again. This was the pattern of those December days. The work was there to be done but the supply of honest labourers was diminishing. The second recce was of the Gazala region, where a great deal of fighting was going on. 13 Corps infantry was advancing towards Derna and Tmimi and a clash was occurring between 4th Indian Division and retreating Italian forces. When we'd finished being debriefed - Masher always kept an eye on the ground and made notes himself, as well as acting as cover - I told him how much I appreciated him. He was the same age as myself, but not being a professional flyer - although 600 hours on Wapitis and Audax hardly made me so - he was my junior in experience as well as in rank. Yet it was clear, after a few weeks in the desert, that he wasn't anyone's inferior. His ability to hit a cricket ball smack in the centre of the bat transposed well to flying. In spite of his untidiness and his slouching walk, he was a neat and accomplished pilot. He was also the least frightened man in the squadron, which made him a sort of king. He didn't have my weakness for making gestures and he didn't seem to require the stimulus of striking back to bolster his morale. A remark of Antoine de St. Exupery in **Wind, Sand and Stars** fits Masher perfectly.

> "There is a tendency to class such men with toreadors and gamblers. People extol their contempt for death. But I would not give a fig for anyone's contempt for death. If its roots are not sunk deep in acceptance of responsibility, this contempt for death is a sign either of an impoverished soul or of youthful extravagance." [3]

Masher's kind of courage was all responsibility. He had no particular philosophy and he lectured no one. His ascendancy was unadvertized. Confronted by danger, he always set out to do the practical and useful thing without fuss or inordinate hurry. On the morning of the "November Handicap" he was the only one of us who thought of the peril to the New Zealanders a

---

3. **Reymal and Hutchwick, New York, 1939, p. 60**

few miles to our north. He was the image of an English peasant, a medieval serf, a bowman at Agincourt, his people might have been farming in Essex for a thousand years; and because of his steadiness he had made himself the most important person in the squadron, doubly important to me because he was English and in the Royal Air Force.

To be fair I must discriminate between my feelings and the facts of the case. The laggards were few indeed - and in cold blood my only solid complaint could be their lack of enthusiasm - but fixed in hectic competition with the Australians, those few were intolerable, monstrous, blocking out the sun. In my imagination they all had the face of Willy Whitlock. They were poised to disgrace me and make my argument a vain one. I wasn't quite sane on the subject.

Walking back to our bivvies from the A.L.O. tent I blurted out the violent truth as I saw it.

"Thank God for you, Masher. You make up for those bastards who walk the other way when the sorties are being dished out."

I said it bitterly, and at once felt ashamed of my tone. He didn't reply. Masher remained friends with everyone, made no judgments on the weaker brethren and didn't have the anger in him to match mine.

Once the battle of Sidi Resegh was over, there was some enthusiasm in the squadron for viewing the scenes of carnage. The battlefield was only ten miles from the perimeter of Tobruk and Doc Reid, when we spoke about it in the mess, was determined to go.

"I'll go out alone, if necessary," he said. "It may sound a bit gruesome to you, but a surgeon has a different point of view. I have a legitimate interest."

"I grant that," I said, "but any operational pilot who goes out there to study dead bodies is not going to help his morale. I've seen enough from a couple of hundred feet to convince me that none of us have any business there."

In the event, Doc took a truckload of ground crews and pilots to this ghoulish tourist attraction. I stayed behind with Murray Gardiner and ground my teeth. I could not understand why a sensible person would put his imagination at such risk. It was bad enough for my mental health to know that Pat Byers had died of burns; I would not have wished to see his charred flesh. Once when we were children, Hugh took Ken and myself up to London to see Madame Tussaud's Wax Museum. Of course, he insisted on frightening us with the "Chamber of Horrors," which we didn't want to see. That year the set piece was the execution of aristocrats by guillotine in the French Revolution. It gave me nightmares for months afterwards. Between Sidi Resegh and Duda I knew they were going to view sights far worse than the sanitized severed head of a gentleman beneath the shadow of a fake gibbet.

I'm pretty sure Ray Hudson went. I can hear his voice, always one of the squadron's predominating sounds, telling horror stories on their return.

In which case Ed Kirkham must have gone, too. Perhaps most of the Australians did. After all, it was Doc Reid's party. A couple of South Africans went. Masher went. I tried to stop him.

"I'll be all right," he said, giving me a twisted grin. "I've been looking down at that graveyard for weeks. I've got to see it close up."

Predictably, they found men - or figures they could recognize as having been men - still in their ruined tanks and trucks. They returned unnaturally excited and talkative, swapping stories loudly in the various No. 451 Squadron dialects - Australian, South African and Masher's rural cockney.

"Jeez! Did you see that poor bastard strung out over the turret?"

"Yiss, man. He was in bad shape."

"When I looked for his face I couldn't find it at first. It was covered with flies. You couldn't see his features Just flies on top of flies."

"The worst thing I saw was was the burned out truck with all those guys flattened out and sort of melted into one another in a corner."

"In one German tank. The one with the big gash in the side."

"Mark four, it was." That was Masher, being knowledgeable.

"Yeh. The driver just sitting there, dead. Still had has hands on the controls."

"Poor sod."

So it went on. I thought of Peter with his brown, unlined face, sitting in a ruined Crusader with flies covering his eyeballs.

No one, except perhaps Doc Reid, was better off for the experience.

In the middle of December, Marshal of the Royal Air Force Lord Trenchard, visited Tobruk. He was the "Father of the R.A.F." for he had formed it as a separate service and commanded it after the Great War of 1914-1918. A tall, impressive figure in blue winter uniform and greatcoat, he was conducted by Wizard through the flights and sections. Apart from myself and Wizard there was no one who knew who he was. Regular officers in prewar days were given a big dose of "Boom" Trenchard in lectures on air history at flying training schools, but to the Aussies, the South Africans and people like Masher, his name meant nothing.

From the very beginnings of air warfare Trenchard had been the prophet of the independent air arm, and had managed to press his ideas on the politicians against the entrenched interests of the army and the navy. For that reason alone he was more responsible for the success of the RAF as a fighting service than any other single person. The Luftwaffe, tied to the German army, had not been free to think in terms of the "air battle." As a consequence it had developed inappropriate aircraft, like Stukas, which could only be used in conditions of air superiority.

He was now doing the rounds of the desert squadrons. In his frail age, with noble height and huge grey moustaches, he was like a Saxon king visiting his subjects. I had been flying when he arrived and had only glimpsed him from a distance. Wizard had sent word that officers were to be introduced to him in the bar.

ROMMEL WITHDRAWS

When I entered I noticed there was a white cloth - a sheet, I think - spread out on Corporal Coffey's usually scrubbed wooden table top, the only time I ever saw such a civilized touch in our mess. Few pilots were present. Either they resented his presence or felt the occasion was none of their business. Trenchard had taken off his greatcoat and peaked hat, and he looked less spiritual and symbolic in his blue service dress. He had so many rows of medals that his pilot's wings, half hidden by his lapel, were barely visible. His sleeves seemed to be entirely taken up by rings, one broad and the rest narrow, indicating his high rank.

Wizard beckoned me over, smiling. I waited while Capitaine Foch was introduced. I remember thinking, as they shook hands, that Trenchard, with his old-fashioned moustache, looked not unlike the captain's grandfather whose visage had glared so ubiquitously out of the pages of my mother's *Les Images de la Guerre.*

Then Wizard turned to me, smiling and avuncular.

"I'd like to introduce you, sir, to a brave young chap."

"Good morning, sir," I said, taking his outstretched hand.

I can remember nothing of our conversation, though we stood by the bar for a while and I drank a glass of beer. Wizard ushered other pilots forward. Sid Cooper was there. Fergie and Ron Achilles were introduced. Today they might not recall the visit. I stood there dazed and reeling, drunk with glory. Wizard's unmodified Welsh voice had made music of his sentence and I can hear it as I write. He may have been merely exercising his political gifts but whether or not what he said was sincere, the effect was to raise my spirits enormously. Inside everyone, I suppose, is a child who wants to do well to please his father. Wizard and Lord Trenchard combining to pat me on the back, satisfied that yearning to perfection.

On the 15th I flew the Trigh Capuzzo again, counting transport. There was a lot more going on at this time. The weather was appalling. It was like a winter's day in England, with low cloud and occasional rain cutting down the light. I don't believe the bombers and fighters were out on either side.

A tremendous battle was being fought at Gazala and most of the squadron effort was devoted to watching it. I flew a recce on 17th. Rommel had begun his pullout and I had the satisfaction of observing some of his armour making off in a westerly direction from a position south of Gazala. On the coast there was a huge movement of trucks north and west, with many men on the ground walking.

Mechili was still in enemy hands and on the 18th I flew down the track once again to check on the situation with Masher as my cover. My log book notes the names of covering pilots more frequently in December than at any other time. The names of Masher and Ferguson alternate. It was a long haul down the desert track and when I arrived at Mechili, being unfamiliar with the area, I blundered on the German landing ground. It was marked on my map and I had planned to give it a wide berth, but the country was so featureless that I couldn't check my position accurately. The field was crammed with aircraft of all kinds.

A twin-engined Me 110 was on the approach with its wheels down, a perfect sitter. I was at about the same height, 600 feet and so close that it would have been easy to shoot it down. We seem to have been unrecognized as British planes and there was no anti-aircraft fire. Mechili had been over a hundred miles behind the lines for the past six months and, apart from a few sneaky reconnaissance sorties, the people there had not seen much invasion of their airspace. The recent fighter sweeps and bomber attacks had all been concentrated in the Gazala region where the ground fighting was taking place.

"I'm going to get this one," I shouted to Masher.

Get close. One burst. Then disappear, I mutter to myself. I was almost within range, tense as a drum, leaning forward against my straps to peer through the sight.

"Three MEs overhead," Masher's voice crackled, spoiling my dreams.

I looked up. They were 3000 feet above us in loose line astern formation.

I cursed and turned steeply away, diving to ground level, watching with increasing bitterness as the fighters flew blandly north, ignoring us. Another thirty seconds and I could have pressed the tit on my spade stick and blown the Messerschmitt out of the sky.

Why didn't I hang on for a few extra ticks and finish the job? I was disgusted with myself. If the MEs had peeled off to attack us, it would have been a different matter. But they weren't even looking at us.

Ray Hudson would have shot the bugger down, I grumbled to myself, as I headed east along the Trigh Capuzzo towards the safety of our own lines. He'd have escaped in the confusion and chalked another one up. I've become too timid. A clapped out recce boy, an escape artist, a Houdini of the airways, a counter of tanks and transport for the army. It was my last chance. Damn those German fighters!

I glanced back at Masher's Hurricane, weaving steadily behind my tail. I pressed my speak button.

"Damn those German fighters," I said.

Masher didn't reply.

XXI

THE END OF THE CAMPAIGN
(18 December, 1941 to 14 February, 1942)

One morning in the last week of December Wizard picked me up in his staff car as I was walking across to breakfast. It was a windy day and he was wearing the strap of his fur felt under his chin to keep it in place. He was in a good mood and had a mischievous look on his face. It wasn't his habit to bubble over with excitement but when he was enjoying himself a sort of devilish humour emanated from him which wasn't always easy to interpret. I wasn't sure whether he'd heard good news or was going to tell one of his uncharitable stories about the army.

"I got a signal last night," he said. "The silly buggers at headquarters have decided we've had enough. They're withdrawing us to Syria." [1]

"Who's taking over our job?"

"208."

"I can't believe it," I said. "So I'm going to live forever, after all."

"I wanted to tell you something privately."

Here he suddenly became solemn.

"I'm recommending two RAF pilots for DFCs. [2] You and Masher. And one of the Australians. Ron Achilles."

Ron Achilles, I thought. How strange. I'd hardly noticed Ron. I knew he was one of the stalwarts but he didn't have the vivid personality of Ray or Ed or Fergie or Colin Robertson. To me he was just there, an icon. I can't recall the sound of his voice. The impression he made on me was purely visual, an image of romantic good looks, as if he were posing for the portrait of a young flier circa 1941. He must have been a fine fellow, a worker, another Masher at heart. I'm sorry I missed him. All I saw was a dumb film star in the middle distance. He had the right name for a hero and was fair-haired like his namesake. I should have taken more notice of him. Someone else will have to sing the praise of Ron Achilles.

By the time we'd climbed out of the car at the mess tent I'd managed to digest the news.

---

1. "The squadron's departure was the occasion of a special message of congratulation from 13 Corps; between 18th November and 18th December No. 451 had flown 128 tactical and photographic sorties and four artillery cooperation, a role which brought it little limelight but which was of considerable importance to the ground offensive." John Herington, *Air War Against Germany and Italy, 1939-1943* , page 209

2. Distinguished Flying Crosses

"Me and Masher," I said wonderingly. "No more Aussies? Ray Hudson or Ed Kirkham?"

"Headquarters types haven't the faintest idea what reconnaissance is. They don't esteem us too highly. Fighters and bombers they know about." His voice rose to an interrogatory whine, very Welsh and ironical. "What is it you fellow do? No raids? No victories in the air? How long do you say you've been doing what you do?"

"As bad as that?"

"I think so."

"Three gongs seems a bit measly." [3]

Wizard pushed at his moustache and fiddled with the strap around his chin.

"It's par for the course, I'm afraid. I wanted to be absolutely fair, so I took the three pilots who'd flown the most sorties. It all boils down to long service and good conduct. That's all we can offer."

I laughed. Long service and good conduct describes the barely average performer who serves out his time until he can hang his hat on a pension.

"A long service medal," I said, "for six months' undetected crime!"

"We're moving back to Sidi Azeiz as soon as we can get organized. Bardia and Halfaya are holding out. We'll be helping with the mopping up operation."

"Artillery shoots."

"And a bit of high level photography."

"Thank God," I said. "I'm going to get married."

I wrote letters that night to Joan and to my parents. We hadn't received any mail for weeks and I suppose the letters just sat there in the Adj's office after I'd written them, but it was good to be able to say I was safe, that I would come home, that I had done well. After my poor start with the Australians, my trouble with Molly and my ineffective handling of the squadron's weaker vessels it was something to have avoided absolute disaster. Neither Joan nor my parents knew anything about my real struggle in the desert. As a matter of fact, they never did. War stories were two a penny at that time. After the war I was disinclined to go over it all again in my head. Thirty years afterwards, when I was a college professor in America, I found that a discussion on the shooting of a deserter in Hemingway's **Farewell to Arms**

---

3. The award of only three decorations still seems, at this late date, very measly for six months of intense operational flying. Ray Hudson and Ed Kirkham had flown three or four sorties less than Masher and me, and it is very difficult to see how they could in justice have been left out. Ray, however, had brushed with Wizard from the start; and Wizard, who had enough to cope with without Ray's constant criticisms, may have felt less than generous when the time came. I think it was particularly deplorable, though, that Ed Kirkham, who was not at all confrontational, had to miss getting a gong because he was a close friend of Ray's. This is something that irks me fifty years later on.

inevitably recalled Willy Whitlock. Soon I found myself adding the story of the "November Handicap" and Pilot Officer Price's shot up Hurricane, the underground hangar in Tobruk. The cry for such tales became a distraction in my classes, but I learned that young people were interested in a war that began long before they were born.

On 24th December the squadron moved back from Tobruk to Sidi Azeiz. I thought I might be seeing Tobruk for the last time. To fix it in my memory, I circled as I climbed to height. The little town above the harbour looked unfailingly pretty. From 6000 feet El Adem airfield appeared as if it were sitting on the perimeter defences. Sidi Resegh still displayed its army of burned out vehicles. I could see that they had taken away the ground markers from my landing strip on the escarpment and it was beginning to fade back into the landscape.

I returned to Tobruk once after the war, on December 8th, 1958, for a Tobruk Day commemoration. I was a wing commander in a planning staff at Episkopi, Cyprus, living in a house on a brown cliff overlooking the Mediterranean. By that time Joan and I had three children who spent most of their days at the beach and swam like ducks. I had been asked by the Air Ministry in London to represent the RAF on this occasion. I presume someone in Australia had mentioned me, because I cannot imagine anyone in the RAF researching who was in Tobruk during the siege and coming up with my name.

It was a solemn affair, held under a bright North African sun, and we stood paying homage to the dead in front of the newly built Tobruk War Memorial. Elderly Australian clergymen, Catholic, Protestant and Jewish, took turns in remembering those who had perished. They each referred to the great events of April, 1941, when Rommel's tanks, supported by Italian infantry, had thrust deep into the fortress. The Australian 9th Division had kicked them out, but it had been costly. Others had been killed by shellfire and bombing during the long siege. British, Polish and Australian troops had been involved in the breakout and in the fighting that took place outside Tobruk in November and December, 1941. They were remembered, too. The cemetery nearby was crowded with white markers. Neat rows of name tabs, giving the same minimum information above each grave.

Most of the visitors were elderly Australians. Retired people, I supposed, who were free to travel. Lined faces, clothes too large for the shriveled frames. They must have been parents of the dead, for they were far too old to have been in the siege. I was in my best tropical uniform, resplendent, a generation younger. I searched obsessively for the gunner colonel and Blue Nelson, without success. I didn't expect to see anyone from No. 451 Squadron, though I thought Bill Langslow might have been in this age group.

When the ceremony was over I took the long walk up to the escarpment and tried to find the underground hangar. The strip was now merely a flat space along the edge of a cliff with clumps of desert grass all over it. It seemed too short for the take off of any modern operational aircraft. Blowing sand had eliminated some of the old contours and I couldn't recognize the crevasse they'd used to set the hangars in. I searched for Tony Barrett's magnificent multi-roomed dugout but failed to find any trace of it. The sand must have filled it in years before and McNamee's metal shield, so effective in keeping out bomb shrapnel and flying nose caps, was buried forever. The view of the harbour from the cliff was as enchanting as I remembered it.

I had flown myself from Cyprus in a twin-engined Pembroke borrowed from the communications flight at Nicosia and I was glad to be able to depart the same evening. I've always hated going over old ground. When I think nowadays of Libya and Qadaffi and the Arab League, it seems strange that we were there at all. In all my months in the desert I did not see a single Libyan Arab.

Sidi Azeiz was a spot we'd often flown over, dodging flak and counting vehicles. Now it was just another landing ground, comfortably situated a hundred miles behind the front lines. Our job was to assist the army in reducing the frontier strong points, still occupied by mostly German troops. The sorties were not at all dangerous. The garrisons were bottled up within their fortifications and the task was to take photographs from a safe height - 15,000 feet - and to assist the gunners in their demolishment of enemy batteries. I flew a number of Arty/Rs on the Bardia and Sollum defences. Apart from steering clear of anti-aircraft shells, the sorties provided no problems. It was just interesting flying in good weather, an exercise of skill. I had begun my operational career between Bardia and Sollum in quite different circumstances and there was a certain charm at first in the contrast. The stretch of road across the Halfaya escarpment where I had blown up the little convoy of ammunition trucks was bare of traffic. There was no sign of human activity even at the heavy gun emplacements we were shooting at. I soon became bored. I flew ten flights in the Lysander for every one in a Hurricane. Masher and I were airborne all day doing useful things, ferrying equipment and people between Fuka and Dekheila and Sidi Haneish and Bir El Thalata. There was no shortage of volunteers for the innocuous operational sorties. I missed the only interesting one. Ken Watts flew a shoot with some 4.5s on Bardia and sank a ship in the harbour.

On 25th December, the day after we settled in at our new location, Bill Langslow drove off to the POW camp nearby and brought back six Italian prisoners as a Christmas present for the Squadron. They were friendly and hard working, singing all day as if they'd never been so happy in their lives. One of them had lived in America and spoke English. He explained that the Italians had no belief in the war and that the soldiers, who had fought hard in the desert, were glad to be out of it, None of us would have felt exactly like that. We were fighting, or so we imagined, for our own liberties and the freedom of Europe too. In that sense we did believe in the war, however much we may have hated the process. Not many of us would have been happy to be POWs.

Bardia fell on 2nd January, 1942, and Micky Carmichael and all his party except Corporal Farr, a wireless operator who had been killed by machine gun fire when the group was initially challenged at Libyan Omar, were released from captivity. None of them returned to the squadron. Micky was hospitalized briefly and sent back to England. He failed to survive the war but I don't know how he lost his life. Probably in the high attrition of recce pilots during the Second Front of 1944.

The garrison at Sollum surrendered on the 12th of January. Naturally Halfaya was the longest to hold out. The white flag went up on the 17th of January, and although I was busy on other missions, I couldn't resist the opportunity of seeing a surrender occur. I grabbed a Hurricane and flew up the wire for the last time. Large numbers of troops clad in German khaki were neatly formed up in units on either side of the road which ran along the top of the escarpment. It looked more like a parade than a surrender. The paved road that snaked up from the coast was filled with marching men, headed by their officers. It was like one of those elaborate war scenes they used to put in Hamley's department store window in London. In these scenarios, which were based on the trenches of the Great War, everything was neater than it could have been in real life. The trucks with fabric tops were lined up in perfect formation, the men in step, the guns protruding immaculately from their sandbagged emplacements. There were little ambulances with big red crosses on them, medical orderlies sat inside, and in between them a wounded soldier lay on a stretcher, his bandaged head showing a star of blood. Halfaya escarpment on that day had the same artificial appearance. It could, I thought, have been constructed for a toy shop out of brown paper and paste, with artistic streaks of ochre paint and shell craters indented with the point of a pencil.

I flew low enough to see the faces, the rifles, the ammunition pouches and the haversacks of the marching soldiers. There was a group of officers in greyish greatcoats and peaked hats standing by a staff car which had a large white flag waving from its bonnet.

No one waved at me.

This had once been dangerous territory and I was viewing it like a tourist who, in a past age, might have hired a felucca to watch the Battle of the Nile or taken a carriage to the field of Waterloo. I flew round and round in childish pleasure, noting the steady progress of troops climbing up the steep pass and accumulating in ordered ranks at the top. I had never before seen so many men on the ground. It was as if a whole army had surrendered.

MESSERSCHMITT ROULETTE

When I landed back from that flight someone remembered that a Tomahawk squadron, then based at our old landing ground near Sidi Barrani, was scheduled to strafe Halfaya that afternoon. We had a sortie laid on to observe it. There was mild panic. Wizard was away somewhere. Sid Cooper kept his nose out of operational matters. Signals communications must have been chaotic or temporarily non-existent.

Jim Leaky nearly went off his head about it. He could see blood spilled, knee deep, on the red earth of Halfaya.

"It'll be murder," he said. "All those poor bastards lined up in files to surrender and twelve Tomahawks blasting away at 'em"

"There are white flags all over the place," I said. "They'd never attack a parade like that."

"Worse things have happened."

"All right. I'll lay them off."

When I landed at Sidi Barrani the pilots were already at their machines, awaiting the word to start up. Their Tomahawks were armed with little bombs suspended below the wings. I passed the message to the nearest pilot within shouting distance and there was much scurrying about. In a few minutes a staff car drove across to my dispersal with a young squadron leader in the back. He was togged up to fly, his flying helmet round his neck. I noticed the big oxygen tube, an unfamiliar sight in No. 451 Squadron.

"They've surrendered?" His look of pain indicated that he didn't want to believe it.

"Yes. I've just been over. They're all lined up on the plateau like a Remembrance Day parade."

"What a bore," he said. "We were all set up to knock the piss out of them."

The sudden slowing of the pace had an amusing spin-off. Doc Reid put his campaign for going solo in a Hurricane into high gear. He'd been studying the Pilot's Handbook ever since the Squadron fell back to Sidi Azeiz. It wasn't easy to convince Wizard, however, that it was a sensible thing to allow a forty-five year old surgeon, who hadn't flown in several years, to take off in a modern aircraft. Doc had many hours on Wapitis and Harts and was no doubt basically a competent pilot, but flying an aeroplane is not exactly like riding a bicycle. It is not quite true that once you have learned you've learned for good. The standard safe way to restore a pilot to the flying condition after a prolonged lay-off is to check him out on a dual aircraft, let him land a few times under supervision and run through the emergency procedures. There was no dual Hurricane, of course. There was no dual aircraft of any kind. Even if there had been it would have been quite illegal to let him fly. There was no justification for risking a valuable, if not priceless, Hurricane to satisfy the whim of a medical officer who once upon a time flew aeroplanes. But Stan Reid was not just a physician in uniform, he was a big chunk of the squadron.

THE END OF THE CAMPAIGN

The ground crew, the riggers, the fitters, the electricians and the armourers who made up nine-tenths of the personnel were Australians, and he was their unquestioned leader. To the Australian pilots he was mediator, judge and father confessor, and for the rest of us he was the one impartial and mature Aussie with the power to influence his own people. Wizard was immeasurably in his debt personally; the squadron couldn't have been run without him. Anyone with their eyes open over the previous six months must have felt grateful to him for his services to the troubled polyglot unit. With my natural tendency towards hero worship, I was in awe of him. Against this background, his open propaganda on his own behalf and his schoolboy enthusiasm for flying proved irresistible.

At lunchtime on 18th January, 1942, matters came to a head.

"I can do it, Wiz," I heard him say. "I've got a lot of experience and I know that Hurricane backwards. Don't I, Sid?"

Sid Cooper, who'd been coaching him, nodded.

"He's word perfect. He knows more about the Hurrybag than Acker Kerr."

"Word perfect!" said Wizard, grinning fiercely. "That's what I'll say at the subsequent Court Martial. Stan Reid, I'll say, was word perfect when he landed on his prop and belly, thinking he was still flying Wapitis with tailskids. That's why I authorized him to fly."

"Oh, come on, Wizard. I'd never do anything like that. I'm a surgeon. As a professional I'm more careful than you lay people."

"In direct violation of Air Council Instructions," Wizard continued, "and the laws of God and man."

"This is the best chance we'll ever have," said Doc. "Bardia and Halfaya are out of the way. We're a hundred miles behind the lines. Bright day. No cloud. Wind five miles an hour. What more do you want? Honestly, give me one landing only. I just want to go solo in a Hurricane. I'm ready for it."

"Let him do it for Australia," I said, thinking of Alan Ferguson. Wizard took his pipe out of his mouth and laughed.

"But Wales may have to pay for it. Oh, I'm probably the biggest tunt in the universe. All right, Stan. Go! I'll position myself in the signals section and talk you round. If I say 'open up your throttle and go round again,' that's what you do. OK?"

"Goodo! I'll be careful, believe me."

The word spread through the camp in minutes and there must have been a hundred people, including nearly all the pilots, crowded round Doc as he walked proudly, his parachute slung over his right shoulder, towards his aircraft. Shouted encouragement and advice was deafening.

"Goodo, Doc, show 'em how to do it!"

"Shoot down a fuck'n Messerschmitt!"

Roars of laughter. Then a barrage of nervous counsel from the pilots.

"Fly a mile downwind and drag her in on the engine."

"Put your flaps and undercart down before you begin your approach. Then you won't have to think about anything but the landing."

"Bring 'er in good and fast, Doc. You've got plenty of room to get down between here and Tobruk!"

Pilots used to simpler flying machines can easily forget things that are vital to their safety. Fine pitch is essential for maximum power, but thrashing around in fine pitch for a long time can damage the engine. Coarser pitch is correct for cruising around, but when you come in to land you must change to fine pitch again in case full power is needed to remedy a bad bounce or to go round again. Better men than Doc have been caught in coarse pitch with "everything hanging down," and stalled out.

One scenario I imagined was that Doc would be so euphoric at getting airborne that he'd completely forget to retract his wheels. The power of the Merlin engine was considerable and he could quickly gain enough speed to bend the undercarriage. I didn't offer any advice myself, but it was a time for anxious thoughts. If Doc pranged it, Wizard would surely be court martialled.

He made a shaky takeoff. He'd been used to less powerful engines and less responsive controls. The tail of his aircraft, instead of rising smoothly, jumped into the air and we could see him zigzagging down his flight path, overcorrecting with his rudder until his wheels left the ground. At 500 feet he raised his undercart and turned port, climbing slowly towards the west.

"He's going to do a recce," Ray Hudson shouted, and a bunch of Aussie pilots collapsed with laughter.

Ten minutes later we saw him some miles to the south and Sid Cooper told an airman to fire off a series of green Very lights to lure him back again. At last he came over the airfield at 1000 feet and made a wide circuit. We saw his undercarriage go down.

His first pass at the ground was awful. He levelled off at twenty feet, and if he'd cut his engine at that point, the Hurricane would have dropped like a stone, making a pancake of the wheels and struts of his undercarriage. I heard afterwards that Wizard had ordered him to open up and go round again. His second approach was better but he chickened out just as he was about to touch down and roared off to try once more. At the third attempt he rammed his wheels in, bounced, bounced again, and then held it down to the end of the strip where he spun out of control, threatening to put his wing in. Luckily no damage was done.

When he taxied in he received the sort of welcome a soccer hero gets when he's kicked the decisive goal seconds before the final whistle. A tide of Aussie ground crews engulfed him and I thought they were going to hoist him on to their shoulders. But Doc never quite lost his Roman gravitas and personal authority. He forbade it with a wave of his hand, although he must have been flattered with the show of love. It was everyone's chance to demonstrate in his favour and the noise was deafening. I bawled my heart out with the rest. The pilots had to struggle to extract him from the hands of the ecstatic technicians.

We finally led him back to the crowded officers mess tent for a drink. He was embarrassed by his performance and his face was uncharacteristically red.

"I really thought I'd be able to fly the kite better than that," he said, shaking his head. "But I was all over the shop. I made an exhibition of myself."

"I told you." Wizard waved a finger and did his Welsh uncle face. "You wouldn't listen to one who knows these tricky newfangled machines. Directly you opened your throttle the tail section shot up above the horizontal and your prop nearly went into the dirt. That Merlin engine has a kick like a mule."

"I know, God's truth! I was just too eager to get into the air. I rammed the throttle against the stop. I made a balls of it."

"The audience loved it," I offered.

"They'd have loved it even better," Wizard added, looking at me with mock severity, "if he'd put his wing in and done a cartwheel. Then they'd have another occasion to cheer as I departed for North Wales as Pilot Officer Williams!"

The fiasco increased rather than diminished Doc's stature and remained part of his legend among the flying and ground crews. It was, however, his first and last flight in a squadron Hurricane.

My personal kit, packed in a black brassbound trunk, had arrived from India by sea and was awaiting collection at Aboukir, an RAF depot near Alexandria. I flew the Lysander to Heliopolis and parked it there for a night, hoping to see Ken and Hugh before picking up the trunk. Hugh was in Syria with his troupe, but Ken met me at Shepheards and we set off down the sunlit boulevards of Cairo.

Ken had decided to give up spying and summarized his reasons.

"The terrible people," he said. "The absence of civilized values. Eventually you get disgusted. Anyway, I can't stand the thought of you and Pete doing all the fighting. The one chance I had to join the resistance in Greece fell through because the navy couldn't spare a submarine - I've applied for a commission in the infantry."

"That sounds dangerous," I said, instinctively believing that to drive a machine into action was preferable to appearing naked to one's enemy. "Dodging bullets? Wouldn't you rather be in a tank?"

"Pete's in tanks," he said, contemptuously dismissing the notion of following in the footsteps of a younger brother.

Within weeks of this conversation Ken was accepted for infantry training in Syria, and shortly after that he joined the London Irish Rifles as a lieutenant. The regiment became part of the British First Division under General Mark Clark's U.S. 6th Corps. On January 22, 1944, the Ango-American force landed thirty miles south of Rome and fanned out to take

MESSERSCHMITT ROULETTE

Anzio and Nettuno, two little fishing villages used by the Romans for holidays by the sea. The landing was fiercely opposed by the German army and the Allies sustained 19,000 casualties. Two thousand died, one of whom was my brother, Ken. At the age of eighteen he had written his own epitaph.

Better to fall like a falling star
Than rise like the pallid moon;
Bright with the sun's reflected light
But never a light of its own.

XXII

GOODBYE TO THE AUSSIES
(15 February, 1942 to 15 March, 1942)

"Wizard," I said to him one night at Sidi Azeiz, "can you invent a reason why my presence is urgently required in India? I want to get married but you needn't mention that."

"I'll put my thinking cap on," he replied, and dropped the subject.

A week later he called for me just as he was shutting up his office for the day. When I walked in he rose from his chair and took me by the arm.

"I've pulled strings for you," he said, "that have never been pulled before, I've sent whining signals, I've bullshitted about your fine qualities and finally" - he paused for effect - "I've got you attached temporarily to the Air Delivery Unit at Kilo 26. They're ferrying Hurricanes to the Far East. You can fly one to Karachi, dump it there, and get married. Three weeks leave. Is that OK?"

For once I was speechless.

The day I took off from Kilo 26 in Egypt, Singapore fell. Twenty-four Hurricanes for the defence of India were led by a single Blenheim across the sandy wastes of Arabia. We looked like a gaggle of geese following a giant condor. Lydda, Habbanya, Sharjah, Jawani, Karachi. I arrived in Lahore by train on 4th March and Joan and I were married in the Cantonment church on 7th before a congregation of dusky Anglo-Indian ladies who had been praying for my survival. Looking back, the wedding had its good points. George Topliss, my best man, and I were dressed modestly in our best blue uniforms and Joan was in a borrowed gown. The poor in spirit and the poor in fact were represented, and we made vows which only death dissolved. What more can the moralist desire?

When I flew back to the Middle East by Transport Command Dakota, the squadron had transferred to Lebanon and was located at Rayak in the Bekaa valley, now famous for Islamic terrorists. Once a French airfield, it was now a busy RAF station which also housed a training unit for reconnaissance squadrons. Nearby was the little village of Zahle, sitting in a fold of the mountains. It possessed a fine square, an imposing Maronite church and a first class hotel, the Kadre.

I stayed at the Kadre my first night, meeting Jasper Brown and Ray Hudson in the bar. They filled me in quickly with what had been going on since the squadron was withdrawn from the Western Desert. Wizard Williams had returned to the U.K. Murray Gardiner and his South Africans were back in their homeland. Doc Reid had been transferred to a hospital job in Egypt. I was no longer a member of No. 451 Squadron, having been posted in my absence to the reconnaissance training unit which was commanded by Sid Cooper.

The popular song that season was "Rum and Coca Cola," which had a catchy Caribbean rhythm.

> *Both Mother and daughtah*
> *Working for the Yankee dollah!*

Jasper ordered one for me. It tasted sweet and innocuous. I felt shamefully at home, talking about the war with my operational buddies. Throughout the honeymoon I'd struggled to drop the obsessions of the past eight months, but it was bliss to take them up again.

Since removing from the dust and fleas of Cyrenaica, Ray Hudson had transformed his appearance. His clean khaki uniform was pressed and he had a prison haircut, fashionable at the time, which made each blade of fair hair stand up from his skull like a brush. He was in fine grumbling form. He complained about the splitting of the squadron between Rayak and Cyprus, the sluggishness of the Australian government in providing pilots to make up their numbers, and the stingy awards, for which he blamed Wizard.

"Can't really fault Wizard," smiled Jasper. "We belong to a poorly-rewarded profession. Recce squadrons never do well for gongs."

"Only one Australian awarded a gong," Ray shouted. "After we were in it from the beginning! Why, if Ed and I hadn't been stuck in Tobruk with two unserviceable kites, we'd have been ahead of the lot of you in sorties flown, and you know it."

"I agree," I said, feeling lucky to be one of the chosen but embarrassed at the truth of his assertion.

We passed on to other more pleasant matters. Molly Malone, Willy Whitlock, the rash of oil pressure drops towards the end of the campaign, the November Handicap, the capture of Micky Carmichael, Doc Reid's first and last solo on a Hurricane.

I had consumed three or four rum and Coca Colas and noticed quite suddenly that I was shouting. I was deliriously happy with my friends in this beautiful foreign place; but something was wrong. I fumbled in my pocket for the key to my room which had an oversized metal ticket attached to it.

"I'm going to bed," I shouted, shifting my buttocks off the high stool and falling to the floor.

Ray and Jasper supported me to the stairs. All I can remember after that is crawling along a dimly lit corridor, drunkenly raising the key, trying to match it up with the number on the door.

GOODBYE TO THE AUSSIES

A week after my arrival at Rayak all the Australian pilots had gone, detached to Cyprus for shipping patrols and submarine searches, and that was the last I ever saw of them. Under the pressures of war I had become an honorary Australian. I had tried hard to gain their respect and they had certainly gained mine. I lost the fur felt they gave me when my kit was transferred to Rayak. Perhaps one of the airmen, thinking it couldn't have belonged to me, purloined it. It will stand as a symbol of the ambiguous relationship between me and the Australians. I was glad to own the felt but I never wore it around the squadron, as Wizard did. Some narrowminded sense of myself, some streetdog competitiveness, held me back. It was unfriendly, and I regret it now. Perhaps this book will be seen as my longwinded apology.

MESSERSCHMITT ROULETTE

XXIII

EPILOGUE

In the late summer of 1947 Doc Reid flew to England to attend an international convention of surgeons. Wizard came up to London to meet him and called me at my office in the Air Ministry. We met in a small French restaurant in one of the streets off Trafalgar Square and talked for an hour in one of those cubicles that seem to shut out the rest of the world. It was as dark as the bar tent at Sidi Barrani and we stared at one another affectionately across the gloom.

All of our previous intercourse had been under tremendous pressure. That was part of our bond. It had been forged in an atmosphere of sand, heat, fleas, the noise of aero engines, anti-aircraft fire, loss of comrades. The peace of an uncrowded restaurant where a foreign waiter fussed over us seemed strange.

Doc was dressed informally and presented the only spot of colour in a roomful of drably attired city types. He was wearing a sports jacket, grey flannels and a gaudy pullover.

"You look wonderful, Doc," I told him. "That sweater really brightens the place up."

"Overseas visitors get a stack of coupons. Bought it this morning in Bond Street. It's a genuine Fair Isle."

"Welcome to this fair isle," said Wizard, with heavy irony.

Bouncy and muscular, Doc's face still showed the tan of an Australian sun. His appearance had not altered since the Western Desert, whereas Wizard and I had paled and shrivelled in the post war climate. 1947 was not a vintage year for Britain. We had a Dickensian, bankrupt economy look about us. The previous era when it had been patriotic to show shiny knees and worn cuffs was over, but clothing was still rationed and the allowance just stretched to buying one suit for best. Mine was a blue pinstripe I never felt right in.

At lunch Wizard was pretty silent. He smiled a lot above and below his black moustache and rearranged his pipe when we weren't eating. He seemed very content, but the occasion had subdued his usual wit. Doc Reid did most of the talking. They were clearly close friends, much closer to one another than either was to me.

"Seven months on continuous ops was too long a stretch by half," Doc said grimly. "It was almost as if they were trying to break us. Along with our

191

other troubles. Our boys weren't happy to be watered down with poms and yarpies."

He made his shark grin.

"And I could see some good lads getting tired by the end of October."

"Willy Whitlock didn't help," I said. The war hadn't ended in my head yet. I still ground my teeth at the memory of Willy and that beautiful ruined Hurricane.

"I should have sent him back before he unpacked," Doc said. "I know that now. Even before he'd drawn his bivvy. Just the look on his yellow face. We didn't understand battle fatigue in those early days."

Mutual congratulations were in order. Doc Reid was voted the greatest aide de camp and factotum in the medical business and the heart and soul of the squadron. Wizard took his bow. I tried to appear modest when they said I was cheerful, even during the bad time. Was I, I wondered? All I could recall was the tension, the rivalry, the discomfort, the weird mixture of fear and rage. If I'd been cheerful it could only have been a reaction to crisis, a nervous tic.

"I've never felt less cheery," I said.

"Come on, Geoff. You were a box 'o birds!"

Wizard rose from his seat after the meal on a call of nature and struggled through waiters and trolleys to the far end of the restaurant.

"What would we have done without old Wizard," Doc said, watching his retreat. "I guess nobody but me knows what he went through. It was no joke keeping that Squadron right side up. I can't imagine anyone else who could have done it."

"What happened to the rest of the Aussies, Doc?' I asked.

"Charlie Edmondson got a DSO in the Med somewhere. Wally Gale was shot down and killed in Italy flying Kitthawks. Ken Watts was captured by the Germans and knocked about a bit. The other boys are fine. I keep in touch."

"You know Masher Maslen was killed?"

"No, I'm sorry."

"Shot down attacking a ground target in Italy. He managed to get the kite down in one piece but landed in a minefield and was blown to smithereens. His parents came up to London to see me. Farming people in their best clothes, awkward like Masher. They were very proud of him and his DFC, but he was their only son."

We kept a two minute silence after that until Wizard returned.

There is a footnote to this memoir that illustrates the complex relationship that exists between monarch and people in Britain. At the war's end I was immediately relegated to the equipment branch, the medical category for pilots once again requiring perfect vision. I questioned the ruling in my case and announced my intention of appealing to the King personally.

EPILOGUE

Lest the reader should think I was tilting at windmills I should point out that there has long been a close and heartfelt connection between the armed forces and the monarch. Queen Victoria began it by reviewing troops dressed in military uniform during the Crimean War. Since that time it has become customary for princes to be trained in the army or navy, and for princesses to be honorary colonels of regiments. King George VI had been the first member of the Royal family to be trained as a pilot. As a consequence, he wore his RAF wings on all his uniforms and appeared most often in public in air force blue, particularly in wartime.

Although in practice Parliament is the supreme authority, the fighting services belonged to the crown. We were all part of "His Majesty's Armed Forces." An officer held his commission from the king. Mine had been signed by George VI. I remember thinking, when I received it, that asking a figurehead king to sign the commission of an individual he would never command was fanciful and romantic. But this was before the evacuation from Dunkirk and the Battle of Britain had drawn monarch and people sharply together. The royal family had stayed in the capital and been bombed with other Londoners. They had become completely identified with the struggle for national survival. And I, of course, had quite recently appeared before this symbolic personage in his own palace and he had shaken my hand and chatted for a minute about the Western Desert.

It was common knowledge that the king identified himself strongly with the RAF, not only because he had been trained in that service but because the pilots of Fighter Command had saved the nation in 1940. The RAF stood in the same relationship to national sentiment as the British Navy after the defeat of the Spanish Armada in 1588. I hoped to be able to use this situation to my advantage.

After six months, and several unsuccessful medical boards, I came before the Air Member for Personnel, Air Marshal "Black Mac" Macdonald. As far as the RAF was concerned he was the end of the line. I saluted him and he ushered me across his large office to a settee. He sat at one end and I sat at the other. He was a man in his late fifties with jet-black hair. He wore a pinstripe suit, a starched white collar and a squadron tie. He smiled broadly, getting ready to exercise his arts of persuasion.

He was selling snake oil and I knew it.

"Well, young man," he said. "I must congratulate you on your persistence. Candidly, most people would not go as far as this. But here is the report of the latest board. They've shot you down again."

He handed me the rejection slip. I'd seen it many times before. It was always worded the same way. "Unfit for flying duties."

"So that's that. I'm really sorry. I'm sure you'll settle down happily in the equipment branch."

I had been rehearsing my next utterance for weeks and I trotted out my lines like a ham actor.

"I understand," I said, "that as an officer in His Majesty's Armed Forces I have the right to appeal to the king personally if I feel I have been unfairly treated in a serious matter. I now want to do that. I have proved my ability to fly under war conditions. I cannot see how I can now be rejected for the peacetime air force. If I am allowed to explain my case to the king, I will be content with whatever decision he makes."

To my surprise the Air Marshal roared with laughter.

"By God," he shouted. "You have got a bloody nerve. I've read your file and didn't believe it. You've held us up to ransom. You're a naughty boy!"

"Am I going back to flying, sir?" I asked.

"Oh, my God, yes," he said. "We couldn't trust you in front of King George. We know exactly what would happen. He'd ask you where you fought. He'd wring all sorts of confessions of heroism out of you. Then he'd call up the Air Council and cane our backsides for not respecting the generation that saved England."

Within three months I was commanding No. 224 Squadron at Gibraltar, the plum posting of my life.

APPENDIX A

WAR CAREERS OF THE AUSTRALIAN PILOTS OF NO 451 SQUADRON

Friendly readers of this account in manuscript have questioned my romantic view of the fighting spirit of the Australians. I was certainly shaken by them from the start and became obsessed with the problem of outdoing them, or at least not being completely outclassed. But was I scared by a few athletic physiques and some tough talk? To satisfy myself on this point I wrote to the Royal Australian Air Force Historical Branch, Canberra, for details of the subsequent operational careers of these men. It was clear from the record provided that the tour in the Western Desert of 1941-42 - which Ray Hudson has described as "worth two tours at least, by far the most lengthy and exhausting in my experience" - was only a beginning for most of them. They had left their native soil in 1940 and from mid 1941 onwards had flown steadily and successfully in front line squadrons until the war was over. What follows here is both a tribute to them and a justification of my high opinion of them as fighters. There were only two casualties - Miller Readett, who was shot down in the Western Desert in September 1941 and Wally Gale, who was killed in April 1944 attacking ground targets on the River Arno in Italy. Because the Historical Branch could only give details of those who had distinguished themselves or been killed in action, this is not by any means a complete record and is bound to leave out the names of those pilots who flew with courage but were never rewarded.

Harry Rowlands, who was shot down with Paddy Hutley during Rommel's probe in September 1941, was commissioned after he had recovered from the cannon shell wounds in his legs. He joined 213 Squadron (RAF) and was cited at the end of his tour for "great keenness and determination. Flight Lieutenant Rowlands has lead formations of aircraft on many sorties over the Castelrosso-Rhodes area. On one occasion twelve Junkers 88 were intercepted. In the ensuing fight three enemy aircraft were shot down, one of them by Rowlands." I didn't know him too well in the desert, partly because he was shot down so early in the campaign. What I do remember is his sharp face, his unruly hair and his big grin.

Alan Ferguson briefly commanded No 451 Squadron while it was based at Rayak in the early months of 1942. In the summer of 1942 he took command of No 450 Squadron RAAF, then operating Hurricanes in the fighter/bomber role in the Western Desert. The citation for his first DFC in the London Gazette of 5th February, 1943, reads that "he personally destroyed six aircraft and has lead large numbers of bombing raids . . . in June, 1942, alone he flew seventy operational sorties." He was shot down over Gambut by a Messerschmitt 109 and was so badly burned that the great RAF surgeon, Archibald McIndoe, was flown in to treat him. He spent twelve days with both hands sewn to the outsides of his hips.

When he had recovered from his wounds in Heliopolis Hospital, he was sent to England to join a special flight which dropped agents into Northern Europe from Beaufighter and Mosquito aircraft. He became engaged to a brave young woman who parachuted from his Mosquito into enemy territory and was never heard of again. After 600 hours of operational flying over France and the Low Countries he was awarded a bar to his DFC. Returning to Australia to fill a staff job, he soon wangled himself into the front line again, commanding No 81 Fighter Wing in the Pacific Theatre. He ended the war in Japan as part of the Allied Occupation Forces. Fergie had a great sense of humour and I owe him a special debt of gratitude for his open support and friendship. His record speaks for itself.

Ray Goldberg was commissioned as soon as the squadron pulled back to Rayak, Syria, in 1942. He joined Hudson and Robertson flying ground attack Kittyhawks in No 450 Squadron RAAF. He was awarded a Distinguished Flying Cross on 9 June, 1944, for "fighter and bomber sorties over the Western Desert, Malta and Sicily. In September 1943 he scored a direct hit on a three thousand ton vessel and later in the same year he made a low level attack on an enemy encampment. Although his aircraft had been hit by a shell from the enemy defences, the officer persisted in his attacks, inflicting much damage on enemy gun posts. In February 1944 he so badly damaged an enemy ship in the harbour of Rogoznica that it had to be beached and was later destroyed." In 1941 he looked too young to be involved in a war. But he had an excellent temperament to withstand stress and showed his paces early. So the placidity of his countenance, which I remember, did not belie him; he was calm and steady by nature and would have done well in any operational role. Persisting in an attack when his aircraft had already been hit tallies with my image of him as a sane version of Molly Malone, a little too brave for my taste but likely to survive.

In January 1944 Colin Robertson led No 450 Squadron (RAAF), flying Kittyhawk fighter bombers, "in an attack on a medium sized merchant vessel which caught fire. He has completed a large number of sorties on a wide range of targets and has displayed great courage, skill and resolution." His D.F.C. was gazetted on 18 February, 1944. Col was a gentleman farmer, very conscious of his roots. Big, omnicompetent and trained in sheep dipping, he was the most likely survivor of any crisis. If there is ever an atomic holocaust, he would be the one to breed from to build a new human race.

Charlie Edmondson flew with 451 Squadron during 1942/3 and then joined 429 Squadron (RAF), a ground attack unit of the Balkan Air Force. He eventually commanded this squadron, earning a brilliant D.S.O. in 1945 for leading attacks on "targets in Yugoslavia, Albania, Austria and the Istrian Peninsular, destroying nine aircraft, 1000 railway waggons and 150 locomotives." Dark haired, low to the ground and always smiling, he was a workhorse in the Western Desert and I revered him for his cheerfulness under dangerous and uncomfortable conditions. It was clear that he would develop into an outstanding leader of men.

Ken Watts was tall, fair and had the best physique in the squadron. I have a photograph of him shaving outside his tent in his briefs that recalls Melville's besotted description of the sailor, Billy Budd. Nowadays his kind of bodily perfection is called beefcake. After his first short tour in the Western Desert he joined No 80 Squadron (RAF), flying Spitfires in the straight fighter role. He went to Italy as a flight commander and, in the early part of 1944, he returned to the RAAF, flying Kittyhawks with No 3 Squadron. He was cited for "completing numerous operational sorties against the enemy, damaging a ME 109, sharing in the destruction of a Junkers 52 near Rimini," and leading "a low level attack on enemy airfields, destroying many enemy aircraft on the ground." In March, 1944 he took command of 112 Squadron (RAF). He was knocked down by flak in his Kittyhawk while attacking a target near the Adriatic coast but bailed out successfully from his blazing aircraft. Italian farmers picked him up, equipped him with a civilian shirt and trousers and gave him elaborate directions for the 160 kilometre walk back to his base at Cutella. He remembers tearing the "Made in Australia" tag off his singlet so that his clothing would not identify him. Unfortunately he was picked up on a country road by a German patrol and taken to Veterbo and thence to Verona. At Verona he fell into the hands of the Gestapo, who were eager for information on his unit. He refused to give them anything but his name, rank and number. Their response was to club him around the head with rifle butts from both sides. He didn't alter his mind, so the unpleasantness was repeated on three further occasions. He ended up in honourable solitary confinement at Stalag Luft 1 on the Baltic, having said nothing.

Years later the effect of these beatings resulted in brain tumours. After five operations Ken is now a paraplegic and has been in a wheel chair for fifteen years. We talk on the telephone, exchange letters, and his recollections have added numerous details to these memoirs.

Ed Kirkham stayed with the squadron but was never decorated. He flew shipping patrols, strikes on Crete, and commanded the unit when it was re-equipped with Spitfires in 1944. Ray Hudson wrote this to me; "Ed held 451 together from the Delta to Corsica, and he took it into action there. A more deserving D.S.O. I never saw." Some things don't add up, do they?

Ray Hudson stayed with the 451 during 1942 and most of 1943, flying standing patrols and convoy patrols from Cyprus. On 24th April 1943 the engine of his Hurricane caught fire over a convoy and he had to ditch. He was picked up by a ship, but suffered superficial injuries and burns. This turned out to be the most relaxed period of his war. Late in 1943 he joined 450 Squadron and was awarded his first D.F.C. on 18th February, 1944 for "leading an attack on a large armed merchant vessel in the heavily defended harbour of Sibinik, Yugoslavia." He commanded 450 Squadron in 1944 and earned a bar to his D.F.C. for "leading attacks on ground targets with courage and the greatest determination, often in the face of intense anti-aircraft fire." His Kittyhawk was shot down in the same minefield in Italy as Masher Maslen. Masher was killed but Ray survived, having the longest and most successful operational career of anyone in the group. After the war he went to New York and learned to fly the new Sikorsky YR4B helicopters. In 1956 he formed the helicopter division of T.A.A. and in 1959 he took the first Australian helicopters to the Antarctic, characteristically distinguishing himself in this pioneer work.

I wrote to Ray Hudson when I had completed the first draft of this book and sent him some chapters to criticize. This led to a back and forth correspondence for two years that was only terminated by his death in 1986. I'm grateful to him for the ferocious energy of his responses. He had cancer of the spine and wrote at the end lying on his face in a hospital bed, cursing the pain and the necessary interference of pain killers, but passionate, coherent and critical always. That was Ray Hudson, the very embodiment of a character I had tried to imagine as a boy, my Uncle Frank's Gallipoli Aussie.

APPENDIX B
ROSTER 451 SQUADRON

RANK	NAME	DATE OF ARR.	REMARKS

ROYAL AIR FORCE PILOTS

RANK	NAME	DATE OF ARR.	REMARKS
Flt. Lt.	Brown, J.	10/41	
Flt. Lt.	Byers, P.	7/41	KIA
Flt. Lt.	Carmichael, M.	7/41	Wounded
Flt. Lt.	Cooper, S.	10/41	
F.O.	Evans	10/41	
P.O.	Graeme-Evans	8/41	KIA
Flt. Lt.	Malone, L.F.	7/41	KIA
P.O.	Maslen, A.V.	8/41	DFC, KIA (Italy)
Flt. Lt.	Morley-Mower, G.F.	1/8/41	DFC
S/L	Pope, V.A.	7/41	
P.O.	Porter, I.	10/41	KIA
F.O.	Strachan,, D.	10/41	
P.O.	Walford, H.	10/41	KIA
P.O.	Whalley, K.	8/41	KIA
S/L	Williams, R.D.	7/41	DFC (Had a DFC before arrival in desert)

SOUTH AFRICAN AIR FORCE PILOTS

RANK	NAME	DATE OF ARR.	REMARKS
Lt.	Andrews, W.	8/41	
Lt.	Campbell, P.	8/41	
Capt.	Gardiner, M.	8/41	
Lt.	Haddon, P.	8/41	
Lt.	Smith		KIA
Lt.	Thomas, T.	8/41	KIA

ROYAL AUSTRALIAN AIR FORCE PILOTS

RANK	NAME	DATE OF ARR.	REMARKS
P.O.	Achilles, R.M.	1/7/41	DFC
P.O.	Ahern, L.N.	27/1/42	
Sgt.	Bartlett, S.J.M.	6/12/41	
P.O.	Baun, J.K.	27/1/42	
Sgt.	Burden, R.H.	1/3/42	
P.O.	Edmondson, C.E.	10/8/41	DSO (Balkan Air Force) 1945
Flt.Lt.	Ferguson, A.D.	29/9/41	DFC & bar (Wstrn Dsrt & UK) 1943
Sgt.	Fisher, D.L.	1/3/42	
Sgt.	Goldman, W.E.	1/3/42	
Sgt.	Gale, W.W.B.	6/12/41	

ROYAL AUSTRALIAN AIR FORCE PILOTS (Cont.)

RANK	NAME	DATE OF ARR	REMARKS
Sgt.	Goldberg, R.G	6/12/41	DFC(Wstrn Dsrt)1944
P.O.	Hudson, R.T.	10/7/41	DFC &bar (Wstrn Dsrt '44 & Italy'44)
P.O.	Hutley, W.D.	4/7/41	WOUNDED
P.O.	Kirkham, E.	10/7/41	
P.O.	Lomas, F.L.	24/1/42	
P.O.	McLean, D.W.	12/3/42	
P.O.	Robertson, C.W.	10/8/41	DFC (Wstrn Dsrt) 1944
Sgt.	Readett, M.	10/7/41	KIA
Sgt.	Rowlands, H.R.	18/11/41	WOUNDED
F.L.	Springbett, K.H.	29/9/41	
P.O.	Schofield, J.E.	27/1/42	
P.O.	Trenorden, L.E.	5/2/42	
P.O.	Terry, W.L.	5/2/42	
Sgt	Watts, W.K.	6/12/41	DFC (Italy) 1944

RAAF Ground Officers

RANK		NAME	DATE OF ARR
F.O.	Signals	Buckland, H.M.	24/3/41
F.O.		Fitzroy, F.	17/3/41
F.L.	Adjutant	Langslow, W.L.	5/3/41
F.O.	Equipment	Miller, H.T.	29/3/41
S/L	Physician	Reid, S.F.	23/3/41
F.O.	Cyphers	Thyer, W.V.	24/3/41

AIRMEN

RANK	NAME
COPPERSMITH	
CPR.	Kelly, J.B.
AC1	McSporran, A.
ELECTRICAL FITTER	
CPL	Dowser, B.E.
CPL	Unsworth, J.
LAC.	Fardell, N.E.
FITTER 11E	
CPL	Foulkes, A.B.
LAC	Davys, R.W.
LAC	Elliott, E.G.
LAC	McClymont, N.V.
LAC	Rabbits, E.
LAC	Reed, E.W.
LAC	Smith, W.H.
LAC	Welsh, J.A.
LAC	Whitford, N.A.W.
AC1	Austin, C.A.
AC1	Chard, G.H.
AC1	Christian, H.I.
AC1	Johnson, H.R.
AC1	Riley, H.
AC1	Rome, S.A.P.
AC1	Ward, J.N.
INSTRUMENT MAKER	
AC1	Andrews, R.D.

RANK	NAME
FITTER 11A	
CPL.	Barclay, J.
CPL.	Fisher, J.T.
CPL.	Townsend, L.J.
LAC.	Cole, J.C.
LAC.	Foyster, A.J.
LAC.	Hemsley, H.C.
LAC.	Mack, B.R.N.
AC1	Anthes, J.H.
AC1	Bailey, W.G.
AC1	Basnett, A.E.
AC1	Bentley, H.W.
AC1	Branch, S.J.
AC1	Guy, N.W.
AC1	Hanney, L.F.
AC1	Hayman, L.W.
AC1	Moeser, C.R.L.
FITTER ARMOURER	
CPL.	Wells, R.
LAC.	Orchard, E.S.
LAC.	Steele, E.D.
AC1	Cox, E.C.
AC1	Kirk, W.J.
CARPENTER GENERAL	
AC1	Burgess, E.L.

RANK	NAME
FITTER D.M.T.	
SGT..	Arnold, W.C.
CPL.	Lyons, E.A.
LAC.	Chadwick, V.A.
AC1	Brenton, K.L.
AC1	Kline, J.K.
PHOTOGRAPHERS	
LAC.	Brady, B.
LAC.	Callaghan, P.N.
LAC.	Green, W.J.
LAC.	Millyard, R.C.
LAC.	Trowbridge, M.
AC1	Isaacs,C.H.
AC1	LeGuay, L.C.
AC1	Owen, C.E.
AC1	Williams, A.F.
ELECTRICIANS	
LAC.	Little, A.M.
LAC.	MCFadden, P.
LAC.	Richardson, A.E.
AC1	Gover, E.A.
AC1	McPherson, G.I.
AC1	Nicholls, K.W.
AC1	Rufus, C.

AIRMEN (Cont.)

RANK	NAME
FLIGHT MECHANICS	
LAC.	Allen, J.L.
LAC.	Bell, A.A.
LAC.	Berglund, R.A.
LAC.	Coote, M.E.
LAC.	Cullen, V.R.
LAC.	Fairhall, H.G.
LAC.	Gornall, J.K.
LAC.	Keelty, F.B.
AC1	Bains, A.
AC1	Barnett, J.
AC1	Baxendale, F.L.
AC1	Bonser, F.W.
AC1	Cummins, J.B.
AC1	Dodd, A.J.

RANK	NAME
FLIGHT RIGGERS	
LAC	Bollard, A.D.
LAC	Ebeling, C.R.
LAC	Honeyfield, G.C.
LAC	Haggard, D.C.
LAC	Hill, B.M.
LAC	Jordan, S.L.
LAC	Kelly, V.W.
LAC	Dohrmann, R.N.
LAC	Lewis, J.C.
AC1	Bignell, R.
AC1	Cross, J.
AC1	Cake, B.G.
AC1	Evans, H.N.
AC1	Gerrard, E.E.

RANK	NAME
INSTRUMENT REPAIRER	
LAC.	Mark, W.R.H.
LAC.	McNicol, K.H.

RANK	NAME
ARMOURERS	
CPL	Lenney, J.A.
LAC.	Barry, L.E.
LAC.	Ifield, M.R.
LAC.	Jaggers, R.C.L.
LAC.	McDougall, D.C.
AC1	Bossley, H.B.
AC1	Cummins, R.A.
AC1	McKensey, J.E.F.
AC1	Porter, W.M.
AC1	Sharpe, G.G.
AC1	Smith, E.H.

RANK	NAME
FABRIC WORKER	
AC1	Brazil, D.F.
AC1	Puller, J.G.

RANK	NAME
CLERK GENERAL	
CPL.	Travers, M.W.
LAC.	Barnes, F.F.T.
LAC.	Griffin, W.J.

RANK	NAME
COOK	
CPL.	Tuckett, K.H.
CPL.	Tier, R.
CPL.	Wilbraham, T.G.
LAC.	Collins, A.C.
LAC.	Connelly, T.L.
LAC.	Goggin, D.J.
LAC.	Haworth, J.E.
LAC.	Jenke, W.E.
LAC.	Sanders, T.R.
LAC.	Shearing, A.L.
LAC.	Skinner, H.A.
AC1	Bertram, D.R.
AC1	Carpenter, R.F.
AC1	Wright, F.M.

RANK	NAME
NURSING ORDERLY	
SGT.	Burge, E.
CPL.	Mear, L.T.
LAC.	Brodie, J.
LAC.	Foulstone, D.J.
LAC.	Maher, W.M.
AC1	Jenkins, H.W.

RANK	NAME
D.M.T.	
CPL.	Taylor, K.A.
LAC.	Bailey, H.W.
LAC.	Griffiths, B.W.
LAC.	Irwin, D.T.
LAC.	McKittrick, T.J.
AC1	Armstrong, J.J.
AC1	Culbert, J.L.
AC1	Cook, F.R.
AC1	Clark, A.A.
AC1	Dorney, J.A.
AC1	Gowland, F.T.
AC1	Halcrow, A.
AC1	Hayes, J.D.
AC1	Davis-Gregory, R.M.
AC1	Robertson, M.B.
AC1	Lamond, A.G.
LAC	Sawrey, A.G.
AC1	Peet, R.F.
AC1	Rowe, J.C.
AC1	Pratt, J.H.
AC1	Stewart, W.G.
AC1	McGann, G.
AC1	Norriss, G.H.P.
AC1	Smith, E.J.
AC1	Towers, A.H.
AC1	Maddison, Q.A.

RANK	NAME
CLERK PAY	
CPL	Adams, I.A.

RANK	NAME
STOREKEEPER	
LAC.	Beresford, J.
LAC.	Cosson, D.W.
LAC.	Harrison, A.W.
LAC.	Lombard, P.J.
LAC.	Morris, J.
LAC.	Raby,M.J.

RANK	NAME
MESSMEN	
LAC.	Andrew, W.R.M.
LAC.	Dalton, D.E.
AC1	Adlard, S.E.
AC1	Bolton, H.
AC1	Buckland, J.H.
AC1	DeLaMotte, A.M.
AC1	Greenwood, L.P.T.
AC1	Hope, R.N.
AC1	McGill, A.R.
AC1	Norman, R.P.
AC1	Nowotna, E.J.

RANK	NAME
MESS STEWARD	
LAC	Atkin, G.H.
LAC	Benger, R.
LAC	Clements, F.L.
LAC	Coffey, L.F.
LAC	Gooday, A.G.
AC1	Amor, W.H.R.
AC1	Boyd, D.B.
AC1	Cardilini, J.M.
AC1	Fisher, L.C.
AC1	Goodsir, D.A.
LAC	Hay, C.B.

RANK	NAME
TELEPHONE OPERATORS	
LAC	Mitchell, M.W.
AC1	Gurran, R.
AC1	O'Brien, G.M.
AC1	Wilson, J.D.

RANK	NAME
SERVICE POLICE	
CPL.	Hammond, H.H.
A/Cpl.	Clarke, G.J.
A/Cpl.	Domeyer, E.W.
A/Cpl.	Northam, C.A.
A/Cpl.	Wigley, F.A.

RANK	NAME
CLERK STORES	
LAC.	Stephens, C.H.
AC1.	Grace, C.B.

RANK	NAME
DISCIPLINARY	
W.O.	HollisT.,H.

AIRMEN (Cont.)
AIRCRAFTHAND

RANK	NAME	RANK	NAME
CPL.	Hayes, P.C.	AC1.	Simpson, L.J.
CPL.	Dryden, D.	AC1.	Gabriel, S.J.
CPL.	Cowan, G.W.	AC1.	Gibb, W.F.
LAC.	Anderson, L.M.	AC1.	Dunger, C.E.,
LAC.	Burslem, R.M.	AC1.	Evans, A.
LAC.	Swinbourne, H.I.	AC1.	Thornton, J.E.
LAC.	Power, M.A.	AC1.	Bradley, W.A.
LAC.	Lewis, K.E.	AC1.	Burnett, N.D.
LAC.	Justin, L.A.	AC1.	King, K.F.
LAC.	Field, K.E.	AC1.	Phillips, D.J.
LAC.	Irvine, W.S.	AC1.	Cooper, S.W.
LAC.	Butcher, L.W.	AC1.	Patterson, R.D.
LAC.	Voss, E.R.	AC1.	Conrad, C.A.
LAC.	Freudenstein, O.K.	AC1.	Guinane, C.V.
LAC.	Tucker. H.	AC1.	Cobby, S.W.
LAC.	Gabriel, H.J.	AC1.	McKay, A.
LAC.	Bellert, J.L.	AC1.	Pearson, J.R.
LAC.	Marsh, J.W.	AC1.	Burgess, J.
LAC.	Lackenby, D.	AC1.	Hayes, F.T.
LAC.	Stevenson, J.	AC1.	Manning, R.M.
LAC.	Crozier, W.J.	AC1.	Preston, J.T.
LAC.	Hine, W.	AC1.	White, R.A.
LAC.	Atcheson, W.B.	AC1.	Edwards, A.R.
LAC.	Pollard, F.H.	AC1.	Price, E.H.
LAC.	Brown, A.A.	AC1.	Olds, R.S.
LAC.	Jarvis, W.R.	AC1.	Morgan, J.A.
LAC.	Miller, J.H.	AC1.	Snowball, J.
LAC.	McRae, M.H.	AC1.	Doyle, E.J.G.
LAC.	Gray, K.P.	AC1.	Bromley, G.W.
LAC.	Curnow, A.E.	AC1.	Hirst, E.A.
LAC.	McPherson, R.O.	AC1.	McArdle, G.N.
LAC	Chambers, J.H.	AC1.	Cox, C.H.
LAC.	Watson, R.C.	AC1.	Street, R.E.H.
LAC.	Norman, G.A.	AC1.	Silvester, A.E.
LAC.	Thornton, B.S.		

RAF Airmen Seconded To 451 Squadron
(Incomplete)

SGT.	Bailey	
SGT.	Buxton	
CPL.	Farr, T.	KIA
	Kelley, A.	
	Spinner, D.	
CPL.	Florey, J.	

DEFINITIVE MILITARY/AVIATION HISTORIES
By
PHALANX PUBLISHING CO., LTD.

The Pineapple Air Force: Pearl Harbor to Tokyo
by John Lambert $44.95

Republic P-47 Thunderbolt, The Final Chapter: Latin American Air Forces Service
by Dan Hagedorn $14.95

Eagles of Duxford: The 78th Fighter Group in World War II
by Garry Fry $29.95

Kearby's Thunderbolts: The 348th Fighter Group in World War II
by John Stanaway $24.95

Wildcats Over Casablanca
by John Lambert $11.95

B-25 Mitchell, The Magnificent Medium
by Norman L. Avery $29.95

Sortie:
A bibliography of U.S. Air Force, Navy and Marine combat aviation unit histories from World War II. $10.95

Pacific Air Combat: Voices from the Past
by Henry Sakaida $14.95

Sun Downers: VF 11 in World War II
by Barrett Tillman

FORTHCOMING TITLES

THE 1ST FIGHTER GROUP IN WORLD WAR II:
The MTO war of the this legendary P-38 unit by one of its pilots, John D. Mullins

FANTAIL FIGHTERS
Battleship and cruiser floatplanes in World War II, by Jerry Scutts

YANKS FROM YOXFORD
The 357th Fighter Group in Europe by Merle Olmsted

MARINE MITCHELLS
U.S. Marine Corps operations with PBJ aircraft in the Pacific, by Jerry Scutts.